FISHES OF THE PACIFIC

Alaska to Peru,
including the Gulf of California
and the Galapagos Islands

507 fishes in full color

GAR GOODSON

Illustrated by Phillip J. Weisgerber

STANFORD UNIVERSITY PRESS
Stanford, California
1988

This book is dedicated to those sane and thoughtful people who fight tenaciously to preserve our beleaguered planet. A holocaust is enveloping the wild creatures and wild places of the world. If the destruction of animals and habitats does not stop, then there will ensue a human catastrophe of even greater dimensions.

Stanford University Press
Stanford, California 94305
© 1988 by the Board of Trustees
   of the Leland Stanford Junior University
Printed in Japan
ISBN 0-8047-1385-5
LC 87-60691
Last figure below indicates year of this printing:

95   94   93   92   91   90   89   88

INTRODUCTION

My initial aim in preparing this guidebook was to familiarize the residents of the Pacific Coast with the magnificent fishes off our shores. But a disturbing fact kept cropping up while researching the book: unless more attention is paid to the protection and preservation of these fishes and the waters in which they swim, it will not be long before there will be very few fishes left to admire.

Eastern Pacific reefs are, or rather were, a fishwatchers' paradise. Older divers remember wistfully the days when reefs and kelp beds swarmed with fishes; rocks, reefs, and dock pilings were caked with mollusks and other marine animals; and the air and water and shoreline teemed with gulls, pelicans, cormorants, and myriad shorebirds. Today, overfishing, pollution, habitat destruction, and the conversion of wetlands have decimated the fish stocks of many coastal areas. There are still places to go, fish to see, but PCB, DDT, sewage, and numerous other poisons are contaminating rivers, bays, and harbors—as well as the fishermen who eat the contaminated fish. Shorelines and beaches are choked with sewage, oil slicks, and plastic residue.

The Pacific Coast is under siege! The Queen Charlotte Islands off British Columbia are now being logged off at a fearsome pace. The troubled waters of Puget Sound and Commencement Bay in Washington, and of San Francisco Bay, are in danger of becoming "dead seas," owing to toxic chemical wastes. The same toxic menace has recently been reported in Santa Monica and San Pedro bays, off Los Angeles, and in San Diego Bay. Purse seining and gill netting in Mexico's Gulf of California are ravaging the resources of this rich sea that was once a living tide of fishes.

Using the pretext of "sustainable yield," some marine biologists and government agencies have given the super seiners, gill netters, and fishing fleets of the world the go-ahead to ravage one fish species after another, to the point of collapse. In the following pages, the reader will see that many fishes—tunas, herrings, sardines, anchovies, salmon, sturgeon, and many, many others—are rapidly diminishing in numbers. Some fishing nations are now beginning to harvest krill, the minute marine larvae that begin the food chain upon which all marine fishes, birds, seals, and whales depend. Mankind's overconsumption, habitat destruction, and pollution put all marine life at grave risk.

Worse, the destruction of the sea beds goes on unseen. If somehow a huge fleet of land-cruising purse seiners scoured the fields and highways of the United States, vacuuming up millions upon millions of birds and waterfowl and wiping out whole species of animals, the public outcry would be deafening. Yet these same purse seiners sweep, decimate, and exterminate great schools of fishes, invertebrates, and even mammals, in all of the world's seas, to the near extinction of many species. But because the carnage is hidden under sparkling, sunlit waves, scarcely a voice is raised.

Biologists and ecologists worldwide now warn that a holocaust is enveloping the wild creatures of this planet. Depredations on the same scale are rapidly destroying the world's great tropical forests. We are witnessing a mass extinction that parallels the disappearance of the dinosaurs 65 million years ago, along with half of all other species then on the earth. No one knows what did the dinosaurs in, but we do know the cause of today's holocaust. The early settlers believed that the wild creatures of field and stream and ocean were inexhaustibly abundant, but five hundred years of harvest and waste have taken their toll, and we can no longer plead innocence or ignorance. If the killing is not brought within sensible bounds, the fate of the animals of the world will be followed by a human catastrophe of even greater dimensions.

There is some evidence that people around the globe are beginning to rebel. We daily discover contaminated fish in river and sea, we turn away from toxic beaches where we used to swim and frolic, and we mourn the birds and birdsongs that once filled field and shore. Many are beginning to protest, calling elected officials and searching for realistic conservation strategies that may check the devastation and preserve at least some small part of our wild heritage. The world's conscience and consciousness are being assailed daily by scientists of international stature. Let us hope that governments begin to listen. Let us hope that we will not have to tell our grandchildren about the wilderness that was, and the underwater world of the reefs that used to be.

Using This Book

It is vital that the residents of the Pacific Coast come to know the splendor and beauty of this threatened under-water realm. There is no other experience in the world quite like a diver's first tour of an underwater reef. Whether in temperate waters or tropical coral reefs, one finds an unforgettable realm of oceanic blue, teeming reef-fish colonies, towering reef formations, and brilliant sea grass and kelp beds, all glistening and sparkling in the sea-filtered sunlight. Many of the fishes shown here can be seen while snorkeling on the surface over shallow-water reefs (in 5- to 20-foot depths) with only a face mask, snorkel tube, and swim fins. (Page 244 gives diving tips for beginners.)

This guidebook is designed for the fishwatcher—whether skin or SCUBA diver, fisherman, aquarist, schoolchild, or casual tourist exploring the shore—who seeks to know more about our marine life. No special knowledge of fishes, other than a general understanding of the parts of a fish identified in the illustration below, is required to comprehend this book.

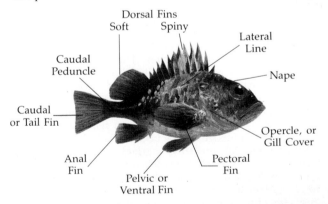

The book is not written in formal academic style—though the ichthyologists and other biologists are likely to find it of considerable interest. Most guidebooks begin with hagfishes, lampreys, sharks, rays, eels, and similar unfamiliar fishes; they proceed, that is, in phylogenetic v order, from primitive species to more evolved species, and only gradually do they get around to such interesting and vital fishes as seabasses, jacks, tunas, mackerels, and surfperches. We have reversed this process, by placing the more interesting and more familiar fishes at the front of the book where they are more easily found and referred to.

For each of the fish families I have provided information (when known) about behavioral and breeding patterns, color variations, feeding patterns, survival techniques, symbiosis, attack and defense behavior, and other distinguishing characteristics. For each fish species I have provided the common name in English, the Spanish common name (in parentheses), the scientific name, maximum size (total length), salient characteristics of the fish, and range. Weight is given for the larger fishes. Edibility ratings are given for those food and game fishes that frequently find their way to the table, as well as for those few fish species (such as the puffers) that are poisonous. Most of the common food and game fishes of our coast have a Spanish common name, and supplying these names may make the book more helpful to Spanish-speaking readers.

As you absorb the information in this book, you will be surprised at how readily you can learn to distinguish one fish family from another, one genus from another, and even one species from another. The identification techniques provided here, much like those in birdwatching guides, are based on visual techniques—not arcane technical or academic data. You will also discover the incredible diversity of life styles and behavior among the fish species. You will learn to recognize a fish by where it is swimming (reef ledge, rocky bottom, kelp bed, sand bottom, or tidepool), how it is marked, how it swims, and where it finds its food. You will learn to recognize courting and breeding behavior, identify fish nestings, even begin to recognize the more secretive fishes (basses, flatfishes, and rays, for example) that are often camouflaged and hiding in reef crevices or on or in sand bottoms. These characteristics and recognition techniques are explored in detail here.

The book treats all the common fishes and a great many of the uncommon or rare fishes of the coastal waters of the eastern Pacific, from Alaska to Peru. North and south of that range, or in the great deeps, there are many fishes we never see along the coast; and in freshwater rivers and lakes, there is still another fish fauna. The book treats 433 species in full, with particular focus on those commonly sighted by divers, taken by fishermen or collectors, or found in the marketplace. Each species is illustrated with at least one watercolor painting. In all, the book contains 507 paintings, and another 46 closely related species (13 of them occurring only in other parts of the world) are discussed in the species texts. We have sought to be as accurate as possible both in describing the fish in words and in illustrating them in pictures.

Much of the material presented appears in a guidebook for the first time. Some species show surprising differences in form and color between juvenile, adult, and breeding adult fishes, and most of these (for example, the salmons and trouts, damselfishes, wrasses, and parrotfishes) have been profusely illustrated here. Many are shown in color for the first time. Most of the fish paintings were commissioned for this volume.

Acknowledgments

I am especially indebted to Phillip J. Weisgerber, who valiantly and expertly painted his way through over 450 full-color fish illustrations, without which this book would be empty indeed. I am very grateful to Dr. Richard Rosenblatt, Professor of Marine Biology at Scripps Institution of Oceanography, La Jolla, California; Dr. Donald A. Thomson, Professor of Ecology and Evolutionary Biology and Curator of Fishes at the University of Arizona; Dr. Camm Swift, Associate Curator of Fishes at the Los Angeles County Museum of Natural History; and Alex N. Kerstitch, Research Associate at the Department of Ecology and Evolutionary Biology at the University of Arizona. These four generously reviewed the entire text and illustrations of this book, and each contributed substantially to its accuracy. Dr. Thomson and Mr. Kerstitch concentrated on southern species, while Dr. Rosenblatt and Dr. Swift covered the gamut of fishes from Alaska to Peru.

I have drawn heavily on the work of previous authors, biologists, ichthyologists, researchers, artists, photographers, and the many specialists who dive and/or research and publish their observations in books or scientific publications. Of particular value in the compilation of this book were the works of William N. Eschmeyer, Earl S. Herald, Howard Hammann, Donald A. Thomson, Lloyd T. Findley, Alex N. Kerstitch, Daniel J. Miller and Robert N. Lea, J. L. Hart, Lionel A. Walford, James E. Bohlke, Charles G. Chaplin, Richard Rosenblatt, Edmund S. Hobson, John E. Fitch, Daniel W. Gotshall, Howard M. Feder, Charles H. Turner, Conrad Limbaugh, W. A. Clemens, and G. V. Wilbey. A bibliography listing most (but not all) of the publications that were used in preparing this guidebook is provided on pages 251–53.

The editors and staff of Stanford University Press were instrumental in assuring that this book got to press in the best possible form, and appreciation is due to William W. Carver, Editor, who patiently and skillfully shepherded the book into safe harbor and final publication, and to Kathleen Szawiola, who laid out the pages. Special thanks for a huge task well and carefully done go to Sarah Redman, the typist, editor, transcriber, nitpicker, and all-around hard worker who helped immeasurably in preparing the book for delivery to the publisher. Finally, I owe deep gratitude to my wife, Queta Goodson, who listened patiently and without complaint to endless readings of tangled fish descriptions, and contributed much in editorial and moral support and companionship during the years it took to prepare this book.

CONTENTS

FISHES OF THE PACIFIC COAST

The Pacific Coast of the Americas is home to an amazing variety of fishes. From Alaska to California to Peru, there is much to see, much to study. We have fishes like the banded cleaner goby, a tidepool specialist that does not exceed an inch and a quarter full-grown; and there are others, like the bluefin tuna, the great white shark, and the Pacific manta ray, that exceed 10 feet and 1,000 pounds, the great white reaching 2,800 pounds. There are the flyingfish, which can cross 450 feet of open water; the anglerfish, a grotesque bottom-sitter that engulfs unwary passersby in a single gulp; the hunters like the sailfish, which can exceed 68 miles per hour in the chase. There are groupers, snappers, croakers, triggers, puffers, and flounders; mackerels, seahorses, sculpins, sturgeons, and sticklebacks; trouts, wrasses, blennies, gobies, and grunions; tiger sharks, hammerheads, skates, and morays.

Many fishes are prime table fare, but most are not; and a few, like the puffers, have poisonous flesh. Most fishes are harmless, but a few have venomous spines or deadly bites; and a handful, like the great white shark and the scorpionfish, should be avoided at all costs.

Like frogs, snakes, birds, whales, and wolves, fish are vertebrates; they have a spinal cord, a brain, and a highly elaborated life history. Some graze on algae and other plants, but most are predators; and most are preyed on by larger predators, including birds, man, seals, squids, other fishes, and even small invertebrates. Like frogs, snakes, birds, and insects, most fishes lay eggs; but a few (like the surfperches and many sharks and rays) are ovoviviparous—the eggs are nurtured in the female's body and the young are born alive. Like mammals and birds, fish have a skeleton, but whereas in most fishes the skeleton is of bone, in the sharks and rays it is of tough cartilage. Fish, then, are as different as mammals and birds, in their form and behavior and in their evolution and life history.

The teeming millions of fishes are not alone in the sea. Besides the mammals, birds, and sea snakes (see p. 243), there are billions and billions of invertebrates and microorganisms, far greater in numbers and varieties than the fishes. But that is another story.

SEA BASSES, GROUPERS, AND
TEMPERATE BASSES

The sea basses and groupers of the Pacific Coast (family Serranidae) are mostly tropical fishes ranging in size from the awesome giant jewfish approaching 8 feet and 700 pounds to the dainty, colorful rainbow basslet of just 6 inches. They include some excellent food fishes—the groupers, sand basses, calico bass, and striped bass—as well as the soapfishes, which secrete a sudsy toxic foam when caught or handled.

Most groupers and sea basses are bottom dwellers, either skulking in caves or reef crevices or roaming across the bottom. Some groupers can change their colors to match their backgrounds, flashing from spots to stripes, blotches, bars, or solid colors as they move from kelp bed to reef rock to sandy bottom. This highly developed changeability protects them from larger predators and enables them to prey effectively on smaller fishes.

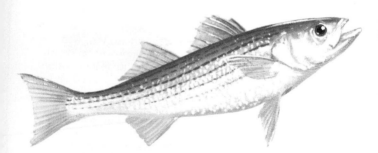

Striped bass, striper *Morone saxatilis*   To 4 feet. A temperate bass of the family Percichthyidae, this splendid fish is anadromous like the salmon, migrating up rivers and streams to spawn. So outstanding are its qualities that it was brought 3,000 miles from its native habitat (Atlantic Coast of North America) by rail in the late 1800's for introduction into the Pacific. Twenty years after 432 yearling stripers were released near San Francisco the annual Pacific Coast catch was well over a million pounds. They are a coastal fish, rarely found more than a mile or two from land, frequenting estuaries, bays, rocky headlands, islets, and ledges. Protected by law from commercial exploitation, they are a prime target of surf fishermen. Unfortunately, lack of spawning grounds has seriously depleted populations in recent years, and the California State Department of Fish and Game reports that sport fishing for striped bass in the Sacramento–San Joaquin Delta system may be nearing an end. It is prized for its tenacious fighting ability, its beauty, and its excellence as a table fish. **Range:** from Barkley Sound (British Columbia) to northern Baja California. **Edibility:** excellent.

Three of the large sea basses shown here—the giant sea bass, the jewfish, and the gulf grouper—are being hunted, speared, fished, and driven to extinction, and without close protection they will soon be little more than a memory for Pacific Coast fishermen and divers. The California Department of Fish and Game has declared the giant (black) sea bass, the gulf grouper, and the broomtail grouper "untouchables," and possession of any one of these can result in maximum fines of $1,000 and/or six months in jail.

ADULT

JUVENILE

Giant sea bass, black sea bass (pescara) *Stereolepis gigas*   To 7½ feet and 560 pounds. This majestic giant lives to 70 years of age and is truly awe-inspiring when seen under water. It seeks rocky reef caves and crevices near shore and is found near kelp beds, ledges, and drop-offs at depths from 20 to 150 feet. Unfortunately the fish has been hunted so close to extinction that, unless it is protected, few divers or fishermen will ever see it in the future. The California Department of Fish and Game has declared this sea bass off-limits for fishermen and divers, and penalties of $1,000 and six months in jail can be imposed on those in possession of it. Juveniles are brick red with irregular rows of black spots on the sides. A temperate bass of the family Percichthyidae. **Range:** Humboldt Bay (northern California) to the Gulf of California, but rare north of the Channel Islands (southern California).

The three characteristics that make large sea basses and groupers particularly vulnerable to extermination by spear fishing are accurately summarized by Carl Roessler, writing in *Skindiver Magazine* (December 1976): "First, groupers are curious, intelligent animals, and on a virgin reef will hover above their caves and crevices, watching the approach of even armed spear fishermen without concern. Second, their defensive techniques are solely 3 adapted to escape from fast-swimming predators such as sharks. When pursued, a grouper will 'go to ground,' staring out at the diver from the presumed safety of a reef cave. This is, of course, no defense at all against a spear gun. Finally, and most tragic for the species . . . most grouper and sea bass species change sex from female to male as they mature into adults. Thus, the rationalization used by many spear fishermen that 'we only shoot the big ones' leads to the extermination of all breeding males."

The sexual life of the serranids is unusual. Most sea basses and groupers are hermaphroditic—either male and female at the same time (synchronous hermaphrodites) or maturing first as females and then experiencing a sex reversal to become functioning males (sequential hermaphrodites). An example of the former is the Atlantic belted sandfish (*Serranus subligarius*), closely related to the barred serrano (*S. fasciatus*) shown here. The belted sandfish became famous for its reproductive powers when, isolated in an aquarium, one managed to fertilize its own eggs. Other basses mature first as females and produce eggs. Later in life they reverse sex to become functioning males, which then can fertilize young females.

The term grouper is usually applied to the larger basses belonging to the genera *Epinephelus* and *Mycteroperca*. Some groupers become quite tame after repeated contact with divers, and will rise from their lairs to meet them for daily handouts.

Panama graysby (enjambre) *Epinephelus panamensis*   To 12 inches. One of the smaller sea basses, with tigerlike stripes, blue and orange spots on the head, and (on adults) a large blue-gray spot behind the eye. It has a tigerlike disposition, hiding in rock reefs and crevices and pouncing on smaller prey and even same-sized prey. Walford (1965) states that the teeth of this graysby are depressible and can be easily pushed over and down to lie horizontally, as do the teeth of the jewfish. This allows the fish to swallow much larger prey. Encountered from shallow reefs out to 250-foot depths. **Range:** throughout the Gulf of California to Colombia, including Isla del Coco and the Galapagos Islands. **Edibility:** good.

Kelp bass, calico bass (cabrilla) *Paralabrax clathratus*   To 28½ inches. A famous bass usually ranking at or near the top of the list of fishes important to the southern California party-boat or charter-boat skipper. In good years over one million kelp and sand basses may be hauled in by trawling, set lines, or spear fishing. Young kelp bass prefer kelp beds and seaweed flats in near-shore rocky areas; larger fish live deeper, usually on patch reef and sand to depths of 150 feet. Not aggressively territorial, but because they seldom wander far, overfishing in an area can seriously deplete them. Easily recognized by the calico white spotting on the back and sides. Sometimes confused with the olive or yellowtail rockfishes (see pages 43–44), but the kelp bass is colored quite differently and has a definite basslike look to the head, jaw, and dorsal spines. In four basses of the genus *Paralabrax*—kelp, spotted sand bass, barred sand bass, and goldspotted sand bass—the first two spines in the dorsal fin are shorter than the elongated third dorsal spine. **Range:** Columbia River (Washington) to Bahía Magdalena (Baja California); most abundant in southern California. **Edibility:** good.

Barred sand bass (cabrilla de roca) *Paralabrax nebulifer*   To 25¾ inches and about 8 pounds. A popular and important catch for party-boat fishermen of southern California. Distinguished from the spotted sand bass by the absence of small black spots on the body, this bass does have small gold-brown spots on its head. The hazy bars on its sides are also distinctive. Found near or on rocky bottoms, and often on sandy bottoms at depths from 4 to 120 feet. Divers occasionally find small groups of four to eight of these cabrillas sitting propped up on their pectoral fins on a sandy bottom, waiting for a meal to swim by. A 25-incher was estimated to be 20 years old. **Range:** Santa Cruz (central California) to Bahía Magdalena (Baja California). **Edibility:** good.

5

Spotted sand bass (cabrilla de roca) *Paralabrax maculatofasciatus*   To 22 inches and about 6 pounds. Handsomely and uniquely covered with small black spots, though the spots tend to cluster in vertical cross-bars, sometimes quite bold. Distinguished from the barred sand bass by the fact that only the spotted possesses small black spots rather than solid bars. The young have two dark stripes across the body. True to its name, this fish prefers sandy bottoms near eelgrass flats, rocky reefs, or breakwaters. Often found concealed in eelgrass clearings, apparently waiting to pounce on smaller prey. A welcome catch for party-boat fishermen. **Range:** Monterey Bay (central California) to Mazatlán (Mexico) and the Gulf of California. **Edibility:** good.

Jewfish (mero, guasa) *Epinephelus itajara*   To 8 feet and 700 pounds. This is one of the largest groupers known, found along both coasts of tropical America, inhabiting caves and crevices from 15 to 100 feet. Like the giant sea bass, it is very scarce near shore, owing to overhunting by spear fishermen. Occasionally some fish retaliate: Alex Kerstitch, writing in *Reef Fishes of the Sea of Cortez* (Thomson et al., 1979) reports having to fend off a huge jewfish with a blow on the snout when the fish seemed to take an interest in him as food. Can be separated from the giant sea bass by the very small eye, short dorsal spines, and rounded fins (jewfish) compared to a larger eye, longer spines, and more square-cut fins (giant sea bass). Jewfishes smaller than $1\frac{1}{2}$ feet are very difficult to distinguish from the spotted cabrilla. Counting dorsal spines (11 for the jewfish, 10 for the spotted cabrilla) is the only way to separate them. **Range:** from the central Gulf of California to Peru.

The temperate basses of the family Percichthyidae are closely related to the true basses, family Serranidae. The two temperate basses covered here (of the 40 species known to exist) are the striped bass and the giant sea bass. The soapfishes (family Grammistidae) are unusual tropical fishes. They are small and secretive, and notable for the sudsy, toxic skin mucus they secrete, hence the name "soapfish." ♦

Goldspotted sand bass (extranjero) *Paralabrax auroguttatus*   To 28 inches. Unmistakable, owing to the golden-orange spots covering its body and most fins. Note that the pectoral fin is a pale, clear yellow, the third dorsal spine is quite long, and a pale stripe follows the lateral line. The gill cavity is a bright orange. Often caught by anglers in the Gulf of California over sandy bottoms, in depths from 150 to 250 feet. **Range:** southern California (one record), the Gulf of California, and the coast of Mexico. **Edibility:** good.

Spotted cabrilla (cabrilla pinta) *Epinephelus analogus*   To almost 3 feet (34¼ inches) and 28 pounds. An offshore grouper inhabiting rocky patch reefs at moderate depths to 210 feet. Quite rare north of Baja California, but plentiful in the upper Gulf of California, where Mexican fishermen take it in quantity on handlines. This cabrilla is similar to the juvenile jewfish. Distinctive for its reddish-brown body and fins covered with spots, the vague dark bars on the side, and the rounded caudal fin. **Range:** San Pedro (southern California) and the Gulf of California to Peru and the Galapagos Islands. **Edibility:** good.

Flag cabrilla (cabrilla piedrera) *Epinephelus labriformis*   To 20 inches. A strikingly handsome sea bass distinctive for the snowflakelike white spots that cover its olive-green to reddish-brown body, and for the black blotch or saddle on its caudal peduncle. This cabrilla is most abundant in shallow water and seeks out rocky crevices and hard substrates where it lives a solitary, predatory existence, dashing out of cover from time to time to gobble down smaller victims. The inside of the mouth is red and the tail fin, anal, and soft dorsal fins are all trimmed in red. **Range:** Bahía Magdalena (Baja California) and the Gulf of California south to Peru and the Galapagos Islands. **Edibility:** good.

Gulf coney (baqueta) *Epinephelus acanthistius*   To over 3 feet. The only southern grouper with a rose-red body, high dorsal spines deeply notched (note the very long third dorsal spine), and a bold ''mustache'' following its upper jaw. Once thought quite rare, it is now known to be a deep-dwelling fish (to 300 feet) common throughout the Gulf of California. It is often taken over reefs and sand bottoms on set lines and by shrimp trawlers. **Range:** the Gulf of California to Peru. **Edibility:** excellent.

Snowy grouper (mero) *Epinephelus niveatus*   To 30 inches. These groupers are found off both the Pacific and Atlantic coasts. The young are easily identified by the pearly white spots on a black or chocolate-brown body and a large dark saddle on the caudal peduncle. On groupers larger than 15 inches, these spots fade. Large adults move offshore to 400-foot depths. Occasionally collected in trawls in the Gulf of California. **Range:** San Luis Obispo (central California) to Peru, including the Gulf of California. **Edibility:** good.

Mutton hamlet (guaseta) *Epinephelus afer*   To 1 foot. A strange little sea bass, closely related to the groupers but more often a resident of seagrass beds than of reef holes and crevices. Hobson (1968) reports that it is a secretive night predator, feeding mainly on crustaceans. During the day it is inactive, often lying among seaweed, sometimes on its side. Also found on the Atlantic Coast and in the Caribbean Sea. Distinctive for the stout, forward-directed spine on its cheek, covered by skin. **Range:** upper Gulf of California to Peru and the Galapagos Islands. **Edibility:** good.

Leather bass *Epinephelus dermatolepis*   To 3 feet. Strikingly colored at virtually all phases of growth. Black-barred juveniles seek shelter in the spines of the long-spined sea urchin, *Centrostephanus coronatus*. Thomson et al. (1979) report that older juveniles and adults form complex feeding associations with shoals of grazing fishes, which they use as a "stalking-horse" or blind to enable them to prey on smaller fishes routed by the grazers. Also very adept at changing color to match the fishes they are swimming with. **Range:** Bahía Magdalena (Baja California) and the Gulf of California to Ecuador and the Galapagos Islands. **Edibility:** good.

9

Broomtail grouper (garropa jasplada) *Mycteroperca xenarcha*   To about 4 feet and 100 pounds. Notable for the ragged, torn, broomlike tail-fin profile. Also note the unusual circular rings and vague blotches and scrawls on the back and sides. Quite uncommon on the California coast and even in the Gulf of California. Said to have a preference for mangrove estuaries. This is another grouper that is closely protected in California; heavy fines and/or jail sentences await those who possess it. Juveniles are mottled with light rings and have a black blotch at the rear of the soft dorsal fin. **Range:** San Francisco Bay to Paita, Peru, including the Gulf of California and the Galapagos Islands. **Edibility:** good.

Gulf grouper (baya, cabrilla de astillero) *Mycteroperca jordani*   To 6½ feet and 200 pounds. Another giant grouper that is rapidly being fished to extinction. Rare in California; possession can cost $1,000 and/or six months in jail. One of the commonest large groupers in the upper and central Gulf of California, but where spear fishing is popular (Guaymas–San Carlos), it too is becoming scarce. Often discovered in underwater caves near shore where it is easy prey for spear fishermen. Can rapidly change color from a striped and spotted livery (shown) to a solid brown or gray. Note the square-cut tail fin and straight-edged anal fin. **Range:** La Jolla (southern California) and the Gulf of California to Mazatlán.

Sawtail grouper (garropa jasplada) *Mycteroperca prionura* To 4 feet. This grouper is so similar to the broomtail grouper that the two were long thought the same. In 1967, Rosenblatt and Zahuranec described the sawtail as a distinct species; it is now recognized to be the only southern grouper with both a serrated tail and dark spots. It seems to prefer deeper water than the broomtail, gulf, or leopard groupers. Compare the evenly serrated tail of the sawtail with the unevenly serrated tail of the broomtail. **Range:** from Islas Santa Inéz through the central and lower Gulf of California to Puerto Vallarta (Mexico). **Edibility:** good.

Leopard grouper, golden grouper (cabrilla sardinera, cabrilla calamarera) *Mycteroperca rosacea* To 3 feet and 40 pounds. A beautiful fish. The small reddish-brown spots over the body enclosed in vague silver-gray reticulations give this grouper a leopardlike appearance. Often has a dark streak or "mustache" above the jaw and white margins as well as stripes and spots on all vertical fins. A few (about 1 percent) of these groupers metamorphose into a golden phase that, when seen in the water even from a nearby boat, is a startling sight—a golden fish! Leopard groupers are shallow-water fishes and tend to cluster in large congregations over rocky reefs toward noon, placid and unperturbed until dusk falls, at which time they become true leopards of the reef, feeding hungrily on sardines, herrings, and anchovies. As one Spanish name indicates, they also favor squid (*calamares*) when available. They will team together to drive shoals of smaller fishes to the surface. **Range:** Bahía Magdalena (Baja California) and the Gulf of California to Puerto Vallarta (Mexico). **Edibility:** good.

SPOTTED PHASE

GOLDEN PHASE

11

Pacific sand perch (cabaicucho) *Diplectrum pacificum*   To 9 inches. A rather plain, drab little fish for a sea bass, but one that blends in nicely on a sandy bottom. Found on soft bottoms from shallow to 100-foot depths. Like its Atlantic cousin, *D. formosum*, it may excavate a burrow or trench in a sand flat near a patch reef from which it will ambush smaller prey. Note the two body stripes and the black spot at the tail base. **Range:** Bahía Magdalena (Baja California) and through-out the Gulf of California to Panama.

Barred serrano (serrano) *Serranus fasciatus*   To 7 inches. This serrano is often found in seagrass beds and around rocks, sandy bottoms, shell fragments, and coral rubble from shore out to 200-foot depths. Like most basses, a solitary hunter, lying in wait to attack smaller prey. Closely related to the western Atlantic lantern bass, *S. baldwini*, with similar habits and coloration, even to the rows of six to eight spots and bars on the back and sides. The lantern bass, however, grows to only about 2½ inches. **Range:** throughout the Gulf of California (quite common in the central and lower parts) to Peru and the Galapagos Islands.

Splittail bass, rose threadfin bass (cabrilla rosa) *Hemanthias peruanus*   To 15 inches. This beauty is well named for its soft rose color tinged with yellow, the greatly extended third dorsal spine or threadfin, and its lavish, flowing, split tail fin. It is unmistakable when caught, which happens rarely. Found from shallow water out to 348 feet. **Range:** Redondo Beach (southern California) and the Gulf of California to Chile. **Edibility:** good.

Pacific creolefish (indio, rabirubia de lo alto) *Paranthias colonus*   To 14 inches. A handsome flame-colored fish closely related to the Atlantic creolefish (*P. furcifer*) but with significant differences in color and body proportions. Often seen in small groups high in the water column picking off plankton that swarm about the surface. Note the five light spots on the back, and the large, lunate tail. Young are bright yellow with five small dark spots on the back. **Range:** central and lower Gulf of California to Peru, including offshore islands. **Edibility:** good.

Rainbow basslet *Liopropoma fasciatum*   To 6 inches. A recently discovered and brilliantly colored little sea bass that unfortunately is rarely seen because it inhabits reef caves and crevices at 200- to 250-foot depths. This fish was thought by one of its first collectors to be a wrasse because of the brilliant, wrasselike colors. It is closely related to the Swissguard basslet (*L. rubre*) and the candy basslet (*L. carmabi*) found in the Bahamas, Florida, and the Caribbean Sea. First encountered in the Gulf of California, collected, and then displayed at the Scripps aquarium in La Jolla, California. **Range:** Central Gulf of California to Cabo San Lucas and south to Panama.

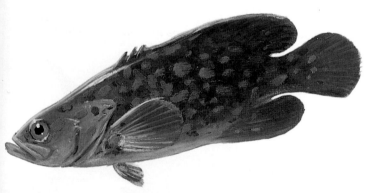

Cortez soapfish (jabonero de Cortés) *Rypticus bicolor*   To 1 foot. The soapfishes are named for the sudslike mucus they produce when caught or handled. This secretion is toxic and is probably useful in warding off predators. The Cortez soapfish is inactive during daylight hours, staying hidden in reef ledges and crevices, but emerges at night when its dark coloration enables it to prey successfully on smaller fishes. Found from near shore to 200 feet. A similar fish, the blackfin soapfish (*R. nigripinnis*) is colored much like the Cortez soapfish and swims over much of the same range. It differs in being smaller (to only about 8 inches), in having only two dorsal spines (the Cortez has three), and in its rounded chin (the chin of the Cortez is pointed). **Range:** both species found throughout the Gulf of California to Peru.

14

TUNAS AND MACKERELS

At the turn of the century, when tuna sportfishing was still in its infancy, Charles F. Holder (1910) wrote stirringly on the joys and terrors of big-bluefin-tuna fishing. "Your boatman is ready for you at six, the lunch is stowed and you pull out into Avalon Bay [Santa Catalina Island] over 'he glasslike sea. The east is a blaze of red, and the placid waters reflect it and the rocks of the precipitous shore. The air is soft, like velvet on the cheek, and there is a crispness in the morning. . . .

"Jim whispers 'look out, sir,' and you turn your head to see three or four flyingfish coming through the air, flushed by the unseen tuna. The blood starts through your veins; your companion, who perchance has never caught a tuna, turns pale and trembles . . . one flyingfish passes over the boat, you duck your head to avoid it . . . and then a mass of white silvery foam leaps upward. There is a blaze of silver, then loud musical notes, z-e-e-e, z-e-e-e, z-e-e-e, rise on the air as the splendid reel gives tongue, and the fight is on. The tuna turns and rushes seaward, tearing at the line, taking feet, yards, and has 500 feet of line perhaps, before the boatman has his boat under sternway, and then begins the contest, ranging ac-

Bluefin tuna (atún de aleta azul, atún azul) *Thunnus thynnus* To 6 feet, 2 inches and 300 pounds. The giant of the scombrid family and among the largest fishes in the world. A 1,600-pound, 14-foot tuna was taken off New Jersey. For some reason, probably diet, our Pacific Coast bluefins grow to only about a third the size of Atlantic Coast tunas. Unfortunately, the efficiency of the modern fishing industry is pushing these magnificent fishes toward extinction and the older fish have long been depleted. Note the short pectoral fin not extending beyond the first dorsal fin, and the white markings on the belly. **Range:** worldwide; in the eastern Pacific from Shelikof Strait (Alaska) to southern Baja California; most common south of Los Angeles. **Edibility:** excellent.

15

cording to the individuals, from 10 minutes to 14 hours. At times the game rushes down into the deep channel; again it plays entirely on the surface, varying the performance by repeated rushes at the boat, to turn and dart away again to the melodious clicking of the reel."

Holder tells of a 125-pound tuna that fought a fisherman for five hours. The fish had towed the boat ten miles off-shore—20 miles in all. The angler gave up, exhausted; the boatman took the rod and continued the battle for two more hours. Then, in a heavy and dangerous sea, out of sight of port, a council of war was held. The anglers could fight no longer—they were too far from shore. They surrendered, and the noble fish was ignominiously pulled in by hand—still so full of vigor that it almost swamped the boat at the gaffing.

The tuna has been a vital resource for man for thousands of years. Above the Bay of Biscay a Spanish cave drawing made during the ice age clearly shows the giant fish. In his *History of Animals,* Aristotle recorded observations about its ages and growth. Yet today the predictability of the bluefin tuna's marathon migrations between its spawning and feeding grounds threatens its very existence. Every year these magnificent fishes must survive voracious fishing with purse seines, gigantic set nets, and fishing traps, superseiner fleets, longline fishing fleets, and fleets of pole-and-line sport fishermen. Fleet capacity far exceeds the potential tuna catch, and the bluefin fishery is in catastrophic decline worldwide. In 1962, Japanese longline fishermen brought in 400,000 tons of tuna on 400 million baited hooks. In 1980 the Japanese longline fleet of 300 ships captured only 4,000 tons of bluefin. A gigantic miles-long fish trap near Gibraltar caught 18,000 bluefin a year from 1929 to 1962. It peaked in 1949 with 43,500 fish. It is now trapping less than 2,000 per year. Other fisheries of the world report the same massive decline. The older fish have been depleted. Prior to 1965, three-to-six-year-old bluefins predominated. Today, one-to-three-year-old fishes are being taken. When the young fish are gone, the end of the bluefin tuna is near.

The tunas and mackerels—members of the family Scombridae—are fork-tailed, heavily muscled fishes built for a roving, predaceous existence near the ocean's surface. All tunas—albacore, yellowfin, skipjacks, and bonitos—and most mackerels are favorite game for shore and offshore

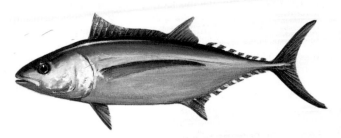

Albacore, longfin tuna (albacora, atún) *Thunnus alalunga* To about 4½ feet and 96 pounds. Considered by Pacific Coast fishermen to be one of the gamest fighting fishes. It is also the finest food fish of all the tunas, especially for canning (the only fish that can be labeled as "white meat tuna"). Albacores make incredible trans-Pacific migrations from Mexican, U.S., and Alaskan waters to Japan and back again—a 12,000- to 15,000-mile journey. Once thought to be drastically depleted after many years of scarcity, populations seem to have replenished over time. The albacore is easily identified by the very long black pectoral fin reaching to the rear of the second dorsal fin, and the yellow sides and finlets near the tail; usually has seven to nine dorsal finlets and seven or eight anal finlets. **Range:** worldwide in temperate seas but rare in the tropics; here, from southeast Alaska to Isla de Guadalupe (off north-central Baja California). **Edibility:** excellent.

Yellowfin tuna (atún de aleta amarilla) *Thunnus albacares* To 6 feet, 4 inches and 450 pounds. A brilliantly iridescent fish when taken from the water, with gold, blue, and yellow reflections pulsing across the body, but these colors fade quickly as the fish dies. The yellowfin differs from the bluefin in having a long pectoral fin reaching but not extending past the base of the anal fin. All fins are tinged with yellow and the finlets by the tail are bright yellow. The second dorsal and anal fins are greatly elongated in large adults, as shown here. Usually found in more-southern waters, it is fished commercially along the Mexican coast, in the Gulf of California, and out to the Galapagos Islands. **Range:** wide-ranging across the tropical Atlantic, Pacific, and Indian oceans; here, Point Conception (central California) to the Gulf of California and Peru. **Edibility:** excellent.

17

fishermen on the Pacific Coast, both for their fighting qualities and excellent food value. They are fast swimmers that strike hard and pull hard. The yellowfin tuna is in the big-game class, reaching 450 pounds, though the average taken is 30 to 50 pounds. The albacore, a smaller tuna, is considered one of the gamest fighting fishes of the sea and the finest food of all tunas, commonly known as "chicken of the sea." Skipjacks are small, almost scaleless tunas valuable for food and fished commercially in Mexican and Central American waters. They have been observed offshore in schools of 50,000 fishes. The bonito tunas delight anglers from Alaska to Baja California with their fighting spirit and splendid colors.

Huge schools of Pacific, frigate, bullet, and sierra mackerels sweep along the Pacific Coast in the summer and fall, and are a bonanza for sport and commercial fishermen. Some, like the Pacific mackerel, may be abundant one year and relatively scarce the next. The wahoo is a fighting fish and a favorite of light-tackle fishermen. It is circumtropical, and acclaimed for its excellent flavor. ◆

Black skipjack, Mexican little tunny (barrilete negro, negra) *Euthynnus lineatus* To about 3 feet, 3 inches. An abundant skipjack in southern waters from Cabo San Lucas and the Gulf of California to Isla del Coco. The flesh of the black skipjack is very dark, but is reported to be very good eating. Note the almost contiguous spiny and soft dorsal fins, the large dark spots under the pectoral fin, and the black stripes on the back. The stripes on the back and the faint stripes on the belly often fade quickly after death. The body is scaleless except for a corselet of scales around the pectoral fins. **Range:** San Simeon (central California) to Colombia and the Galapagos Islands; rare north of Baja California. **Edibility:** good.

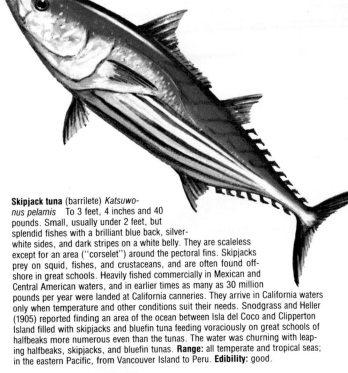

Skipjack tuna (barrilete) *Katsuwo-
nus pelamis*   To 3 feet, 4 inches and 40
pounds. Small, usually under 2 feet, but
splendid fishes with a brilliant blue back, silver-
white sides, and dark stripes on a white belly. They are scaleless
except for an area ("corselet") around the pectoral fins. Skipjacks
prey on squid, fishes, and crustaceans, and are often found offshore in great schools. Heavily fished commercially in Mexican and
Central American waters, and in earlier times as many as 30 million
pounds per year were landed at California canneries. They arrive in California waters
only when temperature and other conditions suit their needs. Snodgrass and Heller
(1905) reported finding an area of the ocean between Isla del Coco and Clipperton
Island filled with skipjacks and bluefin tuna feeding voraciously on great schools of
halfbeaks more numerous even than the tunas. The water was churning with leaping halfbeaks, skipjacks, and bluefin tunas. **Range:** all temperate and tropical seas;
in the eastern Pacific, from Vancouver Island to Peru. **Edibility:** good.

Mexican bonito, striped bonito (bonito) *Sarda orientalis*   To 2½ feet. This wide-
ranging tropical bonito is found in the western Atlantic, in the Indo-Pacific, around
Hawaii, and from the coast of Mexico to Peru. It differs from the Pacific bonito and
skipjacks in having horizontal lines on its back above its lateral line and no spots
under the pectoral fin. Dorsal finlets number seven to nine; anal finlets are six
or seven. The flesh is white and reported to be tasty. **Range:** Bahía Magdalena
and outer Baja California coast to Peru; uncommon in the Gulf of California. **Edibility:** good.

19

Pacific bonito (bonito) *Sarda chiliensis* To 3 feet, 4 inches. A delight for anglers from Alaska to Baja California because of its fighting spirit and splendid colors. The back is brilliant blue with oblique dark slanting stripes, the sides are silvery, and the belly is white. When lifted aboard a charter boat fresh from the sea, it is a beautiful sight. The dorsal fins are set close together; there are seven to nine dorsal finlets and six or seven anal finlets. The body is fully scaled. This bonito is fished near the shore, where it swims in large schools in pursuit of squid and small fishes. In southern California they spawn from January to May. **Range:** two populations, one from the Gulf of Alaska to southern Baja California and Islas Revillagigedo, the other from Peru to Chile; between, from Mexico to Peru, the gap is filled by the Mexican bonito. **Edibility:** fair—a popular canned fish in some areas.

Frigate mackerel (bonito) *Auxis thazard* To 1 foot, 8 inches. Like the Pacific bonito, this mackerel will school inshore in summer and fall, but its appearance is irregular. Although not highly valued as food, it is used as a bait fish. A very similar fish, the bullet mackerel (*A. rochei*), closely resembles the frigate but has 15 or more diagonal bars on its back, whereas the frigate has 15 or more oblique, wavy lines. Both fish usually have eight dorsal finlets and seven anal finlets. **Range** (both species): from Redondo Beach (southern California) to Peru. **Edibility:** poor.

Pacific mackerel, chub mackerel (escombro, caballa) *Scomber japonicus*   To about 2 feet and 6 pounds. This mackerel has the most catholic of tastes and will snap eagerly at anything offered, from live bait to dry flies, squid, shrimps, and even sparerib bones. Huge schools sweep along the Pacific Coast in summer and fall. They are most abundant between Monterey (California) and southern Baja California, often traveling in the company of other fishes, including small bluefin tunas. Quite similar to the frigate and bullet mackerels with about 30 irregular bars on the back, but the Pacific mackerel has scales all over its body, the other two species only in corselets around the pectoral fins. Usually five finlets behind the dorsal and anal fins. **Range:** worldwide in temperate and subtropical seas; here, from Alaska to Cabo San Lucas (Baja California). **Edibility:** good fresh, canned, or smoked.

Sierra mackerel, Pacific sierra (sierra, cero, escombro) *Scomberomorus sierra*   To 2 feet, 8 inches. A handsome, slender mackerel with several rows of golden spots along the sides. These tend to fade as the fish matures. This, the most abundant game fish along the Mexican and Central American coasts, is so common in some areas that anglers out for bigger game consider it a nuisance. It runs in large schools within a mile of shore pursuing smaller schooling fishes. Easily recognized by its slender shape and gold-spotted sides, it is silver-blue above and silvery below. **Range:** La Jolla (southern California) to Peru, including the Gulf of California and the Galapagos Islands. **Edibility:** good.

Gulf sierra, Monterey Spanish mackerel (sierra, cero, escombro) *Scomberomorus concolor*   To 2 feet, 4½ inches. Very similar to the sierra mackerel except that males lack the rows of golden spots on the sides. Females have two alternating rows of brown spots on the sides. During the 1870's this mackerel was common in Monterey Bay, and was an expensive delicacy in San Francisco markets. In the late 1880's it vanished from northern California and has never returned. It is now abundant only in the northern Gulf of California; occasional stragglers reach southern California (most recently in 1958, but apparently not since). They swim in schools, usually inshore. **Range:** Monterey Bay to Baja California and the Gulf of California. **Edibility:** good.

Wahoo (peto, guahu) *Acanthocybium solanderi*   To 7 feet and 100 pounds. This famous fighter takes off so fast on its initial run that light-tackle fishermen must pursue it full throttle to prevent their lines from being stripped. If it can be checked, the wahoo provides a superb battle of great leaps, soundings, and long runs. The wahoo is unmistakable, having a long, slender, cigar-shaped body, sharply pointed head, and close-set triangular teeth. Also note the very long first dorsal fin and series of nine dorsal finlets. The finlets and body shape show a relationship to the tunas and mackerels, but the peculiar gills indicate that it is also related to the swordfishes and spearfishes. **Range:** circumtropical; here, from Cabo San Lucas (Baja California) to Isla del Coco; Walford (1965) reports it as common at Panama and in the Galapagos Islands. **Edibility:** excellent when cut into steaks—in Hawaii its name is *ono*, meaning sweet.

JACKS, AMBERJACKS, SCAD, POMPANOS, AND ROOSTERFISHES

The offshore jacks of the family Carangidae are powerful, fleet-finned, silvery fishes that range the ocean in predatory packs. Frequently they will sweep in over the reefs to feed on resident fishes, depending on their speed of attack to kill. Their swiftness and tenacity provide a real challenge to the fisherman who hooks one, and some jacks are ferocious fighting fishes. They rarely break out of the water, but take punishing runs and dives for deep water. They never give in until completely exhausted, and even small juveniles are dauntless fighters.

Yellowtail (jurel de aleta amarilla) *Seriola lalandei*   To 5 feet and 80 pounds. Truly handsome, powerful, yellow-striped fishes, favorites of party-boats in southern California. Yellowtails school off San Diego in the spring, appear off Los Angeles a month later, and vanish when autumn comes. In the winter, Gulf of California anglers catch yellowtails by trolling off rocky points or by anchoring and jigging among the schools. Hungry packs of yellowtails will drive schools of mackerel, anchovies, smelts, or sardines into tight circles, then eat their way through the massed schools. Today the yellowtail is much reduced in numbers. Holder, writing in 1910, reported such a feeding maelstrom in the Bay of Avalon at Catalina Island, where seemingly thousands of fishes tinted the waters a golden hue. Sadly, those days are gone forever. Note the all-yellow fins and the yellow (sometimes dusky) sidestripe; also a dark stripe slanting obliquely from the nose through the eye. Young under 5 inches have dark bars on the sides. Adults breed offshore, milling in circles near the surface, streaming milt and roe. Called *S. lalandi dorsalis* or *S. dorsalis* by some researchers. **Range:** British Columbia to Chile, including the Gulf of California. **Edibility:** excellent, either fresh or smoked.

Pacific Coast jacks display a wide range of body shapes and sizes. The roving offshore fishes include the moderately deep-bodied jacks of the genus *Caranx*, the amberjacks (*Seriola*), the cigar-shaped scads (*Decapterus*), the jack mackerel (*Trachurus*), and the rainbow runner (*Elagatis*). The deep-bodied and compressed pompanos, permits, and palometas (genera *Trachinotus* and *Alectis*) and the highly compressed and high-browed lookdowns and moonfishes (*Selene*) are inshore fishes that feed on crustaceans, mollusks, and small fishes found over sand flats and beaches, around reefs, and over mud bottoms. Some of the jacks shown here are circumtropical, occurring around the world in warm tropical seas. There are about 200 species of jacks worldwide; 21 are covered here, most of them rare north of southern California.

Many juvenile carangids display bold or light vertical bars. These bars usually disappear as the fish matures.

Roosterfishes, of the family Nematistiidae, are closely related to the jacks. They are one of the outstanding game fishes of the Pacific Coast, with long dorsal fins that are erected when the fish is excited. ◆

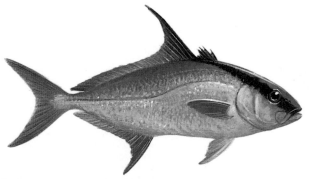

Almaco jack, Pacific amberjack (jurel de castilla, pez fuerte) *Seriola rivoliana*   To almost 5 feet (59 inches) and 126 pounds, usually 50 to 60 pounds. Another roving offshore predator similar to and sometimes confused with the yellowtail, but deeper-bodied, with much longer soft dorsal and anal fin lobes. Most fins are dark or dusky, not yellow. The color is variable, usually metallic bronze, gray, or bluish green. Usually a bold, black stripe extends from the nose through the eye to the upper back, and sometimes a brassy mid-stripe from the nose to the tail. Young (until about 7 or 8 inches long) display five or six bars on the body. A popular sport fish in the lower Gulf of California. In earlier literature called *S. colburni*. **Range:** circumtropical; here, Oceanside (southern California) to Peru, including the Gulf of California and the Galapagos Islands. **Edibility:** good.

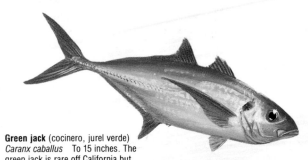

Green jack (cocinero, jurel verde)
Caranx caballus To 15 inches. The
green jack is rare off California but
quite common from Guaymas in the Gulf of California south to Peru. It frequents
shallow reefs but is more often found offshore in schools. Although a small fish, it
is popular with anglers because of its pugnacity on light tackle. Note the slender
body (for a jack), long pectoral fin, spot on the rear of the gill cover, and the scutes
following the rear of the lateral line to the tail. The breast is completely scaled.
Young to 7 inches have seven or eight broad bars on the body and one on the
head. These bars are often seen in larger living fish, but they fade soon after boating. **Range:** Santa Cruz Island (southern California) to Peru and the Galapagos Islands. **Edibility:** fair.

Crevalle jack, common jack, cavally (toro, cavalla, jiguagua) *Caranx hippos* To
30 inches. This jack is very common along the shores of the Gulf of California and
south to Ecuador. A fierce, stubborn, and tenacious game fish, a 20-pounder on
light tackle may fight for an hour. Valuable as a food fish, especially in Central
American markets. Smaller jacks are said to be good eating, but those over 1½ feet
are reputed to be dark and have poor flavor. Note the heavy body, steeply rounded
head, scutes near the tail fin, spot on the opercle, and the light spot on the pectoral
fin. Juveniles, called *tana* in Mexico, have five bars on the body and one on the
head, and are often taken in the surf by adroit net fishermen. Rare north of Baja
California, but one crevalle was taken in San Diego Harbor. **Range:** circumtropical;
here, San Diego to Ecuador, including the Gulf of California. **Edibility:** see above. 25

Black jack, brown jack (jurel negro) *Caranx lugubris*   To 3 feet. An unusual, rare jack swimming worldwide in tropical waters, and almost always taken at isolated or offshore islands. In the Atlantic, it is a sport fish of some importance off the Bahama Banks. Distinctive for the blackish-brown color, deep body, blunt head, and thick lips. Also note the long pectoral fins, the long soft dorsal and anal fin lobes, and the prominent scutes along the rear half of the lateral line. Deep-swimming fishes, they have been taken from 650-foot depths. **Range:** circumtropical; in the eastern Pacific at the Galapagos Islands, Clipperton Island, Islas Revillagigedo, and at Los Frailes near Cabo San Lucas (Baja California). **Edibility:** conflicting reports; in the Atlantic it is called *caranx-le-garbage* because of poor taste, yet in Polynesia it is "the most tasty of all the jacks—never tough and never dry."

Blue crevalle (jurel) *Caranx melampygus*   To 3 feet. A splendid jack with a silvery blue-green body; scattered black and bright-blue spots or stars with golden specks and highlights over head, back, and sides; and brilliant neon-blue color at the bases of the dorsal and anal fins. Pectoral fins are yellow. A pelagic fish that hunts in schools and packs, it likes to sweep into shallow reefs to prey on schools of smaller fishes. A very old fisherman on Rangiroa Atoll in Polynesia remembers that in some years the water of his shallow lagoon would shimmer with blue and gold as thousands of blue crevalles entered the mouth of the reef. Older fish become deeper-bodied, more densely covered with black spots. **Range:** Indo-Pacific and eastern Pacific from Cabo San Lucas (Baja California) to Panama, including Islas Revillagigedo and Isla del Coco. **Edibility:** good.

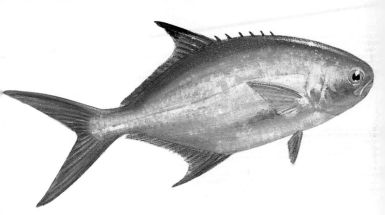

Paloma pompano (pámpano) *Trachinotus paitensis*   To 20 inches and 5 pounds. This is one of the finest food fishes. Excellent game fish on light tackle, they are extremely nervous and unpredictable when stalked; rooting close inshore over sandy bottoms for mollusks and crustaceans, they may show anglers a tail or flank, then bolt. Young are much like adults in form. Adults are similar to the adult permit. Note the black-tipped dorsal fin lobe, rounded head, blunt nose, small mouth, and short, stubby pectoral fin. A close relative of the Florida pompano (*T. carolinus*). **Range:** Redondo Beach (southern California) to Peru, including the Gulf of California and the Galapagos Islands; rare north of Baja California. **Edibility:** excellent.

Yellow jack, yellow-barred jack, golden jack (pompano rayado) *Gnathanodon speciosus*   To 3 feet. These are beautiful golden animals, especially as juveniles when their sides look like hammered, golden plate with 10 to 12 dark stripes, but the colors fade soon after boating. One of the few jacks without teeth as an adult, the yellow jack has a strongly protusible mouth with which it feeds on invertebrates and small fishes. Juveniles are "pilot" fishes, seeking out larger predators such as sharks for protection. I was diving in Kaneohe Bay, Hawaii, when a tiny yellow jack stationed itself just in front of the faceplate of my diving mask. I tried time and again to lose him, but each time I returned to the water, there he was—right between my eyes. Finally, I was laughing so hard I couldn't swim and had to return to the beach. **Range:** Indo-Pacific and in the eastern Pacific from Isla Carmen (Gulf of California) to Guaymas and south to Panama. **Edibility:** excellent.

ADULT

African pompano, threadfin, threadfish (flechudo) *Alectis ciliaris* To 15 inches. This unusual carangid ranges from Mazatlán to Panama in the eastern Pacific and is also found on the Atlantic Coast of America and in Hawaii, central Polynesia, Micronesia and Melanesia, the East Indies, the Indian Ocean, and Africa. The juveniles, as shown, are little diamond-shaped beauties with long filaments trailing from the first four or five rays of their dorsal and anal fins, hence the name threadfin or threadfish. The filaments usually (but not always) become progressively shorter with age. The adult, as shown, is so different from the juvenile that it was at one time classed as a separate species, *Hynnis hopkinsi* or goggle-eye jack. Found along bays and beaches in shallow, clear water. **Range:** see above. **Edibility:** poor.

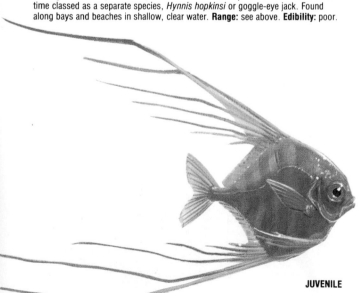

JUVENILE

Pacific permit, palometa, longfin pompano (pámpano) *Trachinotus kennedyi* To 3 feet. The permit is the dedicated angler's delight and agony. Very wary and skittish, they can wear an angler down by their unwillingness to take a baited hook. From 30 minutes to 3 hours may be required to land a large permit on light tackle. A fine food fish, though not as succulent as the paloma pompano. The common name longfin pompano refers to juvenile permits, which have very deep bodies and long, curved, soft dorsal and anal fin lobes extending back almost to the tail fin. The young permits appear quite similar to gafftopsail pompanos except that they lack the bars on the sides. As the permit matures, the long, trailing fins become progressively shorter and the fish becomes the rounded, stubby, short-finned adult shown here. Note the black blotch at the pectoral fin base. Also called Culver pompano, *T. culveri*. **Range:** Bahía Magdalena (Baja California) and the Gulf of California to Ecuador. **Edibility:** excellent.

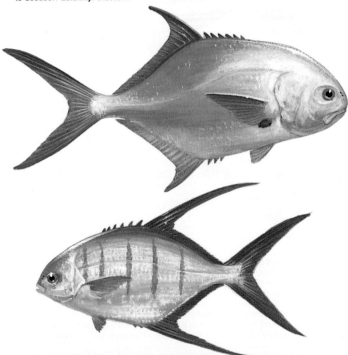

Gafftopsail pompano (pámpanito) *Trachinotus rhodopus* To 2 feet. Very common in the Gulf of California, often schooling in silvery packs of a few dozen to hundreds of fishes—a splendid sight to see. They frequent sandy, exposed shores and inshore reefs, where they have been observed feeding on zooplankton near the surface. Distinctive for the four or five bars on their sides, the very long, soft dorsal and anal fin lobes, and the yellow to reddish fins. A very similar Atlantic Coast relative is the Atlantic gafftopsail pompano (*T. goodei*). **Range:** Zuma Beach (southern California) to Peru, including the Gulf of California and the Galapagos Islands; rare north of Baja California. **Edibility:** good.

Pacific lookdown (jorobado) *Selene oerstedii* To 1 foot. Similar to the moonfish in shape, but with a much deeper body and more steeply sloping forehead. Fishermen also call it moonfish, hunchback, horsehead, dollarfish, and hair-finned silverfish. Juveniles look much like the African pompano juvenile. Note the long, trailing threads on the soft dorsal and anal fins and the long pectoral fin. Lookdowns are very slim, compressed, platelike fishes; when seen from the front they are wafer-thin. Like moonfishes, they swim in large silvery schools near shore. **Range:** Bahía Magdalena (Baja California) and the lower Gulf of California to Peru. **Edibility:** good.

Pacific moonfish (pez luna, jorobado) *Selene peruviana* To 10 inches. The names fishermen give this fish are descriptive and graphic: horsefish, pug-nosed shiner, and blunt-nosed shiner; *jorobado* is Spanish for hunchback. Moonfishes are very shiny, silvery, and platelike, and swim inshore in large schools. They are impressive when seen from the side in schools; if viewed head-on their wafer-thin bodies make them almost invisible. Similar to the Pacific lookdown, but the body is not so deep nor the head so steeply sloping. Also note the very low, soft dorsal and anal fins and the black spot at the upper edge of the operculum. Called *Vomer declivifrons* in earlier literature. **Range:** Redondo Beach (southern California) and the lower Gulf of California to Peru; rare north of Baja California. **Edibility:** good.

Jack mackerel, California horse mackerel (charrito) *Trachurus symmetricus* To 32 inches. These jacks run in large schools offshore to 600 miles and also travel inshore. They feed on krill, squid, anchovies, and lanternfishes, and are a movable feast for many larger predators including yellowtail, sea basses, seals, sea lions, porpoises, swordfishes, and pelicans. Often fished for sport off piers and from boats, they are also a prime target of commercial fishermen and an important cannery fish. Juveniles often school near kelp beds, piers, and breakwaters. Note the large eye, long pectoral fin, scutes along the entire lateral line, and the dip of the lateral line at the tip of the pectoral fin. The spiny dorsal fin is a bit higher than the soft dorsal; there is a black blotch at the top rear of the gill cover. **Range:** southeast Alaska to southern Baja California, the Gulf of California, and the Galapagos Islands. **Edibility:** good.

Bigeye scad (ojotón) *Selar crumenophthalmus* To 16 inches. Easily recognized by its very large eye and often called such names as goggler, goggle-eyed jack, and horse-eyed jack. A slender jack, mackerel-like in form, esteemed as a food fish in Central America. Not much valued as a game fish but a popular live-bait fish. Occurs inshore and on outer reefs in large schools. **Range:** circumtropical; here, from Cabo San Lucas (Baja California) to Panama. **Edibility:** fair.

Pacific bumper (horqueta, monda) *Chloroscombrus orqueta* To 1 foot. A schooling jack usually found in shallow inshore areas, often entering brackish water. Bumpers frequently make a grunting sound when caught on hook and line. Note the long pectoral fin and the long, soft dorsal and anal fins reaching almost to the tail; a black blotch at the top of the gill cover; and a dark spot at the top of the caudal peduncle. Dorsal and anal fins have dark margins. **Range:** San Pedro (southern California) to Peru. **Edibility:** good.

31

Pilotfish (pez piloto, romero) *Naucrates ductor*   To 2 feet. Unique, both as juveniles and as adults, and legends about them are as old as the ancient Greeks. Long thought to guide sharks and whales, and even to steer lost ships and swimmers to land, these jacks do not guide but merely swim in the company of large sharks, whales, rays, various schools of fishes, and sailing ships, usually alongside or following; a pilotfish has been recorded following a sailing ship for 80 days. Why they do so is a mystery—probably it is a way of finding food by hitch-hiking under or alongside the larger animal or ship. Pilotfishes often eat smaller fishes. Strangely, juveniles will shelter under the bells and among the stinging tentacles of jellyfishes in the open sea. Notable for the five to seven bold bars on the sides and the low spinous dorsal fin with four spines. In Hawaii, known as the ''annexation fish'' because it appeared in some numbers around the islands in 1898 at the time of annexation to the United States. **Range:** Vancouver Island to the Galapagos Islands, including the Gulf of California. **Edibility:** poor.

Mexican scad (jurel fino, caballa Mexicana) *Decapterus scombrinus* To 18¼ inches. Swims inshore and offshore in large schools from the surface to 78-foot depths. Distinctive for the single isolated finlets in back of the dorsal and anal fins and for the well-developed scutes along the rear (straight part) of the lateral line. Also note the spot on the gill cover and reddish side stripe. Sometimes mistaken for the jack mackerel, but the jack has scutes along the entire lateral line. **Range:** Pacific Grove (central California) to the Galapagos Islands. **Edibility:** fair.

Yellowtail leatherjacket (zapatero) *Oligoplites saurus* To 1 foot. Leatherjackets are schooling jacks usually found along sandy beaches, inlets, and bays, and often caught in the surf with beach nets. Very sharp dorsal and anal fin spines can inflict injury if carelessly handled: the anal spines are venomous. Not classed as game fishes, large ones can nevertheless be tough and stubborn fighters on light tackle. Three other Pacific leatherjackets are the bigmouthed (*O. mundus*), the smallmouthed (*O. altus*), and the slender (*O. refulgens*). **Range:** *O. saurus*, Gulf of California to Panama; *O. mundus*, Gulf of California to Ecuador; *O. altus* and *O. refulgens*, Panama to Golfo de Guayaquil (Ecuador). **Edibility:** poor.

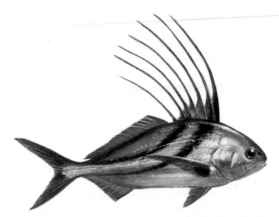

Roosterfish (papagallo, gallo, pez de gallo) *Nematistius pectoralis*   To 4 feet and 100 pounds. A beautiful iridescent animal and one of the great game fishes of the Pacific Coast for light-tackle angling. A 20-pounder will make a startling first run with its roosterlike comb high above the water. Reeled in, it will make several wild dashes for freedom before tiring. Easily recognized, even as juveniles, by the comb of the long threadlike dorsal fin spines. Also note the two dark, curved stripes on the body and the dark spot at the pectoral fin base. Fished in shallow inshore areas, usually sandy shores along beaches. Seems to erect the long dorsal fin when excited, or as offense or defense. When relaxed, the fin is lowered into a sheath along the back. A member of the family Nematistiidae, closely related to the jacks. **Range:** San Clemente (southern California) to Peru, including the Gulf of California and the Galapagos Islands. **Edibility:** excellent.

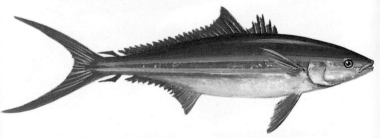

Rainbow runner (salmón) *Elagatis bipinnulata*   To 4 feet. A handsome blue-and-gold-striped fish, physically similar to the amberjacks, wide-ranging but quite rare. It is known from Cabo San Lucas to the Galapagos Islands and Isla del Coco in the eastern Pacific; and it ranges throughout Oceania from Hawaii to Australia, both coasts of Africa, and the western Atlantic from Massachusetts to Venezuela. The rainbow runner is found in bays and along beaches, preferring clear water, swift currents, and sandy bottoms. Distinctive for the blue back, gold midstripe between two light-blue stripes, yellow tail, and the single finlets following the soft dorsal and anal fins. It is often seen swimming with sharks and pilotfishes. An esteemed game fish when taken on light tackle, said to rank with the yellowtail and attracted to the same lures. **Range:** circumtropical; see above. **Edibility:** excellent.

ROCKFISHES AND SCORPIONFISHES

Over 100 years ago a perceptive ichthyologist gave the generic name *Sebastes*, meaning "magnificent," to the rockfishes of the family Scorpaenidae. Rockfishes are not only splendid, but unusual in many ways, and very numerous. The genus *Sebastes* is rich in species—69 so far identified—and new species are still being discovered. Fish experts puzzle over how and why these basslike fishes have evolved into so many separate species; *Sebastes* is the largest genus on the U.S.–Canadian Pacific coast. Like Darwin's finches in the Galapagos, rockfishes seem to have developed a multitude of adaptive types from one or a few common ancestors. Some rockfishes prefer rocky reef caves and crevices, and others float in great schools midway in the water column. Others live almost exclusively in and around kelp beds. Some seek out shallow tidepools and inshore bay areas, and others frequent deep offshore banks over rocky or soft bottoms from 100 to 2,500 feet.

The colors and markings of many of the rockfishes are outstanding; some are almost tropical in their brilliance

China rockfish *Sebastes nebulosus*
To 17 inches. A truly remarkable, unmistakable fish with a bluish-black body slashed, speckled, and spotted with yellow-gold. The broad yellow stripe is unique. The China rockfish hugs rocky reef crevices inshore and out to 400-foot depths, and is quite territorial about its home base.
Range: southeast Alaska to Redondo Beach (southern California). **Edibility:** excellent.

Quillback rockfish *Sebastes maliger*
To 24 inches. A handsome fish that often raises its mastlike dorsal spines high and wide. Notable for very high, deeply notched dorsal spines, and distinctive white, yellow, and orange blotches and spots on a dark-brown body. A shallow-water fish in Canada, it prefers deeper water off California. Some range out to 900-foot depths.
Range: Gulf of Alaska to Point Sur (central California). **Edibility:** good.

Gopher rockfish *Sebastes carnatus* To 15½ inches. This territorial fish prefers rocky bottom caves and crevices, often around kelp beds strewn with boulders and covered with sea urchins. Because it likes shallow habitats—depths usually less than 50 feet—it is popular with shore and boat anglers; but it ranges out to 200-foot depths. Note the two brown stripes fanning out from the eye, the white blotches at the third and eighth dorsal spines, and another spot where the spiny and soft dorsal fins meet. Similar to the black-and-yellow rockfish. **Range:** Eureka (northern California) to central Baja California. **Edibility:** good.

and beauty. The names are indicative of the rainbow of colors, stripes, spots, and speckles that adorn some of them: aurora rockfish, calico, tiger, flag, rosy, China, and chilipepper. Since most of them dwell in marine depths where little light penetrates, such colors are seen only when the fish are hauled up by fishermen or when divers throw lights on them. Because most rockfishes are excellent eating, they are hunted relentlessly off U.S. and Canadian shores by sport and commercial fishermen. To attract and reassure shoppers unfamiliar with Pacific Coast rockfishes, fishmongers, restaurateurs, and supermarket managers will dress up rockfish fillets with such false but familiar names as red snapper, ocean perch, sea bass, or codfish. But rockfishes are not snappers, nor are they perches, basses, or cods (all of these may be found elsewhere in this book). They are properly called rockfishes and, so far as eating is concerned, they need not take a back seat to any other food fish.

Wise fishermen handle rockfishes carefully because the dorsal, anal, and ventral spines are mildly venomous and a puncture wound can cause some irritation and pain, depending on the size of the fish and the depth of the wound. The California scorpionfish (often called sculpin) 35

Copper rockfish, whitebelly rockfish (barriga blanca, Palermotana) *Sebastes caurinus* To 22½ inches. Distinctive for the wide white stripe that runs along the lateral line, the white belly, and the copper-yellow stripes radiating back from the eye. Since discovery more than a century ago, two similar yet apparently different rockfishes have puzzled experts. Both fishes had white bellies and were found from the surface to depths of 600 feet. *S. vexillaris*, called whitebelly rockfish, was configured and colored much like the copper rockfish but with a head and back more yellow or olive-striped than in the copper rockfish, which was more copper or reddish in coloration. The copper rockfish ranged from the Kenai Peninsula (Alaska) to Monterey (California); the whitebelly seemed to range from Crescent City (California) to Islas San Benito (Baja California). Experts now conclude that the two are really the same; the name copper rockfish (first given in 1845) has been retained. Look for this rockfish around shallow rocky reefs and to 600-foot depths. A very popular sport fish. **Range:** Gulf of Alaska to central Baja California. **Edibility:** good.

Bocaccio *Sebastes paucispinis* To 3 feet. *Boccaccio* means ''big ugly mouth'' in Italian; this fish has the biggest, most aggressive mouth and jaws of all the rockfishes. It preys voraciously on smaller fishes—even smaller bocaccio. Its large size makes it a very important market fish in California; anglers catch them happily from Alaska to Baja California. A 30-inch female can produce 2,300,000 young in each of two broods a year—one in November and another in March. Bocaccio range widely and may be found in kelp beds (when young), over rocky reefs, or over hard or soft bottoms at 90 to 1,000 feet. **Range:** Kodiak Island (Alaska) to Punta Blanca (central Baja California). **Edibility:** good.

36

and the spotted scorpionfish are very venomous; the sting from either can be extremely painful. One of the most publicized envenomations occurred when Commander Scott Carpenter, U.S. astronaut and aquanaut, was stung on the finger by a California scorpionfish while emerging from the hatchway of the U.S. Navy Sealab II at a depth of 205 feet off La Jolla, California, in October 1965. Many scorpionfishes were attracted by the lights of the hatchway and became a hazard to crew members exiting and re-entering the underwater laboratory.

All rockfishes are ovoviviparous—females are fertilized internally by males, and the eggs are incubated and ejected by the mother as living embryos, usually during winter months. In this way, large bocaccio females can incubate over two million eggs. Scorpionfishes (*Scorpaena* species) are oviparous—eggs are ejected in gelatinous free-floating balloons that may measure 8 inches in diameter, and develop outside the mother's body. The thorny-heads, *Sebastolobus* species, are related to the rockfishes. They live at great depths (from 300 to 5,000 feet), are bright red in color, and are fished commercially with trawls, traps, or set lines. They are often called idiot fishes or channel rock cod. ♦

Black-and-yellow rockfish *Sebastes chrysomelas* To 15¼ inches. A striking animal, prized as a food fish. When seen under water it is very similar to the gopher rockfish; brought to the surface, the distinctly different colorations are evident. The two species are closely related and share similar habitats, behavior, and range. Yet Feder et al. (1974) report that at Diablo Cove near Morro Bay, California, black-and-yellows were found only from inshore tidal areas out to 30-foot depths, whereas gopher rockfish occurred from 50- to 70-foot depths. **Range:** Eureka (northern California) to Isla de Natividad (central Baja California). **Edibility:** good.

Redbanded rockfish *Sebastes babcocki* To 25 inches. So alike are the flag and redbanded rockfishes that they were originally recorded as the same fish. The redbanded is a more northerly fish, however, and is uncommon south of San Francisco; it lives much deeper (from 300 to 1,560 feet) than the flag. The first broad bar on the body of the redbanded passes behind the gill cover; on the flag its position is on the gill cover. **Range:** Amchitka Island (Alaska) to San Diego (California). **Edibility:** good.

Flag rockfish *Sebastes rubrivinctus* To 20 inches. Five rockfishes have dark bands running across light-colored bodies—flag, redbanded, tiger, treefish, and calico; comparison can facilitate their identifications. The flag rockfish is well named, with a very pale, almost ivory body slashed by three broad crimson bars. It is beautiful, and often confused with the redbanded rockfish. Prefers deep rocky reefs at 100- to 600-foot depths. **Range:** San Francisco (California) to Bahía de San Quintín (northern Baja California). **Edibility:** good.

Tiger rockfish *Sebastes nigrocinctus* To 20 inches. Well named for its stripes and solitary disposition. It frequents rocky caves and crevices at 180- to 900-foot depths, occasionally lying on its side. Because of this habitat, it is rarely taken in trawls but is fished on set lines over deep rocky reefs. The tiger rockfish and treefish have a unique body pattern of five black bars; the treefish has a yellow or olive background color, not pink or red like the tiger. **Range:** Prince William Sound (Alaska) to Point Buchon (Morro Bay, central California). **Edibility:** good.

Treefish *Sebastes serriceps* To 16 inches. One of the most striking, unusually marked rockfishes, with black stripes over a yellow body and red lips and chin. The treefish is quite similar to the tiger rockfish in all but color. It has more southerly range than the tiger, and is rare north of Santa Barbara, California. The treefish seeks out shallower water than the tiger and is found in sea-urchin-carpeted reef caves and crevices at 8- to 150-foot depths. Adults and young alike are very aggressive in defense of their home crevices. **Range:** San Francisco (California) to Isla Cedros (central Baja California). **Edibility:** good.

Calico rockfish *Sebastes dalli* To 10 inches. The only rockfish with three or four broad, oblique bars running backward over a whitish- or yellowish-green body. Also note the stripes on the tail fin. Quite common in southern California and frequently caught but discarded by anglers, owing to its small size. Adults seek soft bottom flats from 60- to 840-foot depths. Rare north of Santa Barbara, California. **Range:** San Francisco (California) to central Baja California. **Edibility:** poor because of small size.

Brown rockfish (rocote) *Sebastes auriculatus* To 21½ inches. Common in shallow water in Puget Sound and a familiar sport fish in central California, recognized by the black spot or "ear" on the gill cover (*auriculatus* means "eared"). Dewees (1984) reports that it is a "homing" fish; when several young brown rockfishes were captured in San Francisco Bay and released more than ten miles west of the Golden Gate Bridge, all quickly returned "home" to the site of their original capture. Adult females can produce 339,000 young. **Range:** southeast Alaska to central Baja California. **Edibility:** good.

Cowcod (rocote) *Sebastes levis* To 37 inches and 29 pounds. Like several other rockfishes, the cowcod has four or five bars on its side, but these are vague and irregular. Note the high, deeply notched dorsal spines. The cowcod's large size makes it a most-sought catch for sport fishermen. Commercial fishermen also pursue it with trawls and set lines; it is often seen in the marketplace. A deep-dwelling fish, adults seek rocky reefs at 500- to 800-foot depths. **Range:** Mendocino County (California) to the Ranger Bank (off central Baja California). **Edibility:** excellent.

Canary rockfish *Sebastes pinniger*
To 30 inches. A brightly colored fish with orange-yellow blotches and spots on a gray-white body. Distinctive for the white streak running along the lateral line, the two or three stripes radiating from the eye, and the black blotch at the rear of the spiny dorsal fin. On older fish (over 14 inches) this spot tends to fade away. A common and tasty market fish, popular with anglers willing to fish deep (from 300 to 900 feet) over rocky reefs. **Range:** southeast Alaska to Cabo Colnett (northern Baja California). **Edibility:** excellent.

Chilipepper *Sebastes goodei* To 22 inches. Similar to the Pacific ocean perch with a projecting lower jaw and knob, but notice that a clear pink stripe follows the lateral line. This is a distinctively slender rockfish with a slender caudal peduncle, dusky caudal fin, and dusky soft dorsal fin. An important market and commercial fish in California, fished from the surface to 1,080 feet. **Range:** Vancouver Island to Bahía Magdalena (southern Baja California). **Edibility:** good.

Pacific ocean perch *Sebastes alutus*
To 20 inches. Filleted ocean perch is one of the finest market fishes, and delicious eating. Consequently, this is commercially the most important species in the northeast Pacific. It is abundant from Oregon northward and heavily fished over its range. An offshore rockfish, it is found in 180- to 2,100-foot depths. Note the projecting lower jaw with a knob on the end; blotch on the gill cover; blotch under the soft dorsal fin; and the black-edged spiny dorsal fin. **Range:** Japan and Bering Sea to La Jolla (southern California). **Edibility:** excellent.

Mexican rockfish *Sebastes macdonaldi* To 26 inches. The projecting lower lip and bright red lateral line help to identify this rockfish. Also note the large spot on the gill cover, the slightly forked tail, and the black pectoral fins. A beautiful fish, though so attached to deep reefs (300 to 780 feet) that it is rarely seen by divers. **Range:** Point Sur (central California) to the Morgan Bank (southern Baja California) and the Gulf of California. **Edibility:** poor.

Yelloweye rockfish (tambor) *Sebastes ruberrimus* To 3 feet. *Ruberrimus*, meaning very red, well describes this fish, which is also called turkey-red rockfish and (erroneously) red snapper. The yellow eye is distinctive, but since this rockfish undergoes three distinct color changes as it matures from juvenile to a 3-foot adult, identification can be difficult. The juvenile, to 1 foot long, has two stripes on the side, white-edged dorsal fins, and a white bar at the base of the tail fin. An early researcher thought it was a separate species and described it as such. Later it was shown to phase into the adult fish shown here with just one stripe along the lateral line. Even larger yelloweyes lose the white stripe altogether and retain only the yellow eyes, orange-red markings, and black-edged fins. Medium- to deep-water fishes, they prefer reef caves and crevices from 50 to 1,200 feet. **Range:** Gulf of Alaska to Ensenada (northern Baja California). **Edibility:** excellent.

Blackgill rockfish *Sebastes melanostomus* To 2 feet. Easily identified by the all-black inner mouth, the black on the rear edge of the gill cover, and the thin black "mustache" on the upper jaw. Fins are sometimes edged in black. A deep-dwelling fish fond of soft bottoms from 700 to 2,500 feet. **Range:** Washington to Isla Cedros (central Baja California). **Edibility:** good.

Splitnose rockfish *Sebastes diploproa* To 18 inches. A good identifier is the deep notch or "double prow" (the meaning of *diploproa*) at the tip of the upper jaw. Similar to the aurora rockfish. Some fishes have a faint dark bar behind the pectoral fin and dark margins on the spinous dorsal. A deepwater fish, found over soft bottoms offshore at 300- to 1,900-foot depths. **Range:** Prince William Sound (Alaska) to Isla Cedros (central Baja California). **Edibility:** good.

Aurora rockfish *Sebastes aurora* To 15½ inches. A splendid fish colored brilliant dawn pink or orangish red from lips to tail. Similar to the splitnose rockfish but with a smaller eye. The jaw of the aurora reaches to the rear of the eye; that of the splitnose reaches only to the middle of the eye. The aurora is fished at depths from 600 to 2,500 feet, and unfortunately, deep-dwelling fishes do not look splendid when brought up from the depths on a line because their internal organs and eyes are ravaged by the effects of the pressure differential. **Range:** southern British Columbia to central Baja California. **Edibility:** good.

Vermilion rockfish (rocote) *Sebastes miniatus* To 30 inches. In general, red rockfishes are deep-water species. The vermilion, the most vermilion of all rockfishes, is rarely encountered (except for juveniles) above 80-foot depths. At 80 feet it is reddish-brown, at 150 feet brick red, and from 150 to 900 feet bright vermilion. Note the three stripes radiating from the eye and the projecting lower jaw. An outstanding food fish usually taken on heavy lines in deep water, and sometimes speared by SCUBA divers. Handle carefully! Spines are very sharp and slightly toxic. **Range:** Vancouver Island to Islas San Benito (central Baja California). **Edibility:** excellent.

Blue rockfish *Sebastes mystinus* To 21 inches. This unique blue-black to bright-blue fish is a familiar sight to sport fishermen and divers. It is often seen in the kelp beds off Monterey County, California, and juveniles are found in tidepools from Pacific Grove to La Jolla, California. A wide-ranging fish of many habitats, the blue is also often seen schooling with other rockfishes. Sometimes called priest fish because of its resemblance to the blue-black frock of a priest. **Range:** Bering Sea to Punta Banda (northern Baja California). **Edibility:** good.

Black rockfish *Sebastes melanops*
To 23¾ inches. Quite similar to and often confused with the blue rockfish. The upper jaw of the black rockfish extends past the eye; the upper jaw of the blue reaches only to the middle of the eye. The black has a rounded anal fin, the blue a straight-edged anal fin. A wide-ranging fish found over shallow-water reefs and in huge schools over deep rockfish banks. Well known to anglers up and down the Pacific Coast and taken from the surface to 1,200-foot depths. Very common around Humboldt Bay and abundant at Sitka, Alaska. **Range:** Amchitka Island (Alaska) to Malibu (southern California). **Edibility:** good.

Olive rockfish *Sebastes serranoides*
To 2 feet. An excellent food fish eagerly pursued by sport fishermen along the California coast, especially off Santa Barbara, where it is abundant. It is found in kelp beds and over rocky bottoms, usually in solitude but sometimes in aggregations, from the surface to 480 feet. Often confused with the kelp bass (*Paralabrax clathratus*), but the olive rockfish has a yellow tail and olive fins, and the kelp bass has a much higher spiny dorsal fin. **Range:** Redding Rock (Humboldt County, California) through Islas San Benito (central Baja California). **Edibility:** excellent.

Widow rockfish (viuda) *Sebastes entomelas* To 21 inches. Gathering in dense schools just off the bottom over rocky banks from about 80 to 1,200 feet, this rockfish is a vulnerable target of commercial fishermen who pursue it with sophisticated electronic gear and midwater trawl. Dewees (1984) reports that in the early 1980's more than 40,000 metric tons of rockfish were landed annually, and at least half were the widow. By 1982, a quota was imposed out of fear the fish would be decimated. The only brass-brown fish with all fins dusky and (often) a rosy belly. Jaw extends only to the middle of the eye. **Range:** Kodiak Island (Alaska) to northern Baja California. **Edibility:** good.

43

Kelp rockfish (garrupa) *Sebastes atrovirens*   To 16¾ inches. Right at home in the kelp forest, and an expert at color-changing and remaining motionless to blend in easily with kelp fronds or the reef face. Divers often see it lying on its side, or tailstanding, or headstanding, apparently trying to resemble its surroundings. Feeds on small crabs, shrimp, squid, and fishes from the surface to 150 feet. As with all rockfishes, the spines are mildly venomous. **Range:** Timber Cove (Sonoma County, California) to Punta de San Pablo (central Baja California). **Edibility:** good.

Rosy rockfish *Sebastes rosaceus*   To 14 inches. Quite similar to the starry rockfish, with four to five whitish spots on the back, but no tiny white spots on the body; notable for the purplish-orange stripes radiating from the eye, purplish band across the nape of the neck, and the purplish blotches along the back. A beautiful fish found at 50- to 420-foot depths, often in reef caves and crevices. **Range:** Puget Sound to Bahía Tortugas (central Baja California). **Edibility:** good.

Yellowtail rockfish *Sebastes flavidus*   To 26 inches. Very similar to the olive rockfish, but the yellowtail has reddish-brown speckles and spots on the back and sides; there is one less soft ray in its anal fin than in that of the olive (eight instead of nine); and it ranges much deeper and farther north than the olive rockfish. A wide-ranging rockfish found in schools over deep reefs from near surface to 900 feet, but usually from 80 to 150 feet. **Range:** Kodiak Island (Alaska) to San Diego (California). **Edibility:** good.

Starry rockfish (rocote) *Sebastes constellatus*   To 18 inches. Six rockfishes, similar in shape and color, all have a series of large white spots on the back: these are the starry, rosy, honeycomb, greenspotted, greenblotched, and bronzespotted. These are treated together for ease of comparison. The starry is unmistakable with its brilliant red-orange body covered with tiny white spots (hence the name), surmounted by three to five larger white spots. Frequents rocky reefs at depths from 80 to 900 feet. **Range:** San Francisco (California) to southern Baja California. **Edibility:** excellent.

Greenblotched rockfish *Sebastes rosenblatti* To 19 inches. The olive wavy lines and vermiculations on its back separate this fish from the similar greenspotted rockfish, which has small green spots. A third species, the pink rockfish, *S. eos* (not illustrated), is almost indistinguishable from the greenblotched and swims over similar depths and range, but grows to 22 inches. To separate the two, look for spines at the lower edge of the gill cover (greenblotched has none, pink has 1 or 2) or count the pectoral fin rays (17 for the greenblotched, 18 for the pink). The gill rakers are long on the greenblotched, short and stubby on the pink. Both species prefer rocky bottoms, at 200 to 1,300 feet (greenblotched) and 250 to 1,200 feet (pink). Named after Richard Rosenblatt, Professor of Marine Biology at Scripps Institution of Oceanography. **Range** (both species): San Francisco (California) to central Baja California. **Edibility:** (both species) good.

Grass rockfish *Sebastes rastrelliger* To 22 inches. This fish is expert at camouflaging its green-black-brown body to blend into kelp and eelgrass beds, tidepools, and rocky bottoms. It swims around shallow reefs and is a favorite catch of pier, breakwater, and rock-shore fishermen. Has been taken at 150-foot depths but usually is encountered at less than 30 feet. **Range:** central Oregon to Baja California. **Edibility:** good.

Honeycomb rockfish *Sebastes umbrosus* To 10½ inches. Though one of the smaller rockfishes, it is esteemed as food. When illuminated under water, the three to five white blotches on the back sometimes glow like light wells. This fish is unique in its honeycomb pattern at midbody, formed by the blackish-olive borders that ring each scale. Adults seek out rocky reefs offshore from 90 to 390 feet. **Range:** Point Pinos (Monterey County, California) to Punta San Juanico (southern Baja California). **Edibility:** good.

45

Greenspotted rockfish *Sebastes chlorostictus* To 19¾ inches. Another fish with three to five white spots on its back, but notice that the back and sides are peppered with numerous small, round, olive-green spots. No other rockfish has quite this coloration. A deep-water species abundant over soft bottoms from 160- to 660-foot depths. **Range:** Grays Harbor (Washington) to Isla Cedros (central Baja California). **Edibility:** good.

Bank rockfish *Sebastes rufus* To 20 inches. A reddish-colored fish (*rufus* means red) with black and gray spots covering its back, body, and dorsal fins. Note the pink stripe along the lateral line and the blackish membranes on the fins. A fairly common fish on offshore banks from 100 to 800 feet. **Range:** Fort Bragg (northern California) to central Baja California and Isla de Guadalupe. **Edibility:** good.

Bronzespotted rockfish *Sebastes gilli* To 28 inches. Another handsome rockfish, lavishly dotted over its dorsal surface, it has a large, sharply upturned mouth, bronze stripes radiating from the eye, and two large orange spots under the soft dorsal fin. A large, tasty fish popular with anglers but dwelling in very deep water—240 to 1,230 feet—especially in its southerly territory. **Range:** Monterey Bay (California) to Cabo Colnett (northern Baja California). **Edibility:** good.

Halfbanded rockfish *Sebastes semicinctus* To 10 inches. One of the smaller rockfishes not favored by rockfishermen, owing to its small size, usually under 8 inches. It is common offshore over soft bottoms from 192 to 1,320 feet. Closely related to the stripetail rockfish, which it closely resembles, and once thought to be the juvenile phase of the stripetail. But this is the only rockfish displaying two distinct dark blotches partway down the body. **Range:** Point Pinos (Monterey County, California) to Punta de San Pablo (central Baja California). **Edibility:** poor.

Speckled rockfish *Sebastes ovalis*
To 22 inches. A tan rockfish heavily speckled with tiny round black spots on sides, back, and up into the spiny and soft dorsal fins. The belly is often pinkish-red and the paired fins are tinged with pink-orange. Young are green with large dark blotches on back and sides. Rare north of Santa Barbara but fairly common over rocky reefs from 100 to 1,200 feet in southern California. **Range:** San Francisco (California) to Cabo Colnett (northern Baja California). **Edibility:** good.

Puget Sound rockfish *Sebastes emphaeus* To 7 inches. Known principally from deep water in the Puget Sound–San Juan area of Washington State. It is one of the smallest rockfishes, too small to be sought by fishermen, but divers report seeing it in fairly shallow reef caves and crevices. It prefers rocky habitats from 35 to over 1,200 feet. The green band running back from the eye and continuing down the lower side of the copper-pink body is distinctive, as are the dusky blotches on back and sides. **Range:** Prince William Sound (Alaska) to Punta Gorda (northern California). **Edibility:** poor, owing to small size.

Greenstriped rockfish (reina, serena) *Sebastes elongatus* To 15 inches. This handsome fish is also known as the strawberry rockfish and poinsettia rockfish by some fishermen. It is a deep-water rockfish (200 to 1,320 feet) commonly trawled commercially. Closely related to the stripetail rockfish, the greenstriped rockfish shares a similar coloration and habitat, but has a slightly wider distribution, and is found over rocky as well as soft bottoms offshore. Easily identified by three or four irregular, broken, green stripes on the pink body. Also note the pink stripe along the lateral line, the striped tail, and the green-blotched dorsal fins. **Range:** Montague Island (Alaska) to Isla Cedros (central Baja California). **Edibility:** good.

Stripetail rockfish *Sebastes saxicola*   To 15¼ inches. This fish is notable for the green stripes on the pink tail as well as for the vague olive-green bars or saddles on its back. Also note the symphyseal knob on the projecting lower lip. An offshore rockfish often taken in deep water (150 to 1,380 feet) by commercial fishermen. This is the original rockfish, at least in name. It was named *saxicola* from the Latin *saxum* (rock) and *colo* (I inhabit) in 1890 by the distinguished ichthyologist Charles Henry Gilbert long before the name "rockfish" became popular. Despite the name, this fish seems to prefer soft bottoms offshore rather than rocky reefs. **Range:** southeast Alaska to Punta Rompiente (central Baja California). **Edibility:** good.

Spotted or stone scorpionfish (lapón) *Scorpaena plumieri mystes*   To 17 inches. Although this common southern scorpionfish is quite venomous, it is not as dangerous as the dreaded stonefish (*Synanceja verrucosa*) of the Indo-Pacific, capable of producing agonizing death soon after a puncture wound. Nevertheless, Thomson et al. (1979) report a snorkeler who mistook a large spotted scorpionfish for a reef rock as he steadied himself in the surge. The painful sting made him almost leap out of the water. His hand swelled up and he felt ill for two days before recovering. Another common scorpionfish in the Gulf and ranging from southern California to Peru is the rainbow scorpionfish, *Scorpaena xyris*. Small (to 3 inches), it is notable for the very prominent spot low on the opercle. Both of these scorpions are inshore fishes often found sitting, well camouflaged, on coral reefs, rocky shelves, or sandy bottoms, waiting to feed on passing crabs, squid, or small fishes. **Range:** a spotted scorpionfish was recently taken at Redondo Beach (southern California); also found along the southern coast of outer Baja California and throughout the Gulf of California to Ecuador and the Galapagos Islands. **Edibility:** stone scorpionfish—good; rainbow scorpionfish—poor.

Shortspine thornyhead *Sebastolobus alascanus*   To 29½ inches. Notable for the bright red color, the spiny, prickly head, and the unusual bilobed pectoral fin. Often caught in trawls and on set lines and important commercially, it prefers deep water, from 100 to 5,000 feet. Also known as the idiot fish or channel rockfish. The closely related longspine thornyhead (*S. altivelis*) is similar except that the third dorsal spine is longest, hence the name longspine. The longspine's gill chamber is black, not pale like the shortspine's, and the longspine grows to only about 15 inches. **Range:** shortspine, Bering Sea to Isla Cedros (central Baja California); longspine, Aleutian Islands to southern Baja California. **Edibility:** good for both species.

California scorpionfish, sculpin (lapón) *Scorpaena guttata*   To 17 inches. A popular and tasty food fish, in spite of its poisonous dorsal, anal, and ventral fin spines. Often found nestling quietly by day on rocky reefs, in kelp beds, and in reef caves and crevices, from 10- to 600-foot depths, the fish becomes active at night and is frequently seen by night divers out in the open near kelp and eelgrass beds. This scorpion can inflict a painful sting and make its victim very uncomfortable, sometimes for a day or two. Often called sculpin, but not in the same family. Capable of spectacular color changes, from rosy red to ash gray, to match its background. **Range:** Santa Cruz (central California) to the Gulf of California. **Edibility:** excellent.

49

SURFPERCHES

An alert fisherman in Sausalito, California, in 1853, glanced into a pail of water where he had placed some adult black surfperches and was surprised to see a number of small fishes also swimming about. Further inspection revealed that offspring—all seeming to be miniature copies of the perch mother—were just being born. The fisherman was astute enough to realize that this was an extraordinary occurrence. He notified authorities who in turn sent word to the celebrated Louis Agassiz at Harvard University. Agassiz published an account of the surfperches, calling them "extraordinary fishes" and giving them status as an entirely new family, the Embiotocidae. He also did not forget the discoverer, A. C. Jackson, whose name is forever immortalized in the scientific name of the black surfperch, *Embiotoca jacksoni.* For some years afterward, a flurry of

Black surfperch, blackperch, butterlips *Embiotoca jacksoni* To 15½ inches. The colors of this fish are variable—from orange-brown to black to light tan to pale greenish white—depending on background and breeding time. The best identifier is the patch of enlarged scales visible between the pectoral fin and the ventral fin. Also note the thick lips and "mustache" (not always visible). Swims in or near eelgrass flats in shallow-water bays; around kelp beds, seaweed, rocky tidepools, breakwaters, and piers; and out to 150-foot depths, often in small aggregations. Mating season brings males and females together into pairs gathered into large, tight schools. Males hang close beside females, fighting off interlopers. Ripe males are easily recognized by the nipplelike organ projecting just in front of the anal fin.
Range: Fort Bragg (northern California) to Punta Abreojos (central Baja California).
Edibility: good.

Striped surfperch, striped seaperch *Embiotoca lateralis*   To 15 inches. A beautiful surfperch sporting a coppery ground color overlaid with sky-blue horizontal stripes from opercle to tail. Also note the blue streaks on the head, black upper lip, and copper-colored fins. Prefers cold water, rocky bottom habitats, and kelp beds from 15- to 70-foot depths. A popular sport fish taken in late winter and early spring around piers and jetties and occasionally in sandy surf lines. Also a frequent target of spear fishermen. **Range:** Wrangell Island (southeast Alaska) to Punta Bunda (northern Baja California). **Edibility:** good.

Rubberlip surfperch, rubberlip seaperch *Rhacochilus toxotes*   To 18½ inches. The largest surfperch of the family and an excellent food fish. The very thick pinkish-white lips—almost twice as thick as on any other surfperch—are good identification, along with the brassy-silvery body and the yellow pectoral fins. Often found in giant kelp beds at mid-depth, as well as near jetties and piers and near the bottom in rocky submarine canyons, out to 150 feet. Abundant throughout its range, it gathers in large schools, and feeds on shrimp, crabs, squid, and octopuses. **Range:** Russian Gulch State Park (Mendocino County, California) to Bahía Tortugas (Baja California) and Isla de Guadalupe. **Edibility:** excellent.

51

papers about this surprising new family of fishes appeared in scientific journals worldwide.

What made the surfperch so remarkable, and even today still is unusual, is that almost all other marine fishes fertilize and scatter large numbers of eggs outside the body, whereas the viviparous perch nourishes her offspring inside her ovary, and spawns them live into the surf. Further, these "babies" are sexually mature at or even before birth, and, even more extraordinary, infant males can inseminate infant females soon after birth.

The number of the young varies with the species and the size of the female, but in general mothers bear from 3 to 80 fry. Incredibly, the barred surfperch produces from 4 to 113 embryos, each measuring from $1\frac{5}{8}$ to $2\frac{1}{8}$ inches long, and all are tightly packed within the ovary. Another surprising characteristic is that breeding surfperches copulate. A small nipple near the anal fin of the male is an organ that transfers milt to the female. Impregnation was suspected and finally observed by Carl L. Hubbs in 1917 when a male shiner surfperch impregnated a female.

Surfperches are also called seaperches and surffishes. All have large fleshy lips, a continuous, unnotched dorsal fin, and a sheath of scales on the back alongside the dorsal fin. Some, like the striped, rainbow, calico, and redtail

Barred surfperch *Amphistichus argenteus*   To 17 inches and $4\frac{1}{2}$ pounds. A true surfperch often found in small schools in the pounding surf zone. The colors of this fish blend naturally with the churning sea. Look for eight to ten rust-colored, irregular bars on the side; all fins are black-edged. Males and females are seen to darken considerably during courtship. Males have been seen to move in figure eights around the female prior to mating. Females can produce from 4 to 113 young, which appear in spring and summer. Surf fishermen reel in this fish in large numbers: about 75 percent of the surf-fishing catch in southern California is made up of barred surfperches. **Range:** Bodega Bay (northern California) to Bahía Playa Maria (north-central Baja California). **Edibility:** good.

Redtail surfperch *Amphistichus rhodoterus*   To 16 inches. A colorful, very abundant surfperch found on exposed, sandy coastlines from central California northward, from shore to 24-foot depths. Like the barred surfperch, this fish is silvery and barred to blend in easily with pounding surf, sand, and foam. Identified by the 8 to 11 bars on the sides, the all-red fins, and the very red tail fin. Feeds on sand-dwelling crustaceans and mollusks. A favorite, important sportfish for surf fishermen (and also for bay and backwater fishermen). **Range:** Vancouver Island to Morro Bay (central California). **Edibility:** good.

surfperches, are strikingly colored, and others are bright, silvery fishes that roam and blend into the pounding surf. They range in size from 4 to 18 inches. There are 21 species, all found off the Pacific Coast of North America except for two that occur off Japan and Korea. One species, the freshwater tule perch, lives in the Sacramento and Russian rivers in California. Surfperches are popular with surf and shore fishermen and are caught from piers and docks, in surf lines, kelp beds, tidepools, and a host of diverse habitats. Most surfperches are shallow-water fishes that live in, exploit, and even spawn their young in the surf zone. Others seek out kelp beds and tidepools. The pink seaperch, *Zalembius rosaceus* (not illustrated), is unusual in living offshore at depths from 30 to 750 feet.

Some surfperches are "cleaners"—specialists at picking parasites off other, usually larger fishes. Observers have seen tiny kelp surfperches surrounded and completely hidden by client fishes waiting to be cleaned. Among fishes that surfperches have been observed to clean are blacksmiths, kelp basses, other surfperches (e.g., the walleye), garibaldis, opaleyes, halfmoons, blue rockfishes, and molas. Cleaners include the kelp, pile, rainbow, and sharpnose surfperches. ◆

53

Calico surfperch *Amphistichus koelzi*   To 12 inches. Very similar to the redtail surfperch, but note the deeper body of the calico, the dusky (rather than bright red) tail fin, and the vague, broken bars on the body, quite unlike those of the redtail. A silvery resident of sandy coastlines and surf lines from shore to 30 feet. Named for Walter Koelz, U.S. ichthyologist. **Range:** Shi Shi Beach (Cape Flattery, Washington) to northern Baja California. **Edibility:** good, though the fish is usually small.

Walleye surfperch *Hyperprosopon argenteum*   To 12 inches. A shiny, silvery perch, very abundant in southern California and frequently the joyful first catch of beginning anglers. Swims in the surf, over sand beaches, near rocky patches, and around piers and jetties. Feder et al. (1974) report that walleyes school in dense packs 6 to 8 feet thick, reaching to within two feet of the surface and perhaps containing several hundred or several thousand fishes. They are an important target of commercial fishermen. Distinctive for the large eye and black-tipped pelvic fins. Males engage in aggressive, swooping courtship displays. Gestation is five to six months with 5 to 12 fry, 1½ inches long, born about mid-April. **Range:** Vancouver Island to central Baja California. **Edibility:** excellent, in spite of small size.

**Rainbow surfperch, rainbow sea-
perch** *Hypsurus caryi* To 12 inches.
A handsome perch distinctive for the
rusty-orange bars flowing down its
back, the iridescent blue and orange
horizontal stripes running from opercle
to tail, the black-tinged anal and soft
dorsal fins, and the black spot behind
the upper jaw. A solitary fish most of
the year, it swims over rocky bottoms,
and occasionally frequents kelp beds
and sandy bottoms (but not surf lines),
from tidepools out to 130 feet. They
have been seen to gather in clusters in
the fall, possibly for breeding pur-
poses. Also observed by Gotschall
(1967) in Monterey Bay, California, to
clean parasites off other fishes. **Range:**
Cape Mendocino (northern California)
to Punta Santo Tomás (northern Baja
California). **Edibility:** good.

Silver surfperch *Hyperprosopon ellip-
ticum* To 10½ inches. Quite similar to
the walleye surfperch, but note the
pink tail fin, the red-orange spot on
the anal fin, the dark-edged dorsal fin;
this fish does not have the walleye's
dark-edged pelvic fin. Seeks inshore
habitats in surf lines, over sandy
beaches, around free-floating seaweed, and among rocks and piers. It
is too small to interest fishermen but
is forage for larger fishes and sea
birds. During mating activity the male
approaches the female from below;
both swim with vents together for two
or three seconds, then separate and
repeat the encounter. **Range:** British
Columbia to northern Baja California.
Edibility: poor, owing to small size.

Kelp surfperch *Brachyistius frenatus* To 8½ inches. These small kelp-colored
beauties make their home in kelp beds, rarely leaving the kelp canopy or the region
just below it. They feed on small crustaceans that live on the kelp fronds. They also
clean parasites from other fishes. Clusters of blacksmith damselfishes have been
seen to surround a solitary surfperch until it is completely hidden; other fishes that
are serviced are garibaldis, kelp basses, opaleyes, halfmoons, and walleye surfperches. Note the sharp snout, upturned, oblique mouth, pale, wide stripe running
down mid-side, and the kelplike coloration. Large aggregations of adults come together in late summer, possibly for mating. **Range:** Vancouver Island to Bahía
Tortugas (central Baja California). **Edibility:** poor, owing to small size.

Sharpnose surfperch, sharpnose seaperch *Phanerodon atripes* To 11½ inches. The sharpnose population seems to experience periodic increases and declines. Today it is rare, seldom caught by anglers, and common only in Monterey Bay; it was formerly much more common throughout California. It swims inshore around reefs, kelp beds, jetties, and piers, and offshore to 750-foot depths. It is distinctive for the sharp, pointed snout, the reddish-brown spots on the sides following the scale rows, and the black-tipped pelvic and anal fins. As the sharp snout indicates, this perch is also a "cleaner" like the kelp surfperch, and Gotschall (1977) reports that it has been observed picking parasites from blue rockfishes, blacksmith damselfishes, and molas. **Range:** Bodega Bay (northern California) to Islas San Benito (central Baja California). **Edibility:** good.

Pile surfperch, pileperch *Damalichthys vacca* To 17½ inches. One of the larger surfperches, often mistaken for the sargo (see page 71) because of the wide black bar on its side. But on the pile surfperch the bar is well in back of the pectoral fin, whereas on the sargo it intersects the pectoral fin. Also notable is the high-peaked soft dorsal fin and the spot below the eye. Feeds voraciously on crustaceans and mollusks and is a frequent visitor around pilings (hence the name), where it pulls free small mussels, barnacles, clams, limpets, and crabs. Young pileperches have been seen picking parasites from other fishes. Also schools in kelp beds just below the canopy and frequents rocky reefs from inshore to 150-foot depths. **Range:** Wrangell Island (Alaska) to Isla de Guadalupe (Baja California). **Edibility:** excellent.

Shiner surfperch, shiner perch *Cymatogaster aggregata*   To 7 inches. One of the most abundant of the silvery, shiny surfperches, easily caught by children using small hooks, from bridges or piers, in eelgrass flats, on bays, and along open coastlines. It prefers the backwaters of bays and estuaries, but is also found in calm deeper water to 450 feet, often in aggregations. The rows of black spots on the sides and the three yellow crossbars are distinctive. Males have yellow bars only in winter, and darken in breeding season, following females closely and fending off other males. A very similar surfperch, found only around the Channel Islands (southern California), where it is quite common, differs in having a larger eye, a more slender body, and yellow ventral markings. It has been called the island surfperch, *C. gracilis*. Some ichthyologists now conclude that it is just a subspecies, that the two are both *C. aggregata*. **Range:** Wrangell Island (Alaska) to Bahía San Quintín (northern Baja California). **Edibility:** poor, owing to small size.

White surfperch, white seaperch *Phanerodon furcatus*   To 12½ inches. This surfperch swims in loose schools in quiet backwater bays, over deep-water reefs, and through combined rock-and-sand areas in quiet water out to 140 feet. It is fished off jetties, piers, and docks but is often discarded because of small average size. Owing to its schooling behavior, it is often taken commercially off northern California. Alone among surfperches are the thin black line at the base of the dorsal fin, the silvery-blue body, and the yellowish fins. **Range:** Vancouver Island to Punta Banda (northern Baja California). **Edibility:** good.

CROAKERS AND CORVINAS

Members of the large and varied family Sciaenidae are called by many names—croakers, drums, corvinas, corbinas, roncadores, kingfishes, queenfishes, seabasses, seatrouts, weakfishes, whitings—but nearly all of them share a common characteristic: they are remarkable for the noises they make. Early submarine commanders were at first astounded to hear the "boop-boop-boop-boop" of schools of croakers, suspecting that enemy craft were near. Later they found that they could hide the sound of their own engines behind the din of the croakers. Some modern fish experts believe that the Sirens in Greek mythology, who tried to lure Odysseus and his crew to destruction with their song, were not half-woman, half-bird creatures at all. Rather, the songs were sung by the meagre or weakfish—a common croaker in the Mediterranean.

The croakers and corvinas of the Pacific usually have blunt, rounded snouts and two almost joined dorsal fins—a spiny dorsal with 7 to 16 spines and a soft-rayed dorsal with one spine and many soft rays. There are usually two anal fin spines. The lateral line extends to the rear edge of

California corbina (corvina de California) *Menticirrhus undulatus* To 28 inches and 8 pounds. A slender croaker with a flattened belly and a blunt nose projecting beyond the mouth. Also note the chin barbel and large, dark pectoral fin. It lacks an air bladder and cannot croak like other sciaenids. These handsome and silvery fish prowl the sandy surf lines in groups of two or three, or schools, probing for sand crabs, worms, clams, and fish eggs with their sensitive barbels. They will accompany a breaking wave high on a beach and have been seen feeding in surf so shallow that their backs are out of water. Highly esteemed by surf, pier, and spear fishermen, they are therefore protected: it has been illegal in California to take them with nets since 1909, or to buy or sell them since 1915. **Range:** Point Conception (southern California) to the Gulf of California. **Edibility:** excellent.

the caudal fin. A muscular, modified air bladder enables most croakers to produce croaking or drumming noises, much like a guitar when a string is plucked. Many croakers are medium-sized, reaching 10- to 12-inch lengths, but some, such as the white seabass, attain 5 feet, and the totuava can reach 6 feet.

The Pacific Coast croakers may be divided roughly into three separate groups with three different life styles: the shore-bottom feeders, midwater feeders, and reef croakers. The bottom-feeding croakers and corvinas hug the shore-

White croaker, tomcod, tommy, kingfish (roncador blanco) *Genyonemus lineatus* To 16¼ inches, usually less than 12 inches. A schooling fish, often swimming with queenfishes and other species in shallow water over sandy bottoms. Not considered a game fish, but is caught in huge quantities by boat, pier, and shore anglers in southern California. Commercial fishermen also harvest it at Monterey in the summer and fall and at Los Angeles in late winter and spring. Consequently the announcement in 1985 that white croakers caught in Santa Monica Bay or San Pedro Bay should not be eaten since they carry trace amounts of DDT and PCB was unwelcome news to local fishermen. For identification, note how the tip of the snout projects beyond the lower jaw. White croakers have small barbels on the chin but not the large, single barbel other croakers have. Also note the small black spot at the top of the pectoral fin base and 12 to 16 spines in the first dorsal fin. The tail fin is usually black-edged. **Range:** Barkley Sound (British Columbia) to southern Baja; rare north of California. **Edibility:** good, but may be contaminated in Santa Monica and San Pedro bays in southern California.

Queenfish, kingfish (roncador) *Seriphus politus*   To 1 foot. These croakers are abundant during summer months, swimming in tightly packed schools, often with white croakers, over sandy bottoms and around piers and pilings in shallow water. They are not esteemed as a food fish but are often used as live bait to catch California halibut. The wide gap between the spiny and soft dorsal fins is distinctive. Also note the large, upturned mouth; the snout does not extend beyond the mouth. The depth of their range is 2 to 70 feet but usually less than 30. At night they migrate seaward into deeper water. **Range:** central Oregon to central Baja California.

Yellowfin croaker (roncador garabato) *Umbrina roncador* To 20 inches and 3.9 pounds. This splendid croaker, a boon to surf, pier, and boat fishermen, is so prized in California that it is protected by law and cannot be netted by fishermen, or bought or sold. Prefers very shallow water close to a sand bottom in the surf zone and near rocks, and in bays and tidal sloughs, where it feeds on small fishes and invertebrates. Ranges from shore out to 25 feet. Identified by the all-yellow fins, wavy stripes on back and sides, a short chin barbel, and a rounded snout projecting beyond the tip of the lower jaw. Blends with and becomes almost invisible against a sand background. **Range:** Point Conception (southern California) to the Gulf of California. **Edibility:** excellent.

Spotfin croaker, golden croaker (roncador) *Roncador stearnsi* To 27 inches and 10½ pounds. Much like the California corbina, these croakers frequent the sandy surf lines foraging for polychaete worms, crabs, small crustaceans, and clams. They also rove over shallow-water rocks, rocky reefs, breakwaters, piers, and bay mouths, sometimes swimming in schools of up to 50 fishes but usually in twos or threes. Unlike the California corbina, the spotfin has no barbel on its chin; it has heavy, crushing pharyngeal teeth, and so can devour heavier-shelled clams than the California corbina. A very popular sport fish and a favorite of surf, pier, and spear fishermen; but it has been illegal since 1909 to net it and illegal since 1915 to buy or sell it. Distinguished by the large black spot at the base of the pectoral fin, the blunt snout that projects beyond the mouth, and the heavy, deep body. Occasionally has a striking golden phase. **Range:** Point Conception (southern California) to Bahía Magdalena (southern Baja California). **Edibility:** excellent.

lines and breaking surf lines. Their silvery, sometimes sandy coloration easily blends with this background, enabling them to pounce on crustaceans, worms, and other bottom-dwelling creatures exposed by the wave action. The mouths of these croakers are beneath the head, an adaptation to their bottom-feeding existence. Some have sensitive barbels with which they probe sand and mud bottoms for food. Examples of these bottom-feeding croakers are the white, spotfin, and yellowfin croakers, queenfish, and most of the smaller corvinas.

The white seabass and the totuava are midwater feeders, especially as adults. They prefer deeper-water habitats where they search the water column for smaller fishes, including other croakers and corvinas, as well as anchovies, squid, sardines, and pelagic crabs.

The rock- and reef-dwelling croakers include the black croaker and rock croaker, which conceal themselves in reef caves and crevices by day and emerge at night to roam the reef and sandy bottoms searching for invertebrates, including worms, crabs, and other small crustaceans.

Unfortunately, because croakers and corvinas are often excellent food fishes, their association with man on the Pacific Coast has not been a happy one for the croakers. The white seabass—a magnificent game and food fish—was decimated by commercial and sport overfishing along the California coast. The fishery for the totuava—a giant

Bairdiella (roncador, corvineta) *Bairdiella icistia* To 12 inches. A common inshore croaker, fond of bays and estuaries. It is especially important as a forage fish for the larger transplanted corvinas in the Salton Sea such as the orangemouth corvina. Recognized by the deep body, gray-to-silvery color, and lack of barbels and spots; the second spine of the anal fin is long, extending beyond the tip of the last soft ray. **Range:** along the Pacific coast of Mexico and abundant in the Gulf of California; introduced into the inland Salton Sea, it is now common and thrives there. **Edibility:** excellent; though small, it is a good panfish.

61

croaker reaching 6 feet and a splendid food fish—has an even more pitiful history. In the early 1900's hundreds of thousands of totuavas were slaughtered and left to rot on the beaches of the Gulf of California. The object of this carnage was the totuava's air bladder, which was removed and sold as a costly soup base. Later, when the quality of the filleted totuava became known, millions of pounds of flesh were shipped by truck to the U.S. from Gulf ports. Today, owing to overfishing and habitat destruction, the fish is close to extinction and on the endangered list.

A recent disturbing development in southern California, the contamination of Santa Monica Bay and San Pedro Bay off Los Angeles, should be taken seriously by local fishermen and consumers. In 1985 the Los Angeles County Department of Health Services posted signs on every pier from Santa Monica Bay to Long Beach warning of the dangers of eating fish contaminated with DDT and PCB, two toxic substances that have been found in local sport fishes. The white croaker and the California halibut were specifically mentioned as containing "trace amounts of DDT and PCB." As this book goes to press, the depressing story of the extent of contamination along the Los Angeles County coast still has not been fully revealed. ◆

ADULT

JUVENILE

Rock croaker (gungo) *Pareques viola* To 10 inches. Like the black croaker, this chocolate-brown croaker makes its home around rocky-shore reef caves and crevices, and has a juvenile phase strikingly different from the adult, as shown. When a juvenile reaches 6 inches, the fish begins to take on the dark adult coloration, and stripes fade. A small school of juveniles floating near a rocky reef, with dorsal fins hoisted high, is a remarkable sight—like tiny drifting oriental kites. Small schools appear only in the summer. Adults are cryptic creatures rarely seen during the day, but emerging from rock caves at night to forage across the reef for food, mostly crustaceans. **Range:** throughout the Gulf of California and south to Panama. **Edibility:** poor.

ADULT

JUVENILE

Black croaker, Chinese croaker (corvina, roncacho) *Cheilotrema saturnum*   To 15 inches. These croakers are rock dwellers along open rocky coasts and bays; large, black adults seek reef caves and crevices where they become almost invisible in the murky light. They can change color to light sandy tan when over a sand bottom or show stripes to match sand-bottom ripples. Note the unique black blotch on the upper edge of the gill cover of the adult, possessed by no other croaker. Snout is blunt and upper jaw projects over lower jaw. Usually a pale bar at midbody. Juveniles appear in August wearing black horizontal stripes on silvery-white bodies, as shown. They closely resemble juvenile sargos and salemas (see pages 71 and 75). They often school over sandy bottoms near rocks in the surge zone. Feder et al. (1974) report that schooling juveniles were seen to stay 6 to 10 inches apart, all facing directly into the constantly reversing surge; schools did not shift position more than 10 feet during the entire season. Adults, larger and blacker, retire from schools into deeper-water caves and grottoes. In California they are protected by law and cannot be bought or sold. **Range:** Point Conception (southern California) to central Baja California and the upper Gulf of California. **Edibility:** good.

White seabass (corvina blanca) *Atractoscion nobilis*   To 5 feet and 90 pounds. Although one of the larger croakers on the Pacific Coast, the white seabass (which is not a true bass) usually weighs 15 to 20 pounds when taken. Unlike other, bottom-grubbing croakers, it tends to feed midway in the water column on red pelagic crabs, squid, anchovies, sardines, and other fishes. White seabass school over rocky bottoms and in and around the kelp canopy. Commercial gill netters used to follow giant kelp cutters, netting seabass where harvesters had cleared away heavy canopy. Unfortunately the white seabass, like the totuava, has been decimated on the Pacific Coast. A prized sport fish, recreational fishermen hooked them by the thousands in the 1950's; in recent years, fewer than 1,000 fishes have been caught annually in southern California. Oceanographers believe that years of overfishing and reduction of habitat are responsible for the decimation. Look for the gray-blue-to-silver body, a black spot at the base of the pectoral fin, and absence of chin barbels. A raised ridge runs down the middle of the belly. Juveniles have four to six dark bars on the sides of the body. **Range:** Juneau (Alaska) to southern Baja California and the northern Gulf of California. **Edibility:** excellent.

63

Orangemouth corvina, yellowmouth corvina (corvina de las aletas amarillas) *Cynoscion xanthulus* To 3 feet. A prized, sought-after game fish, excellent food. On an experimental basis, 275 were introduced into the Salton Sea in 1950 and these have increased to millions today. Fishes weighing 32 pounds have been recorded from this location. The inside of the mouth is bright orange-yellow and the fins are mostly yellowish. Also note the long slim body; prominent lower jaw; and the tail, pointed in the middle. **Range:** throughout the Gulf of California to Mazatlán (Mexico). **Edibility:** excellent.

Totuava (totoaba, machorro) *Totoaba macdonaldi* To 6 feet and 300 pounds. This magnificent animal, the largest croaker in the Americas, is a textbook example of man's obliteration of a fish species that once numbered in the millions. In the original account of the totuava, Gilbert (1890) found it "very abundant along the entire shore of the Gulf of California and [it] congregates in great numbers near the mouth of the Colorado River. . . . Large specimens were seen at Guaymas and the mouth of the Rio del Fuerte." Demand for the air bladders of the totuava for use as a soup base caused extensive depletion of the species in the early 1900's. Walford (1937) reports that "so high a price did the bladders command—sometimes as high as $5 a pound—that it did not pay to bring to market the carcasses of the fish, which were permitted to rot on the beaches. Thus many tons were wasted." The flesh became an export to the United States in 1924 and by 1928 shipments reached 1,838,000 pounds. The totuava was well on the way to extinction; today it is an endangered species protected in the upper Gulf. Note the angular tail, longest in the middle; small eyes; lack of canine teeth; and the dull yellow inside the mouth and opercles. **Range:** middle and upper Gulf of California.

Shortfin corvina, shortfin seabass (corvina) *Cynoscion parvipinnis*   To 20 inches. Common in the Gulf of California, at one time this corvina was also seen and fished along the California shore from Santa Barbara south; but Miller and Lea (1972) state that none have been seen in the northernmost part of its range since the 1930's. Swimming in shallow inshore sandy areas, it is a target of surf fishermen. A mostly silvery croaker with short pectoral fins (hence the name). The lower jaw projects beyond the upper jaw; one or two large canine teeth may be found on each side of the upper jaw. It lacks chin barbels. **Range:** Huntington Beach (southern California) to Mazatlán (Mexico) and the Gulf of California. **Edibility:** good.

Gulf corvina (corvina del golfo) *Cynoscion othonopterus*   To 28 inches. Highly esteemed as food and game, and avidly pursued by anglers. At one time a prime Gulf of California food fish taken commercially on handlines and set lines and shipped overland by truck to the United States from Gulf ports. Like the totuava, however, overfishing took its toll and today the Gulf corvina is greatly diminished. Distinctive for the silvery body, square-shaped tail fin, and yellowish fins. Soft dorsal, anal, and tail fins are covered with scales. **Range:** now apparently restricted to the upper Gulf of California. **Edibility:** good.

Striped corvina (corvina rayada) *Cynoscion reticulatus*   To 2 feet. Handsome, and the only Pacific corvina that has back and sides covered with irregular brown or blackish stripes. All fins are unscaled; the tail fin is slightly pointed in the middle; the lining of the mouth is orange. **Range:** throughout the Gulf of California and south to Panama. **Edibility:** Kumada (1937) reports that it is an important food fish; other sources say the flesh is soft, unpalatable.

Highfin corbina (berrugato) *Menticirrhus nasus*   To 2½ feet. This striking, silvery fish with lancelike second dorsal spine is related to Atlantic Coast kingfishes, including *M. saxatilis*, the northern kingfish, and *M. americanus*, the southern kingfish. All are inshore bottom-grubbers, evidenced by the single short, thick barbel on the chin; occasionally they are seen feeding over sand bottoms quite near shore. Surfcasters bait with shrimp and other crustaceans and hook them off sandy beaches. **Range:** southern California and the coast of Mexico to Panama, including the Gulf of California. **Edibility:** good.

Corvalo (mimis, corvalo, corvina) *Paralonchurus goodei*   To 1 foot. This unusual croaker is notable for the numerous small whiskerlike barbels on the chin, useful when nosing into sandy bottoms for worms, sand crabs, and other crustaceans. Also note the silvery body with the conspicuous crossbars running down the back and sides, and the fan-shaped tail. The soft dorsal and tail fins are sheathed in scales. Prefers shallow inshore sandy areas and surf lines. Not much is known about this southerly croaker; it is described in the Catalog of Mexican Marine Fish (1976) as ranging from Bahía Magdalena (Baja California) and the Gulf of California to the northern coasts of Peru. **Range:** see above. **Edibility:** good.

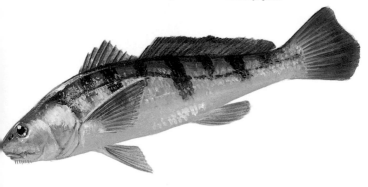

SNAPPERS

The name "snapper" was coined by some early, anonymous fisherman who landed a fish and noted that it tended to open and snap its mouth shut powerfully as it expired. This phenomenon became a valuable lesson for beginning fishermen, since countless unwary anglers were bitten and sometimes badly wounded by thrashing snappers. The jaws of snappers are strong and armed with stout canine teeth. In some ways similar to sea basses, snappers can be separated by noting that the rear of the upper jaw fits into a groove (partially hiding it) when the mouth is closed; it does not in sea basses. Snappers, of the family Lutjanidae, are closely related to the grunts (see page 71). Both have the characteristic sloping head and shovel-nosed appearance known as the "snapper look."

Snappers are avidly pursued by fishermen because of their excellent food quality, and they are relentlessly pursued by bottom fishermen. They are the wariest of game fishes, and some fishermen swear that snappers not only are able to think, but often outthink fishermen. Walford (1937) states that for some reason they will strike a trolled

Yellow snapper, yellowtail snapper (pargo amarillo) *Lutjanus argentiventris* To 2 feet and 20 pounds. This beautiful animal is rare north of Baja California. It is abundant in the Gulf of California from near shore out to 75 feet. Adults stay close to rocky reefs where caves, holes, and crevices provide shelter. They feed on smaller fishes, squid, octopuses, and crustaceans, usually at night, at dusk when daytime fishes are still active, or at dawn. Yellow snappers are able to tolerate fresh water and sometimes enter streams and estuaries. Young appear in late spring near shore in tidepools and estuaries. Larger juveniles are often seen in large schools in summer, hovering near reefs. **Range:** Oceanside (southern California) to Peru, including the Gulf of California and the Galapagos Islands. **Edibility:** excellent.

lure only in the early months of the year. In Central America the snapper trolling season is restricted to December through March. Snappers are stubborn fighters right up to boating and often give a good run or two.

Although primarily marine in habitat, some lutjanids, especially such reef inhabitants as the yellow snapper and dog snapper, readily enter brackish and fresh water. Shallow mangrove areas provide an ideal nursery for many young snappers. Most of the snappers shown here are reef dwellers, usually found skulking in reef caves and crevices by day. The Pacific red snapper is a deep-water fish, however; it is the famed food fish populating the "snapper banks" found at 300-foot depths in the Gulf of California and down the Pacific Coast to Peru. Great schools of Pacific red snappers tend to gather in underwater canyons and depressions, or around deep seamounts or rises where food is plentiful. Commercial and sport fishermen catch them every year by the millions. Snappers are carnivores; most feed mainly on crustaceans and smaller fishes. The larger species, like the dog snapper and colorado snapper, feed heavily on smaller fishes. ◆

Pacific red snapper (huachinango) *Lutjanus peru*   To 2½ feet. This famous fish is so popular and succulent that it is often marketed whole, head and all, to guard against substitution; countless other fishes, from other snappers to basses to snook, have been disguised and sold as red snappers. Red snappers occur in vast schools over deep, offshore "snapper banks" at depths of 300 feet or more, where they are relentlessly fished by commercial and sport fishermen. This snapper is colored a much clearer red than either the colorado or dog snapper. The sides have a pale, silvery color and the belly is whitish. **Range:** throughout the Gulf of California to Peru. **Edibility:** excellent.

Pacific dog snapper (pargo prieto) *Lutjanus novemfasciatus* To 4 feet and 100 pounds. Like the colorado snapper, one of the larger inshore predators; these and other snappers take a heavy toll of such smaller prey as grunts, croakers, wrasses, and crustaceans. At night, particularly at twilight before many of the smaller diurnal fishes have retired, dog snappers become most active, slashing heavily through schooling fishes such as grunts. Most often found from 15 to 40 feet, they occur out to 100 feet. Young school in protected shallow bays and estuaries, and some enter freshwater streams. The dog snapper has the largest canine teeth of any Pacific Coast snapper; both juveniles and adults usually have nine dark bars on the sides. **Range:** throughout the Gulf of California to Peru. **Edibility:** good.

Colorado snapper (pargo colorado) *Lutjanus colorado* To 3 feet. This snapper resembles the yellow snapper in many respects, but its body is mostly red, without the yellow tail of the yellow snapper. Also note the long pectoral fin reaching past the anus. Sometimes confused with the dog snapper, but the colorado snapper has a longer pectoral fin, angular dorsal and anal fins, a blue streak under the eye, and less conspicuous canine teeth. Found inshore over and under reefs and in caves and holes out to 100-foot depths. It emerges at night to feed on smaller fishes and crustaceans. **Range:** Estero Point (central California) to Panama, including the Gulf of California; rare north of Baja California. **Edibility:** excellent.

Blue-and-gold snapper (pargo rayado) *Lutjanus viridis* To 1 foot. Light-blue stripes with a dusky margin over a golden body make the blue-and-gold the most colorful Pacific Coast snapper. Sometimes roaming singly, and often forming into large schools over the reefs, it is a remarkable sight, especially when seen for the first time. Swims from near shore out to 50-foot depths. **Range:** La Paz (Baja California) to Cabo San Lucas, and to Ecuador, Las Islas Tres Marias, Islas Revillagigedo, and the Galapagos Islands. **Edibility:** good.

69

Barred pargo (coconaco) *Hoplopagrus guentheri* To 2½ feet and 30 pounds. A deep-bodied snapper even more wary than most, usually found skulking in reef caves or among crevices of tumbled boulders. In some areas it has been greatly depleted because, when threatened, it dives immediately for a reef hole (as do most snappers), where it is easily speared. A nocturnal feeder that emerges at night to search for small schooling fishes and crustaceans. Distinctive for the tubular nostrils that extend beyond the upper lip. Occurs from near shore to 90 feet, but is most common from 10 to 30 feet. Juveniles are found near shallow patch reefs from August to October. **Range:** throughout the Gulf of California to Panama. **Edibility:** excellent.

Spotted rose snapper (pargo chibato) *Lutjanus guttatus* To 2½ feet. This snapper, found over sandy bottoms as well as patch reefs, is the only snapper on the western coasts of the Americas with a dark spot on the lateral line just below the soft dorsal fin. Three Atlantic Coast species display such dark spots. On some rose snappers the dark spot is obscure and almost invisible. An excellent food fish, it ranges widely down the Mexican and Central American coasts, and is a preferred catch of fishermen. **Range:** both shores of the Gulf of California south to Peru. **Edibility:** excellent.

Mullet snapper (pargo de raizero) *Lutjanus aratus* To 2½ feet. A rather slim-bodied snapper more often found over sandy bottoms than rock or coral reefs; it is also found in estuaries and mangrove sloughs. This snapper can be separated from all other Pacific Coast snappers in having 11 dorsal spines instead of the usual 10. Juveniles are usually much paler than adults, with much bolder, more distinct stripes. **Range:** central Gulf of California to Ecuador. **Edibility:** good.

GRUNTS

One of the pleasures of diving or snorkeling over Mexican and Central American reefs is the splendid sight of a school of silver-striped or -spotted grunts. They are seen almost everywhere off tropical reefs, hovering in small groups or massing in great schools. Sometimes they seem to flow between the reef canyons like a river of gleaming silver. When massed into tight, iridescent schools, illuminated by sunlight under water, the subtly beautiful Cortez grunt, the spottail, or the salema becomes a feast for the eyes; you stop and marvel as these exotic animals pass in tight procession. Unfortunately for the grunts, larger predatory fishes are drawn to these schools as to a food

ADULT

JUVENILE

Sargo (sargo rayado, mojarra piedrera) *Anisotremus davidsonii* To 17½ inches. The largest of the Pacific Coast grunts, this familiar fish is often seen by divers alone and in schools around kelp beds, over rocky or rock-sand areas, and near dock pilings and piers. Sargos range from near shore (young) out to 130 feet, chiefly between 8 and 25 feet. They are often taken by surf, boat, and spear fishermen. Adults are distinctive for the dark, vertical bar running from the dorsal fin to the pectoral fin base; juveniles have two dark stripes running horizontally at mid-body, as shown. One-inch fingerlings appear in late summer, schooling with juvenile salemas and black croakers. In early winter, stripes disappear, the black vertical bar appears, and young adults leave schools and become solitary. They join adult schools at 5 inches in length. Adults are often mistaken for the pile surfperch (see page 56). The dark vertical bar on the surfperch is farther back toward the center of the fish, not under the pectoral fin, as on the sargo. **Range:** Santa Cruz (central California) to Bahía Magdalena (Baja California), with a disjunct population in the upper Gulf of California. Also introduced into the Salton Sea in 1951, where it is common. 71

ADULT

JUVENILE

Panamic porkfish (mojarrón, mojarra rayada) *Anisotremus taeniatus*   To 12 inches.
A splendid gold-and-blue-striped fish that seems to be uncommon over its range
but does appear in large, magnificent schools in some areas, including Cabo San
Lucas. Very similar to the Atlantic Coast porkfish, *A. virginicus*. Young are lemon
yellow and white, with two dark stripes on the side and a round black spot at the
tail fin base. **Range:** Cabo San Lucas (Baja California) to Ecuador.

bank, and they take a heavy toll. Closely related to the
snappers, grunts are also noted for their excellence as
food for man. Early settlers in the Florida Keys virtually
subsisted on a diet of "grits and grunts," and today grunts
still form an important part of the fisherman's catch. Although generally small, and considered a panfish, some
grunts attain 1½ feet (burrito grunt) and 2 feet (sargo) in
length.

Grunts, of the family Haemulidae, are so named because
of the sounds they produce by grinding their pharyngeal
teeth together. The adjacent air bladder amplifies the
sound, and agitated grunts can be quite noisy when they
are taken from the water. Some grunts (genus *Haemulon*)
have mouths that are bright orange-red on the inside.
Grunts look much like snappers—right down to the "snapper look" of the head and mouth. However, they differ
considerably in dentition. In the eastern Pacific, grunts
possess feeble jaw teeth but quite formidable pharyngeal
teeth, whereas snappers have vomerine teeth and sharp,
potent canine teeth. The young of most of the grunts
shown here all look very much alike, with black lateral
stripes and a black spot at the base of the caudal fin, as
72 illustrated for the sargo, graybar, and burrito grunts. ◆

ADULT

JUVENILE

Burrito grunt (burrito) *Anisotremus interruptus*   To 1½ feet. A stocky blunt-headed grunt closely associated with reefs, according to Thomson et al. (1979); large adults often swim solitarily and hide in reef caves. It is a nocturnal benthic feeder fond of invertebrates, but is also active during the day along rocky-shore and sand areas. Striped young appear in late summer, swimming in schools near sheltering reefs. They resemble juvenile sargos (except that young burrito grunts have a large black tail spot that the sargo lacks). **Range:** Bahía Magdalena (Baja California) and throughout the Gulf of California to Peru and the Galapagos Islands.

Blackbar grunt (mojarrón, burro) *Anisotremus dovii*   To 1 foot. A striking, handsome fish easily recognized by the three black bars across the body and one through the eye. A fifth pale bar crosses the caudal peduncle. The body color is grayish silver. Note the very large eye, high dorsal spines, and long anal spines. **Range:** southern Gulf of California to Peru; common at Mazatlán and Panama.

73

ADULT

JUVENILE

Graybar grunt (burro, mojarra almejera) *Haemulon sexfasciatum*   To 1 foot. In the central and lower Gulf of California, a diver may round a reef to find a great school of graybars flowing like a gray and yellow cloud between reef canyons. A handsome fish, the graybar sports a contrasting pattern of six gray and six yellow bars on its back (hence the name *sexfasciatum* or six-banded). *Haemulon* means bloody gums and some *Haemulon* species have mouths that are bright red or orange inside. Graybars feed largely at night and, as the Spanish name implies, on clams (*almejas*), and also on annelid worms, crustaceans, lancelets, and snake eels. Juveniles have two black stripes running from eye to tail with a black caudal spot, as shown.
Range: throughout the Gulf of California to Panama.

Cortez grunt (burro, jiniguaro) *Haemulon flaviguttatum*   To 1 foot. A lovely fish with a pearly blue spot on each body scale and, when multiplied by 50 or 60 other fishes massed in a tight school, a splendid sight. They mingle and swim sociably with the wavyline grunt; small schools are often preyed upon by snappers, jacks, tuna, and other large predators. Ranging from near shore out to 50-foot depths, they seek rocky or sandy shorelines by day and move offshore at night to feed on midwater and bottom invertebrates. Note the large dusky spot on the tail fin. Juveniles have bright yellow fins, two lateral stripes, and a very bold spot on the tail. Formerly *Lythrulon flaviguttatum*. **Range:** Punta San Juanico (southern Baja California) and throughout the Gulf of California to Panama.

Spottail grunt (burrito) *Haemulon maculicauda*   To 1 foot. Similar to the Cortez grunt, but the pearly scales on this fish form a striped pattern unlike that of the spotted Cortez grunt. The conspicuous tail spot is also a good identification mark. During the day, spottails school, hover, and hug inshore reefs and piers. At night they move offshore over sandy bottoms to feed on invertebrates. They range from inshore out to 100-foot depths. Formerly *Orthostoechus maculicauda*. **Range:** throughout the Gulf of California to Ecuador.

Salema (ojotón) *Xenistius californiensis*   To 10 inches. Salema are familiar to divers, who often see them in large, iridescent schools, sometimes swimming with other grunts in a magnificent procession. The six to eight orange-brown stripes on the blue-green and silver body are distinctive. Salemas mill over and among rocks near shore or high in the kelp canopy out to 35-foot depths; nocturnally they swarm about docks and piers, picking off the plankton in the night tides. Note the large eye, deeply notched dorsal fin, and upturned mouth designed for plankton feeding. Juveniles appear in late summer, mixing with young sargos and black croakers, and feeding on amphipod crustaceans. Similar to and sometimes mistaken for the striped bass (see page 2). **Range:** Monterey Bay (California) to Peru, including the Gulf of California; rare north of Santa Barbara (California).

Wavyline grunt (rayadillo) *Microlepidotus inornatus*   To 1 foot. These beauties have seven to nine orange-bronze stripes on a bluish steel-gray body. They hover in large, tightly packed schools by day, purling and weaving through reef canyons and rocks and sandy patch-reef areas. After sunset they lie offshore and feed over open sandy areas. They pick crustaceans out of the midwater tides and probe the bottom for mollusks and other invertebrates. Hobson (1968) reports that wavyline grunts are heavily preyed upon by larger fishes, especially at twilight. Attacks reach a peak 20 minutes after sunset, then abruptly cease. **Range:** Bahía Magdalena (Baja California) and the central and lower Gulf of California, to Mazatlán (Mexico).

SCULPINS

Tidepool explorers who roam rocky Pacific coastal shores marvel at the small fishes that dart, often seeming to jump, from one protective pool to another. Many of these are sculpins, of the family Cottidae. Living as they do in a hostile environment—the intertidal zone—makes special demands of a fish. They must be quite small, fast-moving, and able to take advantage of any available cover in very limited living space. They must also hug the bottom and be expert at lurking in rockpools to pounce on small invertebrates, crustaceans, and mollusks for food. To avoid predators, tidepool fishes must be able to blend into the background by rapidly changing color—from green to brown to red to white—to match the tidepool rocks and algae carpeting. Because they live close to shore, they must be adaptable to a wide range of environmental changes—from the coldest Pacific winters to the hottest southern summers—and to wide variations in salinity.

Cabezon, great marbled sculpin *Scorpaenichthys marmoratus*   To 39 inches and 25 pounds. The largest and best-known sculpin, often caught by sport fishermen yet frequently discarded by cooks when they discover the bluish-green flesh; but the meat turns white after cooking and is considered very good eating. Cabezons inhabit rocky, shell-encrusted bottoms from shore out to 250 feet, where crustaceans and mollusks (their favorite food) are abundant. They also feed on squid, octopus, fish eggs (including their own), and small fishes. Couples return to the same nesting site year after year. The nests are about 8 to 10 feet apart, and each female lays from 50,000 to 100,000 white, pink, or blue-green eggs. Males guard the nests and drive away intruders, and will not budge when approached; they can be pushed, stroked, or even lifted with bare hands. Spear fishing seriously threatens the future of the cabezon, since it is vulnerable when nesting. Capable of changing colors—from green to tan to brown to olive—to match its background. **Range:** Sitka (Alaska) to Punta Abreojos (central Baja California). **Edibility:** good, but eggs are extremely poisonous to humans and can produce violent illness.

Fluffy sculpin *Oligocottus snyderi* To 3½ inches. A bright little tidepool inhabitant, extremely variable in color: green to reddish brown to pink to lavender. In the male, shown here, the first ray in the anal fin is greatly enlarged; the first two or three rays are separated from the rest of the fin. Also note the four to six dark saddles on the back, and the forked preopercular spine. **Range:** Sitka (Alaska) to Rio Socorro (northern Baja California), but not found in southern California.

Calico sculpin, mossy sculpin *Clinocottus embryum* To 2¾ inches. Notable for the feathery cirri that decorate its head. Also note the triangular spot below the eye, the six dark saddles across the back, and the brown to orange bars on all except the pelvic fins. Quite common over intertidal areas and shallow, rocky coastlines. **Range:** Bering Sea to Punta Banda (northern Baja California), but not found in southern California.

Pacific Coast sculpins, especially the "tidepool johnnies" of the genera *Oligocottus* and *Clinocottus,* fill most of the above requirements. Most have large heads, and their bright eyes are perched high on the head to give them the widest possible view of their rockpool world. Some, including the fluffy, tidepool, rosylip, and calico sculpins, usually inhabit homepools in the tidepool zone: they may wander across the reefs at flood tides, but almost all return to "home" pools by low tide. This unusual behavior was established over 50 years ago when biologists tagged a number of tidepool sculpins in the San Juan Islands of Washington. This homing tendency has been noted in parrotfishes (see page 117) and rockfishes (see page 34) as well as others.

The inability of the small intertidal sculpins to move away from home tidepools may have serious ecological implications. If there is heavy collecting or pollution in an intertidal area, the chance of certain fish populations being repopulated from nearby areas is reduced. Surveys have 77

Red Irish lord, bullhead *Hemilepidotus hemilepidotus*   To 20 inches. The Irish lords, including the brown Irish lord, *H. spinosus*, and the yellow Irish lord, *H. jordani*, prefer nearshore rocky reefs and intertidal areas, but they also range out to 160 feet. They are notable for their partly scaled bodies. The scale rows form two main bands, one just below the lateral line and the other on the back surrounding the dorsal fin. Reds spawn thousands of pink eggs in March in conspicuous masses. A popular food fish over its northern range. **Range:** red Irish lord, Kamchatka Peninsula (U.S.S.R.) to Monterey Bay (California); brown, southeast Alaska to Santa Barbara (California); yellow, Kamchatka Peninsula to Sitka (Alaska).

Tidepool sculpin *Oligocottus maculosus*   To 3½ inches. Most tidepool watchers have seen this bright, active, shallow-water sculpin; it is common along rocky shores where it hops and darts from one sheltered spot to another like an arrow. It can return to its home tidepool even when moved up to 335 feet away for a period of six months. Males clasp females with a pectoral fin and fertilize pale green eggs as these are deposited on a rock. Note the single spine of the preopercle, forked at the tip, and the irregular, dark saddles across the back. The body is smooth, with no scales or prickles. **Range:** Sea of Okhotsk (U.S.S.R.) and Bering Sea to White Point (Los Angeles County, California).

revealed as many as 30 school buses in a single day on a Marin County, California, beach, with all children collecting marine life. College students spent nearly 7,000 days collecting specimens at the Elkhorn Slough area of central California. Obviously, coastal areas cannot long withstand this kind of threat. New regulations are needed to protect those intertidal areas that are not already hopelessly damaged; these little animals do not need collectors and pollution to add to their daily battle for existence.

Larger sculpins live farther out in the intertidal zone and some range out to 1,200-foot depths. The cabezon, which grows to over 3 feet, is a popular food fish in spite of its blue-green flesh; the roe is poisonous, however. The Pacific staghorn sculpin and the buffalo sculpin are so named because of the large, hornlike spines on their cheeks; they spread their gill covers wide and menacingly to ward off predators. The grunt sculpin, a short, stocky little creature, popular in aquariums, jumps and crawls along the bottom on the tips of its fingerlike pectoral fins. ♦

Pacific staghorn sculpin, armed sculpin, bullhead *Leptocottus armatus* To 18 inches. An abundant sculpin often caught on baited hooks near shore over sandy bottom areas, in bays and estuaries, and even in freshwater coastal streams. Look for the antlerlike (staghorn) preopercular spine on each side of the head, the dark spot on the rear of the spiny dorsal, and the scaleless body. Hart (1973) states that this sculpin will bury itself up to the eyeballs in bottom sand. When stressed or threatened, it may expand its spiny gill covers and emit a low-pitched humming noise, presumably to ward off predators. A voracious feeder, mostly on invertebrates, it is in turn eaten by sea birds, striped bass, and sea lions. **Range:** Gulf of Alaska to north-central Baja California.

Buffalo sculpin *Enophrys bison* To 14½ inches. Like the staghorn sculpin, this fish has large hooklike spines on its preopercle—one large one pointing upward, the other downward. When disturbed, it can present a formidable appearance by expanding and displaying the large, menacing spines on its gill covers. Large and abundant, it is often caught by fishermen on beaches and off rocky areas. Most common inshore, it ranges out to 65-foot depths. Females lay orange-brown eggs in small clusters in February. Males guard these, fanning with pectoral fins to keep eggs oxygenated. Feeds on crustaceans, small fishes, and algae. **Range:** Kodiak Island (Alaska) to Monterey Bay (California).

Grunt sculpin *Rhamphocottus richardsonii* To 3¼ inches. A very strange sculpin often exhibited in aquariums because of its unusual appearance, strange movements, and bizarre mating behavior. It is called the grunt sculpin because of the noises it makes when removed from the water. The short, stocky body is covered with prickles. The eyes move independently. It moves along the bottom and crawls over rocks on the tips of fingerlike pectoral fins in an odd, jerky way; it is an awkward swimmer. At mating time, the female chases the male until she traps him in a cave or crevice, then lays about 150 eggs there and closely guards the male until he fertilizes the eggs, after which he leaves. Grunt sculpins inhabit tidepools, rocky reefs, and sandy bottoms, and require water temperatures of about 45 to 50° F. In Washington and British Columbia they are found in inshore tidepools, but in the San Francisco region they seek depths of 500 to 600 feet to reach cold water. **Range:** Japan to Alaska and south to Santa Monica Bay (southern California).

Rosylip sculpin *Ascelichthys rhodo-rus* To 6 inches. This is the only sculpin on the Pacific Coast that has no pelvic fins ("legs", and the scientific name means "legless" fish with red margins); it has red-tinged lips and a very low, red-margined spiny dorsal fin, no scales, a very smooth skin, and a single white preopercular spine. Look for it under tidepool rocks at low tide and around rocky inshore areas on exposed coastlines. **Range:** Sitka (Alaska) to Pillar Point (central California).

Sailfin sculpin, sailorfish *Nautichthys oculofasciatus* To 8 inches. A popular fish at coastal public aquariums; it swims gracefully with its saillike dorsal fin erected high. Hart (1973) reports that this is a nocturnal fish found inshore and over rocky bottoms out to 360 feet; nighttime SCUBA divers occasionally see it when it forages for food. Eggs are orange and are laid in late winter or spring. One-inch young appear in late May. **Range:** Japan and Kodiak Island (Alaska) to San Miguel Island (southern California).

Great sculpin *Myoxocephalus polyacanthocephalus* To 2½ feet. One of the largest Pacific Coast sculpins; only the cabezon grows larger. Distinctive for the wide, bull head, large mouth, and long upper preopercular spines on both sides of the head. Like the staghorn and buffalo sculpins, it can expand fearsome, spiny gill covers; these, and its great size, effectively frighten adversaries. Can be confused with the buffalo sculpin, but has a longer jaw (reaching to the rear of the eye); the jaw of the buffalo reaches only to the middle of the eye. Food consists of small fishes, including blennies and other sculpins. Quite common over its range on sand and mud bottoms, especially in British Columbia; often taken near shore and at moderate depths. First recorded in British Columbia in 1866 by J. K. Lord. **Range:** Japan to Alaska, the Bering Sea, and to South Puget Sound (Washington).

Threadfin sculpin, filamented sculpin *Icelinus filamentosus* To 10½ inches. Compared to the tidepool species, this is a deep-water sculpin, found on soft sand and mud bottoms from 60- to 1,200-foot depths. Males are immediately recognized by the two long filamentous dorsal spines, as shown. Also note the large, hooked, antlerlike upper preopercular spine, the two rows of scales close to the dorsal fins, and one scale row along the lateral line canal. Males are sometimes blotched with orange and red spots. Feeds on crustaceans, including shrimps and isopods. **Range:** northern British Columbia to San Diego (California).

Snubnose sculpin *Orthonopias triacis* To 4 inches. A small sculpin rarely caught by anglers but familiar to sharp-eyed divers who find it hiding in rocky areas. Distinctive for the large, blunt head, the black spot at the front of the spiny dorsal fin, and the five dark saddles on the back. The anus is farther forward than on most sculpins. Found among or near rocks between high and low tides and near reefs below the intertidal zone, out to 100 feet. **Range:** Monterey Bay (California) to northern Baja California.

Longfin sculpin *Jordania zonope* To 6 inches. An attractive fish thought to be rare before the advent of SCUBA diving. Divers discovered that it hangs vertically on rock faces, and thus was never taken by early trawling methods of collection. Longfin sculpins inhabit rocky areas and kelp beds, are highly territorial, and can change color easily to match background. Note the unusually long anal and spiny dorsal fins, orange tail fin, six to eight dark saddles on the back, and two or three bars on the cheek. Named for David Starr Jordan, eminent U.S. ichthyologist and first president of Stanford University. **Range:** southeast Alaska to San Luis Obispo (central California).

Lavender sculpin *Leiocottus hirundo* To 10 inches. A brightly colored sculpin thought to be quite rare until SCUBA divers discovered that it was a common fish on sandy bottoms and rocky subtidal areas out to 120 feet. Distinctive for the very long first two dorsal fin spines that are erected like a lance when the sculpin is under stress, and for the blue-spotted dorsal fins. A smooth, scaleless fish with twin points on the upper preopercular spine. **Range:** Santa Barbara (southern California) and Santa Rosa Island to Punta Banda (northern Baja California).

Smoothhead sculpin *Artedius lateralis* To 5½ inches. Very common along the Canadian coast in tidepools and shallow water out to 43 feet. The female lays tiny cherry-red eggs in a mass in February in a sheltered area among the rocky tidepools, and the eggs hatch in about 16 days. Note the pointed head, protruding upper jaw, narrow band of scales on the back, and six dark saddles on the back. **Range:** Kodiak Island (Alaska) to northern Baja California.

Scalyhead sculpin *Artedius harringtoni* To 4 inches. Distinctive for the orange head in both males and females, the red bars radiating from the eyes, and the red spot at the tips of the first two dorsal spines. Clemens and Wilby (1946) report that the mature courting male becomes very robust, develops a large head, enlarged front teeth, and plumed cirri over its eyes. It also assumes colors and patterns that are quite unlike the female and the immature male. Courting males are very territorial, displaying aggressively to repel intruders; so different are they that they were once described as a separate species. Scalyheads prefer intertidal and subtidal rocky reefs and pilings and range out to 70-foot depths. **Range:** Kodiak Island (Alaska) to San Miguel Island (southern California).

GREENLINGS, LINGCOD, AND COMBFISHES

The greenlings and the lingcod are in a small family of North Pacific cold-water fishes—the Hexagrammidae—that are related to the rockfishes and sculpins. Most of them are rocky-bottom dwellers that have mailed cheeks and flaring pectoral fins like the sculpins. Their heads are usually smooth, however—not bony and spiny like those of the rockfishes and sculpins. Some of the larger species are excellent food fishes. The intense green flesh of the kelp or rock greenlings or young lingcod may dismay the uninitiated until they find that cooking dispels the green and the meat is then white, flaky, and delicious. It is often compared to the rockfish in taste and quality.

Greenlings are often brightly colored, and some are adept color changers. The lingcod can change colors in a flash from dark to light: trawl fishermen, when boating a thrashing 3-foot lingcod, often see light-yellow sides flash to dark black or brown, and orange spots turn to brown.

The kelp greenling is distinctive for its bright colors and the conspicuously different color patterns of the male and female. The first record of this handsome fish was made back in 1866 in British Columbia by an early naturalist, J. K.

Rock greenling *Hexagrammos lagocephalus*   To 2 feet. A striking fish with colors that can blend and precisely match sun-dappled rock and seaweed, its customary background. The ground color, as shown, is dark green; brilliant blood red slashes and spots cross the body and fins. The inside of the mouth is blue. Note the large cirrus over the eye. Has five lateral line canals, as do most greenlings covered here. Found in rocky areas along shallow, exposed coastlines where it is a valued catch of shore fishermen. **Range:** Bering Sea to Point Conception (southern California).

83

Lord. He was overcome with the beauty of the animal, and his description has become a classic in fishy literature: "Its sides . . . rival in beauty many a tropical flower . . . [and are] adorned with colors not only conspicuous for their brilliancy, but grouped and blended in a manner one sees only represented in the plumage of a bird, the wing of a butterfly, or the petals of an orchid . . . red, blue, orange, and green are so mingled that the only thing I can think of as a comparison is a floating flower bed, and even the gardener's art, in grouping, is but a bungle contrasted with nature's painting."

Most greenlings have more than one lateral line and some have five. They have a small skin flap or cirrus over the eyes and all have small ctenoid scales; the lingcod has cycloid scales.

The combfishes—members of the family Zaniolepididae—are distinctive for their rough scales and tough skin, which give the body a sandpaper-like texture. They have high, comblike dorsal fins; the first three spines in the dorsal fin of the longspine combfish are extremely elongated. ◆

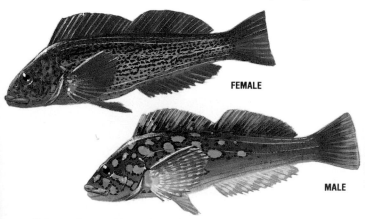

FEMALE

MALE

Kelp greenling, greenling seatrout *Hexagrammos decagrammus*   To 21 inches. A favorite catch of rock-shore fishermen from British Columbia to northern and central California. Once hooked, these greenlings head straight for a hole or crevice or tangle of kelp or seaweed. They are masters at shaking loose from a line, and it takes an expert fisherman to land one. They are often found in kelp beds and over sandy bottoms from near shore out to 150 feet. The male is brown-olive in body color with striking irregular blue spots on the head and the front of the body. The female is peppered all over with small reddish-brown spots on a tan or gray-brown body. Her fins are reddish orange. This greenling has five lateral lines. **Range:** Aleutian Islands to La Jolla (southern California).

Painted greenling, convict fish *Oxylebius pictus* To 10 inches but rarely over 6 inches. Because it is a secretive fish living in rocks and crevices, and does not take bait, it is rarely encountered by shore fishermen. Divers often see it hovering motionless in the water column. It is also seen on the bottom near rocky holes and crevices or hanging vertically on steep rock faces, sometimes near kelp beds. Found from 4 to 120 feet and occasionally out to 160 feet. Strangely, it is immune to the stinging cells of the *Telia* anemones that are common in northern waters. Distinguished by five bold, dark bars on the body, a long, pointed head, two pairs of cirri on the head, a single lateral line (instead of the usual five), and a notched anal fin. **Range:** Kodiak Island (Alaska) to north-central Baja California.

Shortspine combfish *Zaniolepis frenata* To 10 inches. This combfish has much shorter spines in the dorsal fin than does the longspine. The rough scales are set firmly in a tough skin, giving it a sandpaper-like texture. There is a pronounced cirrus above the eye; the second spine in the dorsal fin is longer than the third. Found mostly on mud bottoms from 180 to 800 feet; often abundant in trawl catches. **Range:** southern Oregon to central Baja California.

Atka mackerel *Pleurogrammus monopterygius* To 19 inches. Named for the Aleutian island where it is found in abundance. Jordan and Evermann (1902) reported that on an expedition to the Aleutians in 1892, crew members caught 585 within four hours of handline fishing off Attu Island. Because the ship was out of fresh meat, all of the fish were soon eaten by officers and crew. The forked caudal fin is distinctive (other greenlings have square-cut tail fins), as are the broad dark bars on the side. Found in depths from 15 to 400 feet. **Range:** the Sea of Japan to the Bering Sea and south to Redondo Beach (southern California); fairly rare south of Alaska.

Masked greenling *Hexagrammos octogrammus* To 11 inches. A northern species with greenish-brown coloring (though this varies with background) and a large cirrus over the eye, which can be laid back when the fish is so inclined. Also note the smallish mouth and teeth, and five lateral lines—the first long and the fourth very short. Like other members of its family, it seeks out shallow, rocky areas along the coast. **Range:** Sea of Okhotsk (U.S.S.R.) to Banks Island (central British Columbia).

Longspine combfish *Zaniolepis latipinnis* (above left) To 1 foot. This and the shortspine combfish are closely related to the greenlings. The longspine combfish thrives on mud bottoms at 120 to 660 feet. They are frequently caught in deepwater trawls. Curiously, when dumped on deck from a trawl net, the combfishes try to take their own tails into their mouths, often remaining in a U-shaped configuration. The skin is almost sandpaper-like to the touch; the first three spines in the dorsal fin are very long—the second is the longest. Note the single lateral line, the very small cirrus over the eye, and the black stripe from eye to snout. **Range:** Vancouver Island to central Baja California.

Lingcod *Ophiodon elongatus* To 5 feet, but usually 4 feet or less, and 70 pounds. A valuable, popular sport and commercial species, esteemed by bottom and spear fishermen as excellent food. The flesh of lingcod is often greenish in color like that of greenlings, but it is harmless and the color soon disappears with cooking. It is a voracious predator, feeding on herring and such bottom fishes as flounder, hake, pollock, and cod. Lingcods range from near shore (juveniles) to depths of 1,400 feet (large adults). Tagged fish have been recaptured after years of freedom at the same spot where they were released. Others, however, seem to be migratory. Recognized by its large mouth, long canine teeth, long dorsal fin with a notch, and a single lateral line. **Range:** Kodiak Island (Alaska) to northern Baja California.

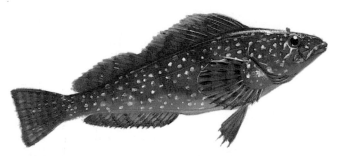

Whitespotted greenling *Hexagrammos stelleri* To 19 inches. Easily recognized by the pearly white spots or "stars" on the body and head. It has five lateral lines, but the fourth is very short and restricted to the breast area. Also note the small cirrus over the eye. Inhabits rocky shores as well as sandy beaches. Young shore anglers in British Columbia catch them regularly, calling them tommycod or rocktrout. A good sport fish that makes excellent table fare. **Range:** Japan to Puget Sound (Washington).

SEA CHUBS, MOJARRAS, PORGIES, SPADEFISHES, AND GOATFISHES

The fishes described here are the nibblers, grazers, rooters, pickers, and bottom grubbers of the reef.

The sea chubs (family Kyphosidae) comprise three subfamilies: nibblers (Girellinae), rudderfishes (Kyphosinae), and halfmoons (Scorpidinae). Nibblers are omnivorous rocky-shore and kelp-bed dwellers that have hinged lips and fine comblike teeth, which enable them to nibble very well. The opaleye and Gulf opaleye, members of this family, roam inshore reefs in large schools, singly and in small pods, feeding on algae, kelp, and invertebrates. Rudderfishes are so called because some species follow ships. The Cortez chub and the zebra perch are both rudderfishes, but neither seems to swim in the wakes of ships. The zebra perch swims near shore in small aggregations, often with sergeant majors. Cortez chubs are found in small schools over rocky reefs and seagrass beds. The halfmoon, tasty and abundant all year around, is valued by southern California rock anglers.

The Pacific flagfin mojarra (family Gerreidae) is a small, silvery fish with large jet-black eyes. Mojarras sometimes

Opaleye (ojo azul) *Girella nigricans*   To 26 inches. In its range, found almost everywhere off rocky shores, kelp beds, piers, and jetties; familiar to southern California shore fishermen, rock anglers, and divers. The oval shape, olive-green color, one or two bright spots below the dorsal fin, and brilliant blue-green eyes are easily recognized; there is often a white bar across the nose. Juveniles are gray-blue above and silvery below. Opaleyes feed mostly on seaweed, occasionally on invertebrates. At spawning time in the spring, they gather into dense schools inshore and in kelp beds. The eggs and larvae are pelagic and have been found miles from shore. **Range:** San Francisco to Cabo San Lucas (southern Baja California).

Gulf opaleye (chopa gris, ojo azul) *Girella simplicidens* To 1½ feet. This opaleye is found only in the Gulf of California; it is very abundant in the upper Gulf and much less common in the lower Gulf. It resembles the opaleye (*G. nigricans*) but has three to four white spots on its back instead of one or two, and is a dark brownish gray. Gulf opaleyes roam the reef in small to large schools, grazing the algae in shallow rocky areas and searching out invertebrates. Young opaleyes congregate in tidepools. Among the hardiest of the Gulf fishes, they can tolerate water temperatures down to 46° F (when other fishes expire from cold) and summer temperatures up to 95° F. **Range:** see above.

Bronze-striped sea chub, blue-bronze chub (chopa rayada) *Kyphosus analogus* To 18 inches. To the diver, these appear silvery or steel gray over the reef; closer inspection reveals fine, brassy pinstripes on the sides. Some chubs will occasionally flash to a white-spotted coloration, especially when distressed. Found in small schools over rocky bottoms, seagrass beds, coral reefs, and often in strong-current areas such as cuts and jetties, chubs are plant and invertebrate feeders. They are powerful fighters when hooked. **Range:** recently reported from Oceanside (southern California), it ranges south to the Gulf of California and Peru.

follow divers over sandy shores hoping for a meal to turn up. They are recognized by the black spot or "flag" on the tip of the dorsal fin. Pacific porgies (family Sparidae) are deep-bodied, silvery fishes that roam sandy shores and patch reefs looking for crabs, shrimp, and mollusks. They can blow jets of water into the sand (much as does the triggerfish) to expose burrowing invertebrates. Spadefishes (family Ephippidae) are large, compressed fishes that swim in great schools. Curious fishes, they will sometimes circle a surprised diver as he watches in awe. Goatfishes (family Mullidae) are the bottom grubbers of the reef. Their distinctive characteristic is long, tactile, highly sensitive barbels under the chin, with which they busily probe the bottom for small crustaceans and worms. Some species also gather into schools; a vast school of yellow-striped Mexican goatfishes is a sight to see—like a shimmering curtain of white, pink, and gold. ◆

88

Pacific flagfin mojarra (mojarra) *Eucinostomus gracilis* To 8¼ inches. A diver may turn while gliding over a sandy shore or patch reef to find himself being shadowed by a small, silvery fish with large, watchful jet-black eyes—this will probably be a mojarra. They feed on such small invertebrates as worms, mollusks, crabs, and shrimp, which they dig out of the sand with long, protrusible mouths; they follow a diver in the hope that he will scrape or plow the bottom, as a ray or a flatfish might do, to expose food. The flagfin mojarra is recognized by the distinct black tip or "flag" on the spiny dorsal fin. A similar species, the spotfin mojarra (*E. argenteus*), has a dusky spiny dorsal, with no distinct black spot at the tip. **Range** (both species): Anaheim Bay (southern California), and the Gulf of California, to Peru.

Halfmoon (medialuna) *Medialuna californiensis* To 19 inches. Tasty and abundant all year around, this is a "bread and butter fish" for the southern California rock angler. Named for the lunate shape of their tails, halfmoons swim high in the water column when over rocky areas; they swim at mid-depth in kelp beds—one of their favorite haunts. They seek cover in kelp and dive into crevices among the rocks when threatened. They feed on seaweed and small invertebrates and range from near shore out to 130 feet, but are most common between 8 and 65 feet. Halfmoons are recognized by their oval shape, dusky patch at the upper rear of the gill cover, and small mouth. A thick sheath of scales covers the soft dorsal and anal fins. Juveniles are blue above, silvery below. **Range:** Vancouver Island to the Gulf of California; abundant in the Channel Islands.

Zebra perch (chopa bonita) *Hermosilla azurea* To 17 inches. A shallow-water schooling fish, the zebra perch is easily recognized by the 11 or 12 bars on the side, the bright blue spot on the gill cover, and the dark patch at the base of the pectoral fin. It is found from near shore out to 25 feet and seems to be uncommon; it is rarely collected and not often seen by divers. It feeds mostly on algae and invertebrates. Juveniles sometimes swim with sergeant majors. **Range:** Monterey (California) to the Gulf of California; common in the upper and central Gulf.

Pacific spadefish (chambo) *Chaetodipterus zonatus*   To 25½ inches. These magnificent fishes grow quite large and are nearly circular, like silvery dinner plates, with five or six dark bars. Seen underwater, a large school of spadefishes is impressive. They are sometimes curious about divers, and have been known to circle one in numbers, walling him in by a silvery, moving cylinder. They are omnivorous, with a special craving for shellfish, and are found over sand and rubble-strewn bottoms as well as around reefs, piers, wrecks, bridges, and offshore oil platforms, where crustaceans are abundant. Tiny coppery-brown juveniles drift motionless near shore mimicking seaweed, leaves, mangrove pods, and floating trash. **Range:** San Diego (California), and throughout the Gulf of California, to northern Peru.

Red goatfish (chivo) *Pseudupeneus grandisquamis*   To 1 foot. Also known as the bigscale goatfish, this fish is not a reef species but frequents moderate depths over soft mud or sand bottoms, probing with its barbels to seek out crustaceans and mollusks and, as a result, often collected in shrimp trawls. **Range:** normally, from the Gulf of California, where it ranges widely, to Chile; one collected at the artificially warm outfall of the San Onofre nuclear power plant in southern California in 1979.

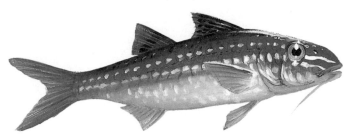

Mexican goatfish (salmonete) *Mulloidichthys dentatus* To 1 foot. These often swim lazily in large aggregations around rocky reefs, or forage singly over sand and mud bottoms, rooting with tactile-sensitive barbels for crustaceans, mollusks, and polychaete worms. They are willing clients to barberfishes or cleaner butterflyfishes (see page 97) that maintain cleaning stations around the reefs. Sometimes several goatfishes, all hanging vertically, head down, may completely surround one or two small cleaner barberfishes, awaiting the cleaner's ministrations. This goatfish is a color changer and may phase from a light to a dark pinkish-red coloration while being cleaned of parasites, or from all-white to rose to pinkish to yellowish silver as the background and occasion demand. Note the yellow stripe from eye to tail with a blue margin, prominent barbels below the jaws, and the bright yellow tail. **Range:** Long Beach (southern California) to Peru, including the Galapagos Islands; in the Gulf of California, from Guaymas to Cabo San Lucas.

Pacific porgy (pez de pluma) *Calamus brachysomus* To 2 feet. Deep-bodied, silvery bottom fishes with firm, moist, white flesh; prime table fare and a fisherman's delight. The young are found in seagrass beds; adults roam sandy shores, patch reefs, and piers over depths from 10 to 60 feet, looking for crabs, shrimps, and mollusks. They devour these with small, powerful jaws armed with canine teeth and strong molars. The forehead is steep, and the mouth set low on the head. Porgies have faint bars on the body but can change color rapidly to dark irregular blotches. **Range:** Oceanside (southern California) to Peru, but rare north of Baja California; common in the northern Gulf of California.

91

ANGELFISHES

One of the puzzles of the marine world is the dazzling beauty and brilliance of certain fish species, including the remarkable angelfishes. The king angelfish, the Cortez angelfish, and the Clarion angelfish—all members of the family Pomacanthidae—have vividly beautiful adult phases as well as brightly colored and completely different juvenile color phases. In a world of dangerous predators, why would a fish species be decorated in lavish, conspicuous colors, easily visible from many yards away? The

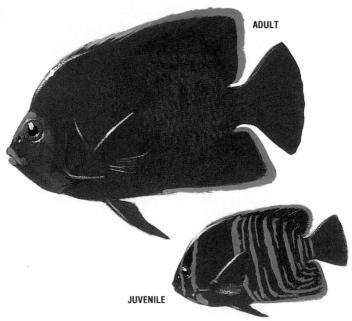

ADULT

JUVENILE

Clarion angelfish (ángel de Clarión) *Holacanthus clarionensis*   To 1 foot. A lovely reef fish, both as juvenile and adult. First found at Isla Clarión, in the Revillagigedo island group where it was thought to be endemic, it has since been found in the lower Gulf of California but is quite rare; fishwatchers keep a sharp eye for additional sightings. The juvenile closely resembles the juvenile king angelfish, but note the predominantly orange head and tail of the Clarion juvenile, compared to the bright yellow tail and head of the king juvenile; also, the clear area on both juveniles running from just behind the eye to the middle of the pectoral fin is wider on the Clarion juvenile than on the king juvenile. They occur around coral and rock reefs out to depths of 100 feet or more. **Range:** Isla Espiritu Santo (lower Gulf of California) to Cabo Pulmo (near Cabo San Lucas), and Isla Clarión (Islas Revillagigedo).

JUVENILE

Cortez angelfish (ángel de Cortés)
Pomacanthus zonipectus To 1 foot.
This splendid fish appears to be a
hardier species than the king angelfish
and can tolerate wider extremes of
temperature. It is quite common over
shallow reefs throughout the Gulf of
California, feeding on sponges—a major diet item—and algae, tunicates, hydroids,
bryozoans, and eggs. Since they share the same food source, Cortez angelfishes
mix and often swim with king angelfishes in feeding aggregations. Thomson et al.
(1979) report that, in contrast to the sociable adults, the juvenile is often solitary,
fiercely territorial, and will attack its own mirror image; juveniles feed on algae and,
to a large extent, parasites they pick from larger fishes. An unusual aggregation of
about 60 half-inch juveniles joined into a tight cluster was reported by Thomson et
al. (1979). Spawning occurs from midsummer through early fall; juveniles are common from August through November. **Range:** Puerto Peñasco (northern Gulf of
California) and Punta San Juanico (southwestern Baja California) to Peru.

93

ADULT

JUVENILE

King angelfish (ángel real) *Holacanthus passer*   To about 14 inches. One of the most gorgeous fishes in the eastern Pacific. The body of the adult is blue-black, flecked with light-blue scale edges and bordered in orange and light blue, with a surprising slash of white near the center. A large school of these fishes is awe-inspiring. Juveniles are brilliantly jacketed in bright yellow or orange and pale blue with shades of black and white. The king angelfish is wary of divers and more difficult to approach than the Cortez angelfish. They seem to prefer fairly shallow reef habitats where the water is clean and clear; they are often found with Cortez angelfishes, sometimes swimming in mixed aggregations. They range out to 250-foot depths, grazing the reef for algae and invertebrates, and consuming great amounts of sponge and plankton. They are frequently seen in pairs at spawning time in late summer; the females, visibly smaller than the males, will defend a territory aggressively. Juveniles are occasionally seen cleaning parasites from larger fishes. **Range:** central Gulf of California to Ecuador and the Galapagos Islands.

answer, according to modern biologists, is that even more important than dangerous predators is the danger of crossbreeding or ineffective breeding.

Because these fishes are precisely evolved to fit a particular niche in the underwater world, the loss of uniqueness and specialization by crossbreeding could spell disaster for the species. To ensure that mistaken selections for mating are kept to a minimum, most angelfish species are distinctly and conspicuously colored. Additional fidelity within the species is gained by the behavior, common among many angelfishes and butterflyfishes, of pairing off and mating for life. One more behavioral trait common among certain lavishly colored reef fishes—including the damselfishes, butterflyfishes, and angelfishes—is territoriality and aggressiveness. Konrad Lorenz observed that brilliantly colored fish were unequivocally more aggressive than less brightly colored kinds. Other researchers have found that this is not necessarily true—some plain-colored fishes are also extremely aggressive. At all events, few dispute the aggressiveness and territoriality of angelfishes, which are almost always directed against competing angelfishes, especially those of the same species and sex. The juvenile Cortez angelfish is fiercely territorial and solitary, and will attack its own mirror image. Many adult angelfishes will pair off and closely patrol their territory in tandem. When neighbor angelfish pairs meet at the borders of their territories, each pair will bristle and display aggressively, asserting dominance on their "homeground."

Angelfishes are closely related to butterflyfishes, and so like them that they are frequently classed in the same family. They differ from butterflyfishes in having a strong, sharp spine at the lower edge of each gill plate. Perhaps because of this extra weapon, angelfishes seem a bit more aggressive than the more timid and retiring butterflyfishes. Most angelfishes feed heavily on small invertebrates, principally sponges and tunicates, but also algae. Juvenile angelfishes have feeding habits quite different from those of adults; some will frequent coral reef "cleaning stations," and pick parasites from larger fishes who come for this service. Angelfishes are abundant in the tropical eastern Pacific but are increasingly rare (and may have been completely eliminated) in some easily accessible diving locales. Their curiosity and boldness make them easy targets for thoughtless spear fishermen. ◆

BUTTERFLYFISHES

The butterflyfishes of the eastern Pacific can boast of some unique and interesting species, although these are less colorful and fewer in species compared to the many-splendored butterflyfishes of the Indo-Pan-Pacific (in Hawaii alone, there are 20 colorful species). The barberfish is one of the few butterflyfish species that seems dedicated to cleaning other fishes. Although juvenile fishes of many species function as cleaners, the barberfish continues this behavior all through its adult life and sets up "cleaning stations" around the reef to service its many client fishes. The scythe butterflyfish is distinctive for the prominent sickle-shaped mark that arcs across its body, and for the surprising depths at which it is found; Richard Rosenblatt of the Scripps Institution of Oceanography, riding aboard a Cousteau expedition submarine, observed one at a depth of almost 500 feet. The longnose butterflyfish is a splendid little visitor from the Indo-Pacific that seems to have

Threebanded butterflyfish (muñeca) *Chaetodon humeralis*   To 10 inches. The most common butterflyfish in the eastern Pacific. It is almost always found in pairs or small groups poking about shallow patch reefs or open sand bottoms from 10 to 40 feet, sometimes ranging out to 180 feet. It has been seen to mingle with schools of small spadefishes. The three black bands across the body are distinctive, the first bar running down through the eye. Juveniles are colored like adults with no color change. **Range:** San Diego (California; one record) to Peru, including the Gulf of California and the Galapagos Islands; abundant along the mainland coast of the Gulf, less so along the Baja side.

Scythe butterflyfish *Chaetodon falcifer* To 6 inches. The name *falcifer* means scythe bearer and this fish is distinctive for the prominent scythelike marking running in an arc from opercle to tail. A beautiful fish but rarely seen by divers because of its preference for deep reefs. It has been found from fairly shallow areas and kelp beds out to 492 feet and has been reported at Cabo San Lucas from 120 to 250 feet. Note the high spinous dorsal fin and long snout. **Range:** Santa Catalina Island (southern California) to the Galapagos Islands, including Cabo San Lucas and Isla de Guadalupe.

Barberfish (barbero) *Johnrandallia nigrirostris* To about 8 inches. This is an industrious cleaner fish with a masked, raccoon-like face. Not unlike human barbers, they set up cleaner stations in or near rock or coral reefs, and larger fishes come to be cleaned of parasites (hence the name). The station may have one or more barberfishes cleaning one or a number of client fishes. Barberfishes also feed on algae, gastropods, and nonparasitic crustaceans. Found over depths from 20 to 40 feet and occasionally down to 130 feet. Distinctive for the black mask over the eyes, the black patch above the eyes, and the black band running from the spiny dorsal to the tail. Named for John Randall, U.S. ichthyologist. **Range:** central Gulf of California to Panama, including Isla del Coco, Isla de Malpelo, and the Galapagos Islands.

97

Longnose butterflyfish *Forcipiger flavissimus* To 6 inches. A splendid little fish, not easy to find in the eastern Pacific but occasionally collected at Cabo San Lucas in the Gulf of California or in the Islas Revillagigedo. It occurs singly or in small groups from shallow reefs to 75 feet, preferring areas with numerous ledges and small caves. It probes with its long, tweezerlike snout for small invertebrates. Note the black-tinged forehead, the ocellus or eyespot on the anal fin, and the black tail. **Range:** through the Indo-Pan-Pacific from the Red Sea to Japan; here, central Gulf of California from Guaymas to Cabo San Lucas and the Islas Revillagigedo.

found a home around the Islas Revillagigedo and at Cabo San Lucas in the Gulf of California.

Hans Fricke, working at Eilat in the Red Sea, marked three neighboring pairs of butterflyfishes and observed them carefully over a two-year period. Each pair closely patrolled its territory and ritually threatened its neighbor pair each time they met, but none ever crossed over the invisible boundary that separated the territories. This preference for a home territory affords the butterflyfishes optimum use of available food and shelter while assuring peaceful coexistence.

Butterflyfishes are members of the family Chaetodontidae. Chaetodonts are disc-shaped fishes with small mouths set with bristlelike teeth (*chaeta* = bristle, *odont* = tooth). Some, like the longnose butterflyfish, have highly adapted snouts for picking small invertebrates from coral crevices. Although seemingly fragile and defenseless against the numerous predators of the reef, butterflyfish are able to survive by their rapidity, agility, defensive shape, and coloring. Most have a dark stripe or patch passing through and concealing the eyes. This confuses attackers trying to strike at the head of the butterfly. These fishes rarely stray far from shelter and their narrow bodies fit easily into cracks and holes in the reef. If cornered, they lower their heads and spread their dorsal and anal spines, presenting the attacker with a difficult, prickly meal to swallow. ◆

DAMSELFISHES

Occasionally divers find themselves ferociously attacked by a dusky little fish that dashes from its rock or coral cranny and insistently rushes forward, sometimes nipping lightly at the divers' arms, legs, or fins. This tiny reef marauder is the damselfish, a member of the family Pomacentridae and one of the most territorial, pugnacious residents of shallow tropical rocky shores and coral reefs. Damselfishes are sometimes seen attacking and driving off entire schools of surgeonfishes or parrotfishes that come too close to their crevices or nests. The pomacentrids are small tropical fishes distinguishable from most other marine species in having only one nostril on each side of the

ADULT

JUVENILE

Garibaldi *Hypsypops rubicundus* To 14 inches. These brilliant, highly visible fishes are so resolutely orange that they are easily seen in clear water from docks, piers, and the decks of boats. Their bright color makes them easy prey for spear fishermen and they are now protected in California, where it is illegal to catch, spear, or retain this fish; it should be released if hooked inadvertently. Because of this protection, garibaldis are quite numerous along the coast from Monterey (California) south to Baja California. The juvenile has a shimmering orange-red color with iridescent blue spots and trim; it is one of the loveliest of all reef fishes. Garibaldis inhabit clear water near rocky reefs and kelp beds and closely defend a reef hole or crevice. They range from near shore out to 95 feet. Garibaldis swim with a sculling motion of the pectoral fins. **Range:** Monterey Bay (California) to Cabo San Lucas (Baja California), including Isla de Guadalupe off central Baja California; juveniles have been found at Cabo San Lucas.

snout, instead of the usual two. Pacific Coast damsels range in size from the 4-inch beaubrummel to the 1-foot giant damselfish and the garibaldi, which grows to 14 inches. Most damselfishes are omnivorous, feeding on benthic algae, plankton, crustaceans, and other invertebrates. They inhabit inshore reefs, rocky flats, coral reefs, and tidepools to depths of 50 feet. Some range out to 250 feet and greater depths.

Most pomacentrids spawn on the bottom, and complex mating behavior has been reported among some species. The male fish clears a strongly defended territory on a section of rock, and begins a series of looping motions over the territory to indicate to passing females that he is ready to spawn. When an egg-bearing female accepts his invitation, she is led to the cleared area. But each damselfish species performs the mating ritual a little differently. The

BREEDING MALE

ADULT

Panamic sergeant major (pintaño, chopa) *Abudefduf troschelii*   To 9 inches. Easily recognized by the six dark bars bordered by yellow resembling the chevron of a sergeant major in the army. It is very common and familiar to divers in the Gulf of California, occurring close inshore in small and large aggregations around rocky reefs, piers, and breakwaters; juveniles are frequently found in tidepools. They feed on plankton from the surface to the middle of the water column, and on invertebrates and algae across the reef. The breeding male darkens in color as shown and becomes very pugnacious. Unlike other species, however, adult male sergeant majors defend their territories only at breeding time, swimming sociably at other times in loose aggregations. Also found to be a cleaner fish. Two-year-old juveniles have been observed picking parasites from schools of mullet, halfbeaks, and needle-fishes in the Gulf. **Range:** throughout the Gulf of California, and Punta San Juanico (southern Baja California), to northern Peru and the Galapagos Islands.

garibaldi courts the female by rushing her while making thumping noises. The female deposits her eggs in the nest using an adhesive that attaches the eggs in clusters. The male then fertilizes the eggs with his spawn. The nests are pugnaciously defended by the male alone in some species. In others, both male and female guard the eggs and some species live permanently in pairs.

Damselfishes can be quite noisy when disturbed. Some express aggressiveness by making clicking noises with the pharyngeal teeth. Others, like the garibaldi, produce thumping sounds so audible that they are clearly heard by approaching divers. Some species of male damsels emit a distinct churring sound—brrrrr—during spawning. This sound is probably an important component of mating, without which the female would not lay eggs. After days of constant activity in defense of the nest and vigorous fanning of the eggs to keep them oxygenated, hatching time arrives. The vigil ends when the tiny hatchlings are left to fend for themselves on the vast, teeming reef. ◆

ADULT

JUVENILE

Cortez damselfish (pez azul de Cortés) *Stegastes rectifraenum* To 5 inches. One of the most territorial damselfishes in the Gulf of California. Adults sometimes attack entire schools of surgeonfishes or parrotfishes who swim too near to a home rock or crevice. They will vigorously strike at Panamic sergeant majors—a closely competing species—large basses, wrasses, and even divers who get too close. The electric-blue-and-black-jacketed juvenile is common in small aggregations over rocky flats and shallow shore bottoms. As they mature, they become solitary and select a home territory in some rocky cranny, which they defend against competitors. During courtship, males darken noticeably in coloration and females take on a light tan hue around the head with bright yellow lips. **Range:** northern Gulf of California to Cabo San Lucas (commonest in the central Gulf); strays along the outer Baja coast to Bahía Magdalena.

ADULT

JUVENILE

Pacific beaubrummel (pez de dos colores) *Stegastes flavilatus*   To 4 inches. The Spanish name, fish of two colors, describes the juvenile, which, with its sky blue dorsal surface and bright-yellow lower body, is a truly splendid little fish to see. Note the black ''eye'' spot ringed in blue on the rear dorsal fin, and the smaller spot near the tail. As it matures, the beaubrummel turns light brown in color with yellow fins. Like the Cortez damsel this fish is strongly territorial and pugnacious toward other species, especially competing damselfishes. It swims over a depth range from 5 to 30 feet and has been seen at depths of 125 feet. Omnivorous, it feeds on algae and invertebrates. **Range:** central Gulf of California to Ecuador.

Clarion damselfish *Stegastes redemptus*   To about 5 inches. Named after Clarion Island, where this damsel was first discovered, one of the most remote islands of the remote Revillagigedo chain off the Mexican coast. It was subsequently collected at Cabo San Lucas, and so appears to have a wider range than first seemed evident. Adults are unique for their gray-blue body, pale caudal peduncle, and yellow fins; juveniles, also distinctive, have an all-yellow body, spots on the soft dorsal fin and caudal peduncle, and dark margins on the body scales. Found around shallow reefs feeding on algae and invertebrates. **Range:** uncertain; to date, collected from Cabo San Lucas (Baja California) and Islas Revillagigedo.

ADULT

JUVENILE

ADULT

JUVENILE

Whitetail damselfish *Stegastes leucorus* To 5 inches. Distinctive for the white tail in both juvenile and adult, and for the greenish back. In the Gulf this species inhabits deeper water and is not encountered at less than 20-foot depths (adults). Evidently most abundant around Cabo San Lucas at 30 to 40 feet, with juveniles encountered at 10 to 15 feet. **Range:** Cabo San Lucas (southern Gulf of California) to Mazatlán, Isla de Guadalupe (off west coast of Baja California), and Islas Revillagigedo.

Dusky sergeant major (pintaño) *Nexilarius concolor* To 6 inches. Closely resembles the Panamic sergeant major but differs in having six to seven dark bars that are less distinct, a much steeper head profile, and overall much darker coloration. The dusky sergeant major is found along rocky shorelines with a strong surge zone; it usually hugs the surf zone. **Range:** Bahía Magdalena (outer Baja California coast) to Peru and in the Gulf of California, from Guaymas to Cabo San Lucas.

103

Blacksmith *Chromis punctipinnis* To 1 foot. Abundant over steep rocky banks and kelp beds year-round in southern California, but rarely taken on a hook because they are, for the most part, plankton feeders with very small mouths. Sometimes large schools of blacksmiths are seen together with senoritas and topsmelt picking and filtering small organisms from the currents around kelp beds. At spawning time, the female lays masses of salmon-pink eggs in a nesting area cleared by the male. The male guards the nest aggressively, driving off all interlopers. Year-old young are gray-blue anteriorly and yellow-orange posteriorly with blue margins on dorsal, tail, and anal fins. Adults are distinctive for the perch shape, an undivided dorsal fin with more spines (13) than rays (11), and the dark greenish-blue or violet-blue body with a series of dark spots from head to tail. **Range:** Monterey Bay (California) to central Baja California.

Scissortail damselfish (castañeta) *Chromis atrilobata* To 5 inches. Look for the scissortail damsel in the blue water high above the deep outer reefs. These handsome fishes cluster together, sometimes in great clouds, feeding on the zooplankton in the prevailing current. You may see them all facing in the same direction, picking copepods, one by one, from the flowing water mass. They are not pugnacious or territorial like other damselfish species. Juveniles and adults are colored much alike. They are easily recognized by the long, slim body, deeply forked tail, black margins on the tail fin, and a conspicuous white spot near the tail under the last dorsal ray. There is a dark blotch at the pectoral fin base. They are common at depths from 20 to 65 feet and are found out to 250 feet. **Range:** upper Gulf of California to northern Peru and the Galapagos Islands.

ADULT

JUVENILE

Silverstripe chromis *Chromis alta* To 5 inches. A very flashy damselfish that sports a diagonal, silvery racing stripe from the front tip of the dorsal to the tail. Alex Kerstitch reports that the silver stripe is evident only on the living fish. The stripe always fades away soon after the fish is collected (personal communication) Juveniles, also striking, with iridescent blue spots over the body, are quite similar to Cortez damselfish juveniles. This fish is found around deeper reefs (75 to 250 feet). **Range:** Islas San Benito (outer Baja California coast) to the Galapagos Islands, and (in the Gulf of California) from Guaymas to Cabo San Lucas.

Blue-and-yellow chromis *Chromis limbaughi* To about 6 inches. A striking, beautiful fish, spotted in electric blue and bright yellow. In older adults, these colors fade slightly. They range over 60- to 250-foot depths and occur in aggregations around large and small patch reefs. Juveniles are often found in shallow water (10 feet). **Range:** apparently endemic to the Gulf of California and to date found only through the central and lower Gulf from Bahía de Los Angeles to Cabo San Lucas.

Bumphead damselfish *Microspathodon bairdi* To about 1 foot. Similar in some respects to the giant damselfish, but bumphead damselfishes are dark brown and have bright-blue eyes; and adults have a pronounced hump on the forehead. The bumphead also lacks the long trailing fin rays of the giant damselfish. Juveniles, rarely seen, resemble young beaubrummels with iridescent blue tones above the lateral line and bright yellow-orange below. Adults are common around Cabo San Lucas and frequent rocky bottom and patch reef areas. **Range:** central Gulf of California to Ecuador, including Islas Revillagigedo and the Galapagos Islands.

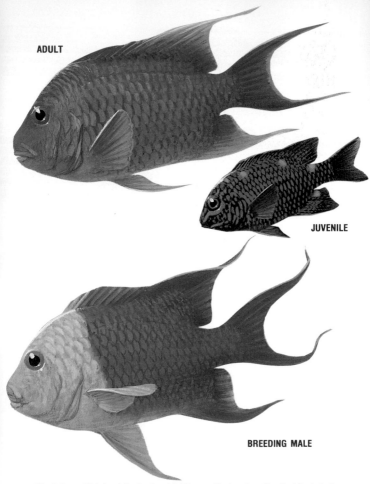

ADULT

JUVENILE

BREEDING MALE

Giant damselfish (castañuela gigante) *Microspathodon dorsalis*   To 1 foot. A diver new to the Gulf of California investigating a tumbled, rocky flat near shore may be surprised to see many giant blue-black fishes busily darting from boulder to boulder. Because these are such large fishes, they suggest some new angelfish species, but they are giant damselfishes. Filaments stream off the dorsal, anal, and caudal fins of some older, larger fishes. Some adults are deep blue or pastel blue from nose to tail. Even juveniles are adorned with iridescent blue spots and markings as shown. Giant damselfishes are aggressive herbivores, and breeding males have been seen to attack large fishes and even divers that venture too close to their nests at spawning time. During courtship, the breeding male often turns silvery white on the head and front half of the body as shown. Both male and female adults develop large humps on their foreheads as they mature. **Range:** Bahía Kino (central Gulf of California) to Isla de Malpelo (Colombia) and the Galapagos Islands.

WRASSES

While diving around shallow reefs in the Gulf of California you may see a gaudy, cigar-shaped fish busily paddling about with its pectoral fins, dragging its tail behind. If so, you are watching a member of the wrasse family (Labridae). Pacific Coast wrasses range in size from the flashy 6-inch Cortez rainbow wrasse to the 3-foot California sheephead. They are often brilliantly colored, usually buck-toothed, and always voracious, opportunistic predators. The California sheephead roves across rocky flats and through kelp beds searching out crustaceans and mollusks, which it will pry off rocks with its protruding canine teeth. The hogfish roots about happily in sand flats

Senorita *Oxyjulis californica*   To 10 inches. Cigarlike in shape and size, the senorita is found almost everywhere by divers—from rocky tidepools out to 140 feet; in and around kelp beds, among seaweeds, and over rocky bottoms and reefs; and in dense schools, small scattered groups, or by itself. It is a successful cleaner fish; a lone senorita may be surrounded by dozens of fishes waiting to be cleaned of parasites. Sometimes many senoritas work as a team to clean a giant sea bass, a large ray, or a mola. They also clean garibaldis, blacksmiths, opaleyes, halfmoons, surfperches, and sargos, removing such ectoparasites as copepods, isopods, and bacteria. Voracious carnivores, senoritas constantly feed on almost any small invertebrate or scrap of food found anywhere in the water column or on the bottom. Feder et al. (1974) report that, when incoming currents flowing into kelp beds, lagoons, or bay entrances are heavy with larval fishes, squids, and crustaceans, large schools of senoritas and blacksmiths can be seen picking the plankton out of the water. When frightened, senoritas will dive for cover into a sand bottom or dive through kelp fronds or seaweed. They often burrow into the sand bottom and sleep there at night. This labrid does not reverse sex as most wrasses covered here do— males and females retain one gender throughout life. Note the large black spot at the base of the caudal fin, the small buckteeth, and the large cycloid scales. **Range:** Salt Point (northern California) to Isla Cedros (central Baja California).

after worms, crustaceans, and mollusks. Razorfishes are found over sand flats or seagrass areas where they can dive quickly for cover into the sand. Most of the smaller cigar-shaped wrasses seek out shallow rocky reefs with sand patches where they can dive for cover. The Cortez rainbow wrasse seems to move easily in all habitats.

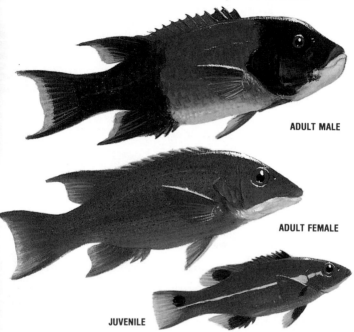

ADULT MALE

ADULT FEMALE

JUVENILE

California sheephead (vieja) *Semicossyphus pulcher*   To 3 feet. This splendid fish grows quite large, is very good eating, and, much like the giant sea bass (see page 6) and the white seabass (see page 63), its numbers have declined drastically off southern California, because of heavy fishing pressure, especially spear fishing, and reduction of kelp beds—the favorite haunt of the sheephead. Moreover, like many groupers and sea basses, this wrasse changes sex from female to male during maturation (at a length of about 1 foot) and mature males fertilize the young females; since many spear fishermen rationalize that they "shoot only the big ones," they effectively exterminate many breeding males. Large males, which can live to 50 years of age, are now very rare. They frequent kelp beds and rocky reef areas where they feed heavily on sea urchins, mollusks, lobsters, and crabs. With their prominent canine teeth, they are experts at prying mollusks off rocky reef faces and bottoms. Note the prominent white chin on both male and female and the dark-spotted fins of the rose-colored juvenile. Some sheepheads, especially juveniles, will secrete a mucous cocoon or "sleeping bag" at night that presumably protects the fish as it sleeps. **Range:** Monterey Bay (California) to Isla de Guadalupe (off north-central Baja California) and the Gulf of California.

Most of the wrasses shown here are adept at diving into the bottom, where they disappear instantly into the sand. All wrasses are diurnal and become inactive at night. Many of them have the ability to sleep buried in the sand. An aquarium full of fifty 8-inch senoritas that swarm about the tank by day will be deserted at night—all are sleeping soundly in the bottom sand. Certain wrasses, including the Mexican hogfish and juveniles of the California sheephead, secrete a mucous cocoon "sleeping bag" at night. No one is sure what purpose it serves, but one the-

Cortez rainbow wrasse (arco iris, viejita) *Thalassoma lucasanum*   To 6 inches. This brilliant fish takes its name from the rainbow stripes of young males and females. As they mature, some females reverse sex and join some males to metamorphose into the secondary-phase colors. The large secondary males mate one-on-one with females, and do not join the group spawning rushes of the younger males and females. Strangely, the large secondary males are rare and only moderately successful in mating, according to Warner (1984), for there is simply not enough territory for them to mate individually with females. Young primary males are very common, and nearly all mating takes place in groups. At night rainbow wrasses lie wedged into rock crevices, often partly covered with sand. Juveniles sometimes perform as cleaners, picking parasites off other fishes. Very common in the Gulf of California; colorful swarms frequent shallow reefs and feed on algae, crustaceans, and soft coral. **Range:** central and lower Gulf of California to Panama, including the Galapagos Islands and Isla de Malpelo.

JUVENILE AND ADULT MALE AND FEMALE

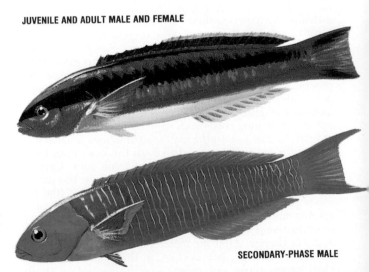

SECONDARY-PHASE MALE

ory holds that it protects the sleeping fish against such nighttime marauders as the moray eel, which relies on scent to locate its prey.

Another behavior trait that serves as a meal ticket is picking parasites off other fishes. Adult senoritas, juvenile Mexican hogfishes, and Cortez rainbow wrasses function as cleaner fishes to remove ectoparasites from other fishes. One opportunistic fish, the sabertooth blenny (see page 200) has gone to great lengths to mimic the Cortez rainbow wrasse as a false cleaner fish in order to facilitate attacks on other unsuspecting fish.

Like their cousins the parrotfishes, many wrasses undergo startling changes in color and form as they mature into adults. For many years, the process by which this occurred was wrapped in mystery. Confusion in the identification of wrasses was manifest when, time and again, fishes thought to be separate species turned out to be male and female or adult and juvenile of the same species. It now appears that virtually all wrasses are protogynous hermaphrodites—that is, females are capable of turning into males, and all males are either born with that gender or are sex-reversed females. In most wrasse species, like the genus *Halichoeres* covered here, all start out life as females; then, at a certain point, they reverse sex to become males—which then fertilize the young females. The sheephead wrasse and the rock wrasse reverse sex when about 1 foot in length. (The sea basses and groupers—family Serranidae, see page 2—also reproduce in this manner.)

In other species, such as the Cortez rainbow wrasse, the process is somewhat different. Young juvenile wrasses, both male and female, mature when as small as 1½ inches, and mate in groups. Such mating usually begins with an upward spawning rush by an egg-laden female. She is followed by numerous young males, all of whom assist in fertilizing the eggs. The eggs drift with the tides until fully developed larvae emerge about one week later. Certain males and females of this species seem to reject this mode of reproduction, however. They metamorphose (the females reverse sex) and become "secondary males" at a specific point in their maturation. It appears that age, size, reproductive potency, and other factors all dictate the incidence of change. After the metamorphosis, the males and ex-females emerge, peacocklike, in the brilliant colors— blue, green, pink, and yellow—of the secondary-phase 110 male Cortez rainbow wrasse. These large, colorful sec-

MALE

FEMALE

Rock wrasse (cocinero) *Halichoeres semicinctus* To 15 inches. Likes rocky habitats, locating its home near rocky bottoms with small patches of coarse sand. It ranges from tidepools out to 78-foot depths and is often a solitary wanderer across the reef searching for such preferred food as amphipods, small crustaceans, and dove and slipper shells. When frightened or disturbed, it will quickly dive into a patch of sand. At night, like the senorita, the rock wrasse sleeps buried in the sand; sometimes it is stranded by low tides. Distinctive for the small mouth equipped with sharp, protruding canine teeth used for picking small invertebrates from the bottom. The male shows an unmistakable large dark bar under the pectoral fin. The female has dark spots on scale rows of the back and midbody, as shown. The juvenile is brown with a broad cream stripe from mouth to tail and, occasionally, a fine cream stripe running across the upper back. All rock wrasses are born as females; when about 1 foot in length, they change to males, and fertilize young females. **Range:** Point Conception (southern California) to Isla de Guadalupe (north-central Baja California) and throughout the Gulf of California.

Sunset wrasse (viejita) *Thalassoma lutescens* To 7 inches. A beautiful fish under water with its blue-green body, orange-red head, and curved lines radiating out from the eyes. Note the yellow pectoral fins edged in black, the black spot at the front of the dorsal fin, and (in adult males) the flowing, lunate tail. Small 1- to 2-inch juveniles are green with a silvery stripe running from eye to tail. The stripe is bordered by maroon on the upper margin. As they mature they phase to a yellowish-brown color, changing to a reddish-orange when about 4 inches in length, and phasing to green in the adult coloration. **Range:** common around rocky shores in the lower Gulf of California, especially from La Paz to Cabo San Lucas; it ranges to Panama and is found around major offshore islands; abundant in the Islas Revillagigedo. Quite common also in the Indo-Pacific, it is found in Hawaii, Japan, Micronesia, Melanesia, Polynesia, and to Australia.

ondary males also mate with females in upward spawning rushes, but one-on-one in male-female pairs, rather than in group matings. There is one exception, so far as is known, to the protogynous mode of reproduction among the Eastern Pacific wrasses. The senorita (*Oxyjulis californica*) does not reverse sex—all are born either male or female and they retain that gender all their lives.

The flesh of the wrasse is generally soft and pasty, and unattractive as food, with a few exceptions. The California sheephead, which grows to 3 feet, and the Mexican hogfish, reaching $2\frac{1}{2}$ feet, are considered good eating and are prize catches for fishermen. Unfortunately, sheephead populations off southern California have declined drastically because of spear and boat overfishing. Large males are now quite rare. ♦

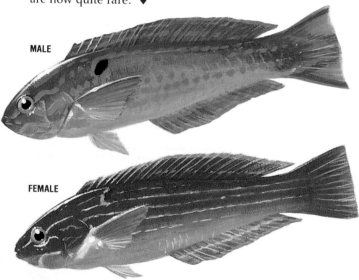

MALE

FEMALE

Chameleon wrasse (señorita camaleón) *Halichoeres dispilus* To about 8 inches. Frequents rocky shallow reefs surrounded by sandy bottom. As the name implies, it is an accomplished color changer: Hobson (1968) reports that both males and females can expertly match the background color. Often salmon-red in color over rocky reefs, they will switch in a flash to pale blue or striped coloration over a sand bottom. Like other wrasses, they dive for cover into sandy bottoms if alarmed, and sleep buried in the sand at night. Occasionally they find themselves perilously stranded on exposed sandbars at extreme low tides. Adults may be identified by the blackish spot below the fourth and fifth dorsal spines. Juveniles have two dark lateral stripes running from eye to tail. **Range:** throughout the Gulf of California to Peru.

ADULT MALE

JUVENILE

ADULT FEMALE

Spinster wrasse (soltera) *Halichoeres nicholsi* To 15 inches. A wrasse of subdued colors but quite handsome at all phases. Males are bluish-green with a large black bar behind the pectoral fin flanked by a conspicuous yellow spot. Females also show the black bar, which joins a broad black stripe at midbody. Young are pale yellow, boldly marked with black blotches and a distinctive, large "eye" spot on the soft dorsal fin. Fairly common in the Gulf of California from 10 to 40 feet; some have been recorded out to 250 feet. Solitary adults poke about the reefs feeding on mollusks, brittle stars, sea urchins, and crabs. Juveniles swim in small groups, often mingling with other juvenile wrasses. **Range:** throughout the Gulf to Panama, including the Islas Revillagigedo; also in the Galapagos Islands.

Banded wrasse (señorita de cintas) *Pseudojulis notospilus* To 10 inches. Males, females, and juveniles all have very similar coloration except that the young have a large "eye" spot on the rear of the dorsal fin. A rocky reef dweller that feeds on mollusks, crustaceans, urchins, and brittle stars. **Range:** throughout the Gulf of California (though uncommon) and Bahía Magdalena (Baja California) to Peru, including the Galapagos Islands; abundant south of Mazatlán (Mexico).

ADULT MALE

ADULT FEMALE

JUVENILE

Wounded wrasse (señorita herida) *Halichoeres chierchiae* To 8 inches. The adult male is brilliant and distinctive, with what almost appears to be a spear wound in its side. The mature female is also colorful, with yellow and reddish-orange stripes and reticulations from eye to tail. Both the juvenile and adult female have a black "eye" spot between the second and third dorsal spines. Found around shallow rocky reefs with adjoining sandy patches, feeding on crabs, mollusks, urchins, and brittle stars. **Range:** throughout the Gulf of California to Acapulco (Mexico).

Galapagos hogfish, harlequin hogfish (vieja colorada) *Bodianus eclancheri* To about 20 inches. These splendid wrasses are colored almost like goldfishes in sparkling, harlequin patterns of orange, black, and white. Apparently every fish is colored differently—some almost completely black, others solid orange with count-less patterns in between. Note the hump on the head common on both males and females. The black spot at the base of the pectoral fin is also evident on all of these wrasses. These fishes spawn in groups, with no pattern of domination by large, territorial males. The population is equally divided—half male and half female. **Range:** once thought to be found only in the Galapagos Islands but now known to range from Ecuador to central Chile, including the Galapagos Islands.

MALE

FEMALE AND JUVENILE

Mexican hogfish (vieja) *Bodianus diplotaenia* To 2½ feet. Not abundant anywhere, but not uncommon over rocky reefs from 15 to 60 feet in the Gulf of California and, occasionally, at 250-foot depths. This fish usually works singly, rooting about hoglike in sandy bottoms and scouting the reefs for crustaceans, mollusks, and small fishes. Sometimes they follow parrotfishes or groupers, snapping up scraps of food left over from the meal of the larger fish. Large male Mexican hogfishes dominate spawning by setting up restricted territories over closely guarded areas of the reef. Each defends his spawning site against younger males. Each day, females come and select the largest and most colorful male for mating. Very young (1-inch) juveniles are bright lemon-yellow; they industriously clean their own and numerous other species. Young often seek cover in the branches of black coral. **Range:** throughout the Gulf of California to Chile, including most major offshore islands. 115

ADULT

JUVENILE

Pacific razorfish (viejita) *Xyrichthys pavo*   To 15 inches. The name razorfish comes from the very compressed, razorlike head and dorsal surface possessed by most razorfishes. Shaped almost like the prow of a ship, they can dive into the sand and even swim along under the sand to escape predators. Both adults and juveniles have another defense. The first two dorsal spines can be pointed forward, lancelike, to repel predators. Commonly seen over open sandy bottoms near rocky reefs from 15 to 40 feet. Tiny juveniles mimic leaves, floating seaweed, and debris, and are very difficult to recognize as they drift back and forth with the tide. This razorfish is quite common in Hawaii and is a valued food fish there. **Range:** lower Gulf of California to Panama, including most offshore islands.

Clown razorfish, pearlscale razorfish (viejita) *Novaculichthys taeniourus*   To 12 inches. Like the Pacific razorfish, this wrasse has a narrow razorlike forehead, which can be a distinct asset when burrowing into gritty reef sand and gravel. It frequents patch reefs and will dive swiftly for the sand if threatened. Note the four or five lines radiating from each eye (hence, clown) and the white area in the center of each scale (hence, pearlscale). The young are so different from the adults that for many years the two were classified as separate species. Tiny juveniles undergo a number of changes in color and form as they metamorphose into the adult phase at about 4 inches. Unlike the adults, young are found among fronds of seaweeds, relying on their green coloration for camouflage. **Range:** central and lower Gulf of California to Panama; a common Indo-Pacific and Hawaiian wrasse.

JUVENILE

ADULT

PARROTFISHES

If you dive off any shallow coral reef as the tide is coming in, you are likely to encounter dozens of gaudy parrot-fishes (family Scaridae). They swarm in over the reef in blue-green, gray, and rust-colored waves, grazing like Guernsey cows through the coral. Many parrotfishes are large and bulky, and must wait for high tide to flood the close-packed coral reefs to give them room to maneuver and feed. They are single-minded, gentle creatures of habit, and have set patterns of travel. Occasionally I have come nose-to-nose with a large parrotfish in a narrow de-file, and had to back off respectfully to let it pass. They are not easily deterred from their feeding routes, and they seem to regard the curious diver with tolerance and some irritation for interrupting their nonstop, movable feast.

Although closely related to the carnivorous wrasses, parrotfishes are grazing herbivores. They are named for their gaudy colors and the parrotlike beaks with which they scrape off chunks of reef rock and coral, leaving distinct beak marks on the reef. In their constant quest for food, they are highly efficient recycling mechanisms. As

Bumphead parrotfish (guacamaya, perico) *Scarus perrico* To 2½ feet. The largest of the genus in the eastern Pacific. Large males and females are easily identified by the massive, fleshy hump on the head over the eyes. The bumphead is the only Pacific Coast parrot in which there is no substantial difference between the sexes. Note the dark blue stripes fanning out from the eyes, the blue stripes around the lips, and the bluish-green body with predominantly blue fins. The tooth plates that form the large beak are also blue. Bumpheads are seen in small aggregations over coral reefs from 10 to 100 feet. They feed largely on coralline red algae. **Range:** central Gulf of California to Peru and the Galapagos Islands.

ADULT MALE AND FEMALE

Bicolor parrotfish, red-lipped parrotfish (perico, pez loro) *Scarus rubroviolaceus* To about 20 inches. This wide-ranging parrotfish is found from the Indian Ocean and East Africa to Hawaii to Panama and the Gulf of California. Color and form differences between adult male and female and the secondary male of the species are very striking. The name bicolor applies quite well to the two-toned female and primary males, but the secondary-phase male is mostly green. The name red-lipped parrotfish is used in some parts of the world and this name fits the secondary-phase male very well, while having no relation to the adult female and primary male. They are very handsome fishes, whatever they are called. The secondary-phase male has green teeth, as shown, while the female and primary male have white teeth. Bicolor parrotfishes are found in areas where coral reefs are abundant, from near shore out to 100 feet; they scrape algae from the coral with their large beaks. **Range:** lower Gulf of California to Panama and the Galapagos Islands.

they graze algae off the reefs, they turn coral and rock into fine sand. They extract the algae by crushing the rock-hard coral with powerful platelike pharyngeal teeth located in the back of the throat, then pass this stony rubble down an apparently cast-iron digestive tract. Because of their set patterns of travel and almost constant defecation, they leave mounds and floors of fine sand and undigested 118 coral rubble throughout the reef. Experiments at Bermuda

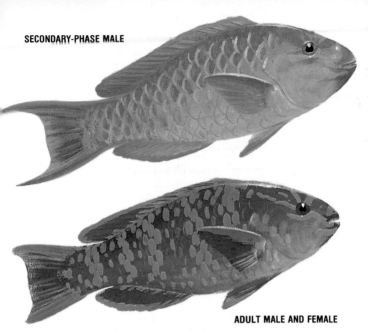

SECONDARY-PHASE MALE

ADULT MALE AND FEMALE

Bluechin parrotfish (pez loro, perico) *Scarus ghobban*   To 1½ feet. The adult males and females and secondary-phase males of the species are starkly different in color. The secondary-phase male is the one with the blue chin, not to mention a striking pink, blue, and green body, and handsome blue and pink fins. Adult females and primary males have a delicate beauty, too, with harlequin-spotted scales forming vague bars on the sides of the pale orange-brown body. This parrotfish is more slender than other species covered here and has a more conical head. **Range:** Indian Ocean and Red Sea to Panama and the central Gulf of California, including the Galapagos Islands.

indicate that some parrotfishes may use the sun for navigation; the rainbow parrotfish (*S. guacamaya*) traveled a good distance from its nocturnal home cave to feed by day and returned at evening by the same route, on a direct course to its cave.

Recent interest and knowledge of the scarids, speeded by the advent of SCUBA diving, has revealed that parrotfishes undergo profound color changes as they mature. The reasons for these changes and the processes by which they occur are not well understood, but it now appears that—like wrasses—most parrotfishes are protogynous hermaphrodites, and females are capable of reversing sex to become males. Most species mature through three different color phases, including juvenile, adult, and male 119 secondary-phase colorations. Adult male and female parrotfishes often share the same color pattern, but some males, and certain females that have reversed to male gender, will mature into large secondary-phase males and sport gaudy peacock- or parrotlike colors and long, flowing tails. Much new information has brought clarification, realignment, reduction of species, and order to the colorful parrotfishes. Of some 350 scarid species previously recorded throughout the world, a recent study reduced this number to 80, and some of these are in doubt.

The considerable difference between male and female parrotfishes is clearly illustrated here by the bicolor, blue-chin, and azure parrots. In general, it is safe to say that most of the brilliant blue, green, pink, and lavishly striped or mottled parrots are adult secondary-phase males, whereas most of the dull gray, blue, red, or brownish-colored parrots are females or primary males. Juvenile parrots $1\frac{1}{2}$ to 4 inches long of most tropical eastern Pacific species are colored a light green or brown, with stripes, spots, bars, or other body markings that differ according to the species.

In a recent study and generic rearrangement of the eastern Pacific parrotfishes, Rosenblatt and Hobson (1969) report finding three basic sequences of color change in these fishes. In the bumphead parrotfish (*Scarus perrico*), the simplest, the dark-colored juvenile phases to the greenish adult; there is no great difference between male and female fishes. In the bicolor (*Scarus rubroviolaceus*) and blue-chin (*Scarus ghobban*) parrotfishes, the juvenile coloration is followed by an adult phase that is the same for both male and female; many adult females keep this coloration throughout life, but certain males and sex-reversed females phase into yet another distinctive coloration, the secondary-phase male, with brilliant green, blue, or pink coloration and flowing, lunate tails.

The azure parrotfish (*Scarus compressus*) is even more complex in transformation as it matures. The juvenile coloration phases to another color pattern in which both sexes are similar. Then, both sexes transform, and each has distinctive male and female colorations as large adults. Small wonder that fish experts have had such a problem in pinning names to the incredible parrotfishes—there are so many of them and they undergo such marvelous, magical sea changes!

120

The loosetooth parrotfish of the subfamily Sparisomatinae is smaller and more wrasselike in shape and habits than any of the other parrotfishes shown here. It is usually found in *Sargassum* and other seaweed habitats, where its kelplike coloration blends perfectly with the seaweed. ♦

ADULT MALE AND FEMALE

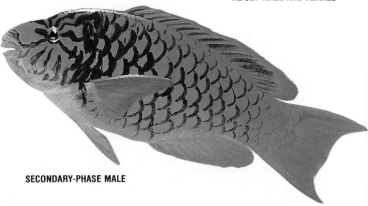

SECONDARY-PHASE MALE

Azure parrotfish (perico, pez loro) *Scarus compressus* To 2 feet. Large males are distinctive with bright green bodies and scales outlined in orange-brown. Note the green stripes radiating from the eye. Similar in many ways to the bumphead parrotfish, especially in shape. Large females are light metallic-blue to azure to gray. Juvenile males and small females are reddish-brown with dark streaks running along the scale rows. Teeth are green in all phases. They graze algae over shallow reefs from near shore out to 75 feet. **Range:** Guaymas and Bahía Concepción (central Gulf of California) to Panama and the Galapagos Islands.

SECONDARY-PHASE MALE

ADULT MALE AND FEMALE

Stareye parrotfish, halftooth parrotfish (pez loro) *Calotomus carolinus* To 18 inches. Named for the distinctive bands radiating from the eye of the male. This fish seems to be a recent immigrant from the Indo-West Pacific and is quite rare in the eastern Pacific. Rosenblatt and Hobson (1969) report it being collected only at remote Isla Socorro (in the Islas Revillagigedo group), though recently two stareyes were seen at Bahía de Las Palmas (near Cabo San Lucas, Baja California). It is related to the loosetooth parrotfish but differs in having overlapping teeth with free tips on both jaws and canine teeth in the upper jaw. **Range:** see above.

Loosetooth parrotfish (loro) *Nicholsina denticulata* To 12 inches. The smallest parrotfish in the eastern Pacific; in size, shape, and habits it resembles a wrasse more than a parrotfish. It is called loosetooth because its teeth are not completely coalesced into a beak as are those of most parrotfishes. Often found in small aggregations in seaweed and is most abundant in winter when *Sargassum* seaweed and *Padina* and other algae growth is full. It is colored much like its habitat, drab seaweed brown. **Range:** throughout the Gulf of California and the outer Baja coast from Bahía Magdalena to Peru and the Galapagos Islands.

SALMONS, TROUTS, AND CHARS

Picture the lone fly fisherman standing in a stream or by a river, locked in battle with a splendid, silvery salmon or trout. Dedicated anglers leave families, jobs, even television sets for the unique joy of hooking them, and they grow panic-stricken in the face of someday losing these lordly fishes. "I desperately want to see the salmon survive as a species," says Prince Charles of Great Britain, and he describes the "excitement, tranquility, and appalling despair" brought to him by the noble animal. The species he had in mind was the Atlantic salmon, *Salmo salar*, much venerated by anglers in the North Atlantic. Izaac Walton called it "the King of freshwater fish." Overfishing has long been a bane of salmon fishermen. Who should fish them? How many fish should be taken? When to stop fishing? An early Scottish king, Robert III, sentenced to death any fisherman taking a salmon out of season. For the past 100 years most countries have enforced laws aimed at controlling the salmon catch so that remaining stocks can replenish themselves. But today the ecological deck is so heavily stacked against the salmon that its extinction may not be far off. Salmon stocks along the Pacific and Atlantic coasts have diminished, especially over the southern parts of their ranges, because of overfishing, pollution, habitat destruction, and barrier emplacement. Acid rain is now having a devastating effect on Atlantic Coast salmon. In time, it will also take its toll on Pacific Coast species.

There are five species of salmon in the eastern Pacific—the pink, sockeye, coho, chinook, and chum. As it matures, each species phases from juvenile form to the sea-run, breeding male, and breeding female forms, and the unique shape and coloration of each phase are illustrated in the following pages. The five species range from Korea and Japan to Baja California. Salmon feed and spend most of their lives in the sea, and spawn in freshwater streams and rivers, a migratory behavior called "anadromous," from the Greek for "running upward." Some, like the chinooks from the Columbia River, may travel over 2,500 miles to the Aleutians during their sea migration. Sockeyes swim more than halfway to Asia and back to British Columbia. When ready to spawn, they miraculously find their home rivers again. Research demonstrates that migrating salmon can maintain widely divergent courses while hundreds of 123 miles at sea, yet strike land with precision at their place of origin. Chum salmon, after the rigors of their seaward migration, travel nearly 2,000 additional miles upstream in the Yukon River to their spawning grounds in Teslin Lake—a truly incredible journey. Some salmon exhaust 96 percent of their fat and 53 percent of their protein reserves in the battle upstream.

Salmons, trouts, and chars are coldwater fishes, members of the family Salmonidae. They are native to the northern hemisphere, but many have been introduced worldwide to such places as the high mountain lakes of Ecuador and the streams, rivers, and lakes of Europe and New Zealand. All salmonids have a small adipose fin near the tail and small cycloid scales. There are no spines in any of the fins—just soft rays. The body is usually robust, and there is a well-defined lateral line.

Our five Pacific salmons spend from one to several years at sea, depending on the species, before returning to spawn in the streams where they were born, and then all adult males and females die. For a period of several months each year each Pacific salmon family is represented only by a network of eggs, because both parents have died and no offspring have yet hatched. However, the

Dolly Varden *Salvelinus malma*   To about 3 feet and 40 pounds (average: 1½ to 2 feet). Species lacking teeth on the rear roof of the mouth count as chars (genus *Salvelinus*), not as pure trout. The Dolly Varden, a troutlike char, is closely related to two other chars—the brook trout (*S. fontinalis*) and lake trout (*S. namaycush*) —and it, too, is usually found in fresh water. Some populations, however, are anadromous, and the sea-run Dolly Varden is dark blue above, silvery on the side, and silvery to whitish on the belly, with creamy white spots on the side. In cold, mountainous headwater streams the color is quite different, with bright orange or red spots on the sides. The ventral and anal fins are whitish on the leading edges. The fish is named after a character in Charles Dickens's novel *Barnaby Rudge*. Miss Dolly Varden's pink-spotted dress was so vividly described that the name sprang to the mind of the very literate angler who named this fish. **Range:** Korea to the Bering Sea and to Oregon, including freshwater populations in California and other western states. **Edibility:** the flesh is delicious—often pink in color. (See also the closely related Arctic char, p. 132.)

life cycle of trouts and chars is different: after spawning they do not die. Female salmon deposit large ($\frac{1}{8}$- to $\frac{1}{3}$-inch) eggs in depressions or nests (redds) in the gravel of cold-water streams. Eggs are fertilized by the male and covered with gravel. Several months pass until the salmon larvae wriggle up through the gravel. Some juveniles move down to the ocean soon after emerging, and others may remain in fresh water for months or even a year or two, depending on the species. All salmon juveniles (except for the pink salmon) and all juvenile trouts have parr marks on their sides, which aid considerably in their identification.

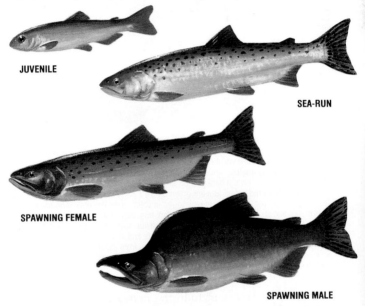

JUVENILE

SEA-RUN

SPAWNING FEMALE

SPAWNING MALE

Pink salmon, humpback salmon *Oncorhynchus gorbuscha*   To 2½ feet and 12 pounds (average: 3–5 pounds). The smallest Pacific salmon, and caught by fishermen in the greatest numbers. The pink flesh obtains a lower price than the rich, red, and delicious sockeye salmon, but pink salmon are more abundant than any other Pacific salmon—and are therefore the most valuable to commercial fishermen. Look for the large, black, oval spots on the back and covering the caudal fin. Pink salmon spawn in late summer only slightly upstream from the sea. Spawning males develop a large humped back (hence the name) and a hooked upper jaw (or kype). Juveniles are the only salmon young with no parr marks. **Range:** anadromous in sea, rivers, and small streams from Japan to the Arctic Ocean and Bering Sea, Alaska, British Columbia (over 700 streams in B.C.), Washington, Oregon, and northern California to La Jolla (southern California, as a stray); also successfully introduced into the upper Great Lakes. **Edibility:** excellent.

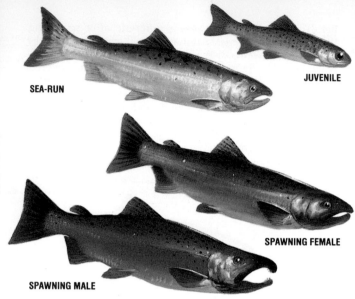

SEA-RUN

JUVENILE

SPAWNING FEMALE

SPAWNING MALE

Coho or silver salmon *Oncorhynchus kisutch*   To 3 feet, 2 inches and 33 pounds (average: 6–12 pounds). A favorite of sport fishermen because they strike hard, run, leap, and fight hard when hooked. They are second only to the chinook in numbers caught by anglers, and are also heavily fished commercially. Note the irregular black spots on the back and on the upper lobe of the tail fin. Spawning males have bright red sides, and are green on the back. Females are similar but less brightly colored. The flesh is pink to red in color. Juveniles have long narrow parr marks and an elongated anal fin. Offshore migrations take some fishes as far as 1,000 miles; they feed on herring, kelp greenling, rockfishes, and sand lance. Spawning occurs in the headwaters of large rivers and in over 970 small streams. **Range:** anadromous in sea and freshwater streams from Japan to Baja California, with center of abundance between southeast Alaska and Oregon. Also introduced into the Great Lakes. **Edibility:** excellent.

Pacific sea trouts include the famed rainbow trout or steelhead and the cutthroat trout (sometimes called the coastal cutthroat trout to separate the anadromous form from the landlocked, non-anadromous form). The rainbow trout is one of the most popular game fishes in the world. Most juveniles remain in fresh water for two to three years before moving to the sea. A sea-run rainbow or steelhead will remain for two to three years in the sea, after which it returns to spawn in coastal streams in the fall or winter. Cutthroat trout are usually freshwater fishes but some populations are anadromous. They resemble the rainbow 126 but have a red or orange "cutthroat" stripe on their lower

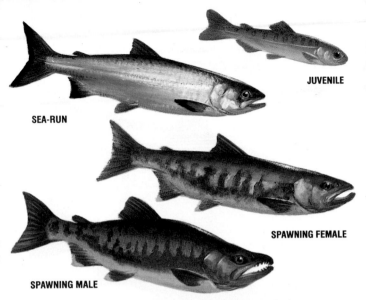

JUVENILE

SEA-RUN

SPAWNING FEMALE

SPAWNING MALE

Chum salmon, dog salmon *Oncorhynchus keta*   To 3 feet, 4 inches and 31 pounds (average: 10–15 pounds). Distinctive for the fine speckling on the back, but it has no black spots. There are dark tips on pectoral, anal, and caudal fins. The leading edges of the pelvic and anal fins are pale white, especially in males. In autumn, after their sea run, chum salmon move into some 800 rivers and streams on the Pacific Coast. Despite ocean migrations of hundreds of miles, some chum salmon travel nearly 2,000 additional miles up the Yukon River to spawn in Teslin Lake. Breeding males have brick red sides and develop large canine teeth, which may have earned them the name dog salmon. The parr marks on juveniles are mostly above the lateral line. **Range:** anadromous in sea and freshwater rivers and streams from Japan to the Bering Sea and Alaska, British Columbia, Washington, Oregon, California's Sacramento River, and to San Diego (southern California). **Edibility:** good, but less pink than the pink salmon and lacking fat content, so canned chum salmon is not highly regarded. It is often called "silverbright" salmon when marketed. It smokes well; favored by Pacific Coast Indians.

jaw. The body and fins are covered with dark spots. The European brown trout was introduced almost 100 years ago to all continents. It is a real challenge to fly fishermen because it is a difficult fish to catch.

The Dolly Varden is a troutlike char closely related to the brook trout and lake trout and, though some populations are sea-migratory, it is often found landlocked in freshwater streams and lakes. The Arctic char resembles the Dolly Varden in many respects, but it is found in the frigid waters of Alaska, Siberia, Norway, Iceland, Greenland, and northern Canada.

127

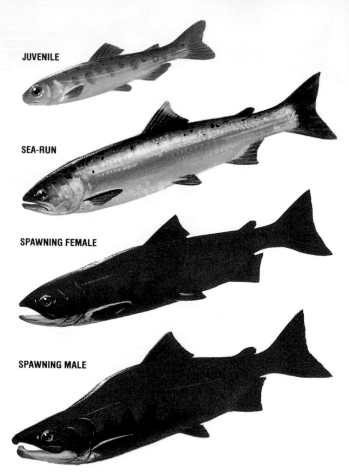

JUVENILE

SEA-RUN

SPAWNING FEMALE

SPAWNING MALE

Sockeye salmon, red salmon, blueback salmon *Oncorhynchus nerka*   To 33 inches and 15 pounds (average: 5–8 pounds). One of the tastiest fishes and commercially the most valuable Pacific salmon, but second to the more abundant pink salmon in the U.S. fishery. Sea-run fishes have greenish-blue backs (hence blueback) with fine black speckling but no black spots on back or tail fin. Spawning males have a green head and a bright red body. The female is similar to the male. The spawning female scoops out one nest after another with great effort, while the male drives off intruders. Juveniles have variable parr marks. Sockeyes make long, tiring migrations to and through lakes to spawn. Some exhaust 96 percent of their fat and 53 percent of their protein reserves in the struggle. **Range:** anadromous in sea and freshwater streams from Japan to the Bering Sea and Los Angeles (California); center of abundance between Bristol Bay (Alaska) and the Columbia River (Oregon).
Edibility: highly prized for its flavor, high oil content, flesh color, and uniform size.

128

JUVENILE

SEA-RUN

SPAWNING FEMALE

SPAWNING MALE

Chinook salmon, king salmon *Oncorhynchus tshawytscha*   The largest of the salmons, to almost 6 feet (58 inches) and 135 pounds (average: 10–15 pounds). Any salmon caught that weighs over 30 pounds is probably a chinook. Also called *tyee*, the Chinook Indian term for large. It was critical to the diet of the Pacific Northwest Indians, and probably kept Lewis and Clark from starvation on their westward journey in 1805. Note the irregular black spots over the back, dorsal fin, and caudal fin. The gums are black at the base of the teeth. Parr marks on the young are large and well defined. The chinook is the fish most often caught by sport fishermen, surpassing in numbers and pounds any other salmon. It is the most highly prized of all the salmons for the fresh fish trade. They enter streams in the fall to spawn, often in large rivers, and some travel 600 miles inland. Young quickly go to sea after hatching and return to spawn after four or five years. **Range:** anadromous in sea and freshwater streams from Japan to the Bering Sea, British Columbia, Washington, Oregon, and California; rare in streams south of the Sacramento–San Joaquin River systems. **Edibility:** excellent—especially when fresh.

129

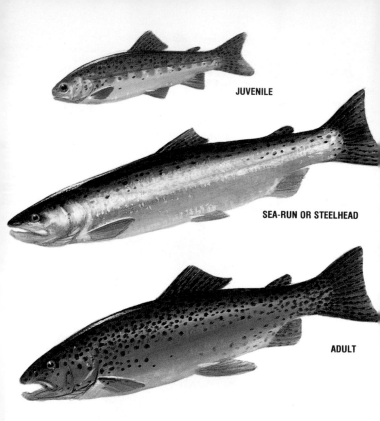

JUVENILE

SEA-RUN OR STEELHEAD

ADULT

Rainbow trout, steelhead *Salmo gairdneri*   To 3 feet, 8 inches and 52 pounds (average: under 10 pounds). A native American trout widely acclaimed as one of the world's finest game fishes. It has been introduced worldwide to such diverse places as the high mountain lakes of Ecuador and the streams and lakes of Europe and New Zealand. The rainbow trout loves fast water, and is fished by enthusiastic fly fishermen in the swift runs and riffles of large streams. Often it has a red to pink side stripe, which gives it the name rainbow. A sea-run rainbow is called a steelhead—also a splendid game fish; steelheads reach 40-pound weights after feeding voraciously during extensive ocean migrations, and are silvery and "steelheaded" when returning from the sea. As it battles its way upstream and spawning time nears, the steelhead becomes dark and spotted, the pink rainbow band appears, and it begins to resemble the adult nonmigratory rainbow trout. On all rainbows and steelheads, note the small black spots on the back and most fins. The head is short and the inside of the mouth is white. Steelhead juveniles are distinctive for the many specks and spots on the back and dorsal fin, and distinct, regular parr marks. Like most trouts, but unlike Pacific salmons, adults usually survive spawning. **Range:** anadromous in sea and freshwater rivers and streams from Japan to the Bering Sea and south to northern Baja California. **Edibility:** excellent.

130

Brown trout *Salmo trutta*   To 27½ inches and 8 pounds (average: 1 to 4 pounds).
A European trout introduced worldwide to all continents, and now a favorite of fly
fishermen the world over. It was broadcast across North America beginning in
1883. It is not an easy fish to catch compared to the rainbow or brook trouts. Even
where equal numbers of brown and rainbow trout were stocked in Oregon rivers,
only one brown was caught for every four rainbows taken. In many areas it is
confined to inland lakes and streams and is valued because its seagoing tendencies
are reduced compared to other species. Nevertheless, there is a limited spread of
brown trout along the Pacific Coast. Sea-run populations and those found in very
large lakes (the Great Lakes, for example) resemble sea-run salmon: they are
silvery in color and speckled with black spots, and have recognizable large dark
spots, some surrounded by pale halos, on back, sides, and dorsal fin. A lesser
number of red or orange spots are usually visible along the lateral surface. There
is an absence of teeth on the back of the tongue. In older males, anal fins are
rounded; older female anal fins are falcate (curving inward). **Range:** a limited sea-
run population from British Columbia to Washington and Oregon; widely distributed
across the United States in inland lakes and streams. **Edibility:** good.

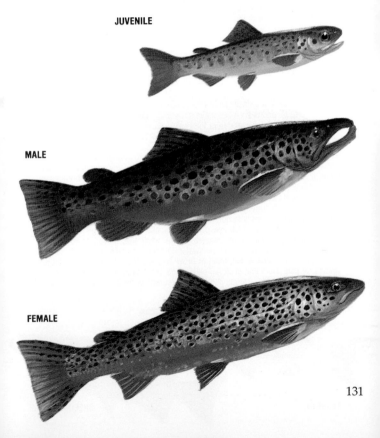

JUVENILE

MALE

FEMALE

131

ADULT

JUVENILE

Cutthroat trout, coastal cutthroat trout *Salmo clarki*   To about 2½ feet and 17 pounds (sea-run trout)—freshwater cutthroats reach 41 pounds. Named after Captain William Clark of the Lewis and Clark expedition. Recognized by the red or orange "cutthroat" streak on the lower jaw. The body and all fins except the pelvic are covered with small dark spots. The inside of the mouth is white and there are small teeth at the rear of the tongue. The cutthroat is usually a freshwater fish distributed in lakes and streams up and down the Pacific Coast and as far inland as Wyoming and Montana. There is a Yellowstone cutthroat, a Snake River cutthroat, and numerous other races and forms. In some areas the cutthroat hybridizes with the rainbow; the cutthroat-rainbow cross, quite common, looks much like a pink-striped rainbow trout with a red streak on its lower jaw. Some cutthroat populations are anadromous. The anadromous fish is often called the coastal cutthroat trout and especially in British Columbia is recognized as a subspecies, *Salmo clarki clarki*. The sea-run trout spawns in coastal streams in late winter and spring. Unlike Pacific salmons, adults usually survive spawning. **Range:** anadromous in sea and freshwater rivers and streams from the Gulf of Alaska to the Eel River (northern California). **Edibility:** good.

Arctic char *Salvelinus alpinus*   To about 3 feet and 25 pounds (average: 2–8 pounds). Similar to the Dolly Varden (p. 125) and also closely related to the brook trout. It is found in the frigid waters of the northern hemisphere. Anadromous as well as landlocked, Arctic char range from Alaska to Siberia, Norway, Iceland, Greenland, and northern Canada. The sea-run Arctic char has colors similar to the Dolly Varden, with larger cream, pale pink, or orange spots on the side. A good way to separate the two is to note the size of these spots: on the Dolly Varden, they are smaller than the iris of the eye; on the Arctic char, they are larger than the iris. Sea-run Arctic char are almost completely silver when they move into rivers and streams to spawn. Gradually the freshwater coloration replaces the silvery phase. The back turns to olive-green, blue, or brownish, and the sides may be bright red, orange, or pale. Note that pectoral, pelvic, and anal fins have white leading edges like the Dolly Varden's. **Range:** see above; circumpolar for both anadromous and freshwater forms. **Edibility:** good.

SEA-RUN

BREEDING MALE

BARRACUDA, SILVERSIDES, GRUNION, SMELTS, MULLETS, AND THREADFINS

Vast, silvery clouds of silversides, smelts, and mullets school, race, and leap in Pacific coastal shallows, providing a feast for such predators as barracuda, jacks, mackerel, and man. The striped mullet (family Mugilidae) ranks as a leading food fish. Like many of the fishes in this group, the mullet is so rich in oil it can be fried in its own fat. Also called "jumpers," mullets leap from the water to escape nets or predators, or seemingly for the joy of jumping. At certain times of the day, coastal shallows, bays, and inlets come alive with leaping mullets.

Silversides, of the family Atherinidae, are named for their brilliant, flashing lateral stripe, and they share with mullets such characteristics as widely divided dorsal fins, pelvic fins placed at mid-abdomen, small, weakly toothed mouths, and tasty, oily flesh. Strangely, silverside fry start life shy and antisocial, carefully avoiding each other. Half-inchers may aggregate for a few seconds only. At $\frac{3}{4}$-inch size, ten fry may assemble in ragged formation, and from then on they school easily with increasing discipline. Threadfins, of the family Polynemidae, are much like

Striped mullet (lisa, liseta) *Mugil cephalus*   To 3 feet. Fishermen pursue this fine food and bait fish avidly. Since mullet feed on algae and detritus, however, scooping up mouthfuls from the bottom, they are rarely taken on a hook. In Central America they are often snagged with treble hooks or taken with throw nets or other entrapments especially adapted to thwart their skill at jumping to freedom. They are inshore fishes that school in sandy or muddy bays and estuaries where they are often seen leaping out of the water. They also cruise rocky bottoms and patch reefs, sometimes seeking out "cleaner" fish like the sergeant major and barberfish to relieve them of parasites. They range from shore out to depths of 400 feet. Spawning is thought to occur well offshore. **Range:** circumtropical; from San Francisco Bay to Chile, including the Gulf of California and the Galapagos Islands; rare north of Southern California.

mullets, but the unique pectoral fins are split into two parts, the lower of which is composed of threadlike rays. Threadfins are beautiful silvery fishes often seen over sandy beach areas.

The California grunion, a member of the silversides family, is famed as the little "fish that dances on the beach." Thousands of fishermen, children, and beach-goers throng California beaches on spring and summer nights from March through August when the grunion

California barracuda, Pacific barracuda (picuda, agujón) *Sphyraena argentea* To about 4 feet and 18 pounds. Although the barracuda is sometimes described as a fearsome fish, the California barracuda is quite harmless because of its small size (usually less than 11 pounds) and habit of swallowing its food whole. They are splendid food fishes and California charter boat fishermen pursue them along the fringes of kelp beds by trolling and with live-bait fishing. Barracuda are pelagic fishes that range from the surface to deep water. They will frequently sweep inshore in large schools to chase anchovies, sardines, and other small schooling fishes. Note the two widely divided dorsal fins, long snout, and large mouth filled with sharp teeth. **Range:** Kodiak Island (Alaska) to Cabo San Lucas (Baja California) and the Gulf of California.

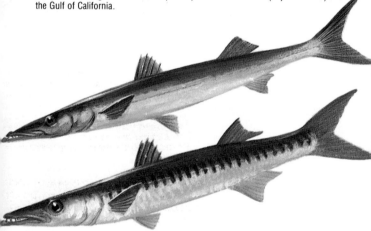

Mexican barracuda (picuda, agujón, buzo) *Sphyraena lucasana* To about 2 feet. Easily recognized by the 20 or so dark bars on the side, especially on larger fishes. It can be separated from the California barracuda by the placement of the ventral fins, which are attached directly below the pectoral fins. On the California bar-racuda, the ventral fins are placed well behind the tips of the pectoral fins. The Mexican barracuda is a schooling fish, frequently joining into large schools or small clusters of a dozen or so to drive schools of smaller fishes into a compact ball and then seizing mouthfuls of prey. As a game fish, Walford (1974) reports that it strikes hard and runs longer than the California barracuda and anglers give it a much higher rating. **Range:** Bahía Magdalena (central Baja California) and the Gulf of California to Panama.

are running and spawning, to catch these delicious food fishes by hand. Scientists puzzle over the incredible ability of the fish to know the exact time in the shifting cycle of moon and tides to spawn in the beach sand. Jacksmelt and topsmelt, not true smelts but also members of the silverside family, also make excellent table fare; in the fresh fish markets they are sold as "smelt."

True smelts are in the family Osmeridae, and are superficially similar to the silversides except that, unlike her-

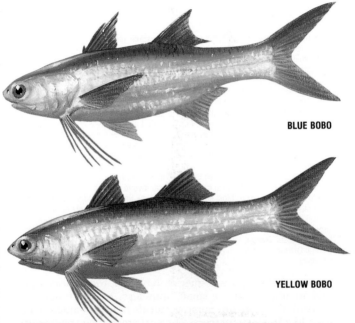

BLUE BOBO

YELLOW BOBO

Blue bobo, threadfin (barbudo) *Polydactylus approximans*   To 14 inches. Found near river mouths and in the surge zone where the surf is breaking. They are sometimes seen in the company of croakers or mojarras probing the sandy bottom for organisms. Their silvery bodies change color to blend perfectly with the white sand, surf, and bubbles, and they can disappear in an instant—as you look at them. Unique for the inferior anchovylike mouth and separated pectoral fin with the lower rays developed into five or six threadlike filaments. These rays may be held against the body or extended out, and they are thought to have a tactile function. Also note the widely separated dorsal fins and the deeply cleaved swallowtail. A very similar threadfin, the yellow bobo (*P. opercularis*) differs in having eight to nine threadlike rays on the lower part of the pectoral fin instead of the five or six of the blue bobo. **Range:** blue bobo, Monterey Bay (central California) to Peru and the Galapagos Islands; yellow bobo, Los Angeles Harbor (California) to Peru; both fishes rare north of Baja California.

135

Jacksmelt (pejerrey, gruñón) *Atherinopsis californiensis* To 17½ inches. Quite similar to topsmelt but the anal fin begins behind the first dorsal fin (not below it, as on the topsmelt). There are 10 to 12 scales between the dorsal fins. Jacksmelt school in murky water over sand bottoms from shore out to 95 feet, most commonly between 5 and 50 feet. Although jacksmelt and topsmelt are silversides, not true smelt, the jacksmelt forms the largest part of the California "smelt" catch and is sold as smelt in fresh fish markets. The heaviest landings are in San Francisco. Most silversides over 1 foot are jacksmelt. Eggs are laid all year and are attached in large masses to seaweed and other floating objects. **Range:** Yaquina Bay (central Oregon) to southern Baja California.

Topsmelt (pejerrey) *Atherinops affinis* To 14½ inches. These are silvery surface-schooling fishes found along sandy beaches and around rocky reefs, kelp beds, bays, and piers. Often seen jumping from the water when pursued by larger fishes such as jacks or mackerel. Spawning occurs in spring and summer in shallow water when a female followed by numerous males makes repeated passes through a clump of red algae. The eggs stick to the algae and are fertilized by the males. Note the small first dorsal fin with five to nine spines. There is no adipose fin; the anal fin begins below the first dorsal fin. There are five to eight scales between the two dorsal fins. Fished commercially, especially around San Francisco. **Range:** Vancouver Island to the Gulf of California.

rings and silversides, osmerids have a spinous dorsal fin and an adipose fin—a small, spineless, rayless finlet just in front of the tail fin. Some osmerids have a characteristic odor like fresh cucumbers. The surf smelt also spawns up on the beach like the California grunion, but it spawns during daylight hours and is often called "day smelt."

The specter of a 2- or 3-foot barracuda following closely and watchfully as a diver makes his rounds can be disconcerting. But the barracuda (family Sphyraenidae) is rarely as dangerous as some early tales of fish ferocity made it seem. The California barracuda is quite harmless, since it is usually small, weighs less than 11 pounds, and swallows its food whole rather than tearing or slashing at the prey. The Mexican barracuda, also relatively small, is easily recognized by the 20 or so dark bars on its side. ◆

Surf smelt (pejerrey) *Hypomesus pretiosus*   To about 10 inches. Not a silverside but a member of the family Osmeridae—the true smelts. Unlike silversides and herrings, true smelts have a spinous dorsal fin and an adipose fin—a small fleshy finlet with no spines or rays—just in front of the tail fin. Surf smelts are fishes of the surf line and they are often taken during spawning runs in simple A-nets, used by the Indians long before the white man came. A fisherman allowing the surge of an oncoming wave to wash through an A-net can catch many fish. Surf smelts bury their eggs on the beaches like the California grunion does. They spawn during daylight hours, however, and are often called day smelt. A surf smelt can lay from 15,000 to 20,000 eggs in coarse-grained beach sand. They hatch in high tides about two weeks later. **Range:** Prince William Sound (Alaska) to Long Beach (southern California).

California grunion (gruñón) *Leuresthes tenuis*   To 7½ inches. This is the famous little "fish that dances on the beach" and it is celebrated each year in California when the grunion run and spawn in March, June, July, and August (no grunion may be taken in April and May). Fishermen with a California license, and children under 16, may catch them in unlimited numbers—but only as the law specifies, with bare hands. California and Baja California beaches teem with people, waiting in the darkness (grunion run only after dark) for the first sight of the wriggling silversides. Females swim onto the beach on advancing waves, and, sparkling like jewels in the moonlight, they do their mysterious little dance, and then quickly drill tail first into the wet sand to lay eggs. One or more males join in the dance and release milt that sinks through the sand to fertilize the eggs. The female pulls herself from the sand and rides the next wave back into the sea. Females can spawn up to eight times per season. Scientists puzzle over the ability of the grunion to time spawning exactly to assure the survival of the eggs buried in the beach sand (from 2 to 6 nights after the full moon and new moon). Eggs hatch about 15 days later, which coincides with the next series of high tides. Even more unusual, the Gulf of California grunion (*L. sardina*) must synchronize its beach-spawning runs with the more variable and extreme tides of the Northern Gulf. How they accomplish this is a mystery to marine biologists. Smaller and more slender than the topsmelt or jacksmelt. The mouth is highly protrusible, almost like a tube. **Range:** California grunion, from San Francisco (California) to Punta Abreojos (central Baja California); Gulf of California grunion, endemic to the northern Gulf from the Colorado River delta to Guaymas (Mexico).

137

HERRINGS, SARDINES, ANCHOVIES, BONEFISHES, MILKFISHES, MACHETE, AND STURGEONS

Even more than the cod, the herring has had a marked influence on the course of human history. Owing to its great abundance and its importance as a food fish, some early coastal settlements were first established as herring fishing villages. Burton and Burton (1975) report that, wherever shoals of herrings approached the coast of Norway, there a village sprang up. The same was true in Scotland and Newfoundland, as well as in Alaska, Japan, and Siberia, where the Pacific herring ranges. Charlemagne founded Hamburg, in A.D. 809, as a herring port. Ostend, Dunkirk, and Dieppe were all founded by the Normans as herring ports. As herring-based trade developed, armies and navies were assembled, and wars and naval engagements were fought to protect the fisheries. In later centuries, Dutch fishing for herrings in English waters led to war with England. Protection of fishing rights led to the foundation of the British Royal Navy and the war of 1652–54, when England fought for and won sea power from Holland.

Pacific sardine, pilchard (sardina del Pacífico) *Sardinops sagax*   To 16¼ inches. The collapse of the 50-year-old Pacific sardine fishery in the 1940's was an early lesson in overfishing that somehow never got learned. From its zenith in 1936, the catch declined until, by 1967, a moratorium on sardine catches, even for bait, was necessary. Hart (1973) states that since 1939 the sardine population has been unsuccessful in producing a big brood of young—no one knows why. Distinguished from the herrings by its spindle shape, black spots on the side under the scales, and the fine striations on the gill cover. **Range:** Kamchatka (U.S.S.R.) to southeast Alaska and south to Guaymas (Gulf of California); most common from California southward. **Edibility**: good, especially when canned; also an important bait fish.

American shad *Alosa sapidissima*   To 2½ feet. Much like the striped bass (see page 2), the American shad was so esteemed by fishermen on the Atlantic Coast that they introduced a number of them to the Sacramento River in 1870 to see if they would thrive, and today they range from Kamchatka (U.S.S.R.) to Alaska and down the Pacific Coast to northern Baja California. They are excellent game fish, especially for fly fishermen, and good eating, said to be delicious when smoked. Shad are anadromous and swim up rivers to spawn each year. They are fished heavily during these late spring and summer runs. One of the largest herrings, the shad is recognized by the row of dark spots on the side, sharp keeled scutes along the belly, and the deep, compressed body. **Range:** see above. **Edibility:** good, see above.

Closer in time and closer to home is a town that sardines built—Monterey, California, the focus of the vast and once seemingly inexhaustible Pacific sardine fishery. The first cannery was built there in 1889; by the 1930's, 18 canneries were pouring rivers of sardines into cans and out to the world. At the apogee of the fishery in 1936, 78 purseseiner fishing boats unloaded 800,000 tons of sardines onto the docks of Monterey. This incredible machine vacuumed shoals of fish from the Pacific for a few more years until the fishery collapsed. By 1953, the catch was so depleted that only 10,000 tons were taken. In 1967 the evervigilant California Department of Fish and Game declared a moratorium on fishing for Pacific sardines. By then, nobody cared. The fish were gone.

But even though the sardines were gone, the fishermen, ships, nets, and factories were ready, willing, and loaded for action—all they needed was prey. Though not so toothsome as the sardine, the next-best fish was the Pacific herring. At one time, vast silvery shoals of herrings flashed and swam on both the Atlantic and Pacific coasts of North America. Through the 1960's, the huge reduction industry processed millions of tons of raw herring for sale as oil and fish meal. The incredible wastefulness of this indus- 139 try is evident when one considers that 100 pounds of live fish are required to yield animal food sufficient to produce one pound of chicken or beef. Used as fertilizer, 200 pounds of fish meal will yield little more than three pounds of vegetable protein. By the 1970's, the herring fisheries on both coasts had collapsed. Hart (1973) states that from 1961 through 1966, 467.4 million pounds of Pacific herring were taken. By 1969 the catch had dropped to 4.4 million pounds. Fishery experts said the herring had "probably altered their migration patterns and would undoubtedly return." They never have.

Again, the rich and fecund ocean revealed another little fish that held promise of endless exploitation. The anchoveta (*Engraulis ringens*), which schooled in countless millions off the coast of Peru, became the next "catch of the day." A. W. Simon (1984) reports that, starting from scratch in the early 1950's, the anchoveta fishery exploded by 90-fold in nine years to become the largest fishery in the world. Over 12 million tons were taken off Peru in 1970 alone. Like the herring, anchovetas fed the giant reduction plants for processing into livestock feed for poultry and pigs. Seeing the handwriting on the wall, experts recommended a limit of 9.5 million tons, but the fish pro-

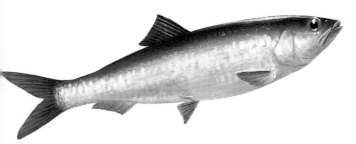

Pacific herring (sardina) *Clupea pallasi* To 1½ feet. At one time great schools of these herrings were widespread on the Pacific Coast. At spawning time they deposit sticky eggs on seaweeds, eelgrass, and kelp in shallow water around bays, harbors, and estuaries. Hordes of predators from fish to seagulls descend on the eggs. Through the 1960's, millions of tons of raw herring were processed for oil and fish meal, and this overharvesting led to the collapse of the Pacific herring fishery, like the Pacific sardine fishery before it. Some remaining stocks are still fished north of San Francisco and shipped to market either fresh, cured, or salted. There is a sizable fishery in San Francisco Bay for herring eggs, which are sold in Japan for *sushi*. Note the single short dorsal fin at the middle of the back, just over the pelvic fin. There are no black spots on the side. The scutes on the belly are weak, not strong. **Range:** Japan to Alaska and south to northern Baja California. **Edibility:** fair when fresh—popular in some areas when salted, kippered, or pickled.

140

cessors would have none of it. Twice the limit was proposed and twice it was rejected. In 1972 the anchoveta catch dropped to less than half its former peak. By 1980 it collapsed to 0.72 million tons. The fishery never recovered and no more anchovetas come from Peru. Fishery experts talk about an unusual change in the Peruvian coastal current, *El Niño*, as being responsible for the disappearance of the anchovetas. This seems unlikely. More to the point, Richard Hennemuth, director of the Woods Hole Laboratory of the National Marine Fisheries Service, says, "There is some doubt that man can be a prudent predator."

Herrings and sardines of the family Clupeidae are compressed, silvery fishes with sawtoothed scutes on the belly, a short, stubby dorsal fin near the middle of the back, and abdominal pelvic fins. The tail fin is deeply forked. They are pelagic, schooling fishes, usually found swimming near the surface. The round herrings of the family Dussumieriidae differ from the clupeid herrings in having rounder abdomens and lacking the sawtooth ridge of scutes on the belly. The round herrings school, but not in the vast numbers common to the clupeid herrings. Anchovies (family Engraulididae) are closely related to the herrings, but the anchovy mouth is set far back on the underside of the head; the lower jaw is small and inconspicuous. Anchovies are small, usually less than 5 inches, and are always found in schools, never singly.

Pacific thread herring, deepbody thread herring (sardina machete) *Opisthonema libertate* To 10 inches. A brilliant, pelagic herring found in silvery schools close to shore. It is abundant in the upper Gulf of California, and is heavily preyed upon by jacks, tuna, and marine mammals and birds. Easily recognized by the greatly elongated, threadlike, last ray in the dorsal fin. Usually has one or two rows of spots on the sides running along the scale rows. A similar fish, the middling thread herring, *O. medirastre*, is almost indistinguishable from the Pacific thread herring in all respects except that it is not so deep bodied. **Range:** (both species): Los Angeles (California) to Peru, including the Gulf of California. **Edibility:** fair—used as bait.

The machete (family Elopidae), milkfish (family Chanidae), and bonefish (family Albulidae) are primitive fishes with long, deeply forked tails and a single dorsal fin of soft rays. The machete and bonefish larval forms are eel- or ribbonlike and transparent. They shrink radically in length during the metamorphosis to the juvenile stage. In Asia the milkfish is valued as food and cultivated in ponds until large enough for the table.

Sturgeons (family Acipenseridae) are also primitive fishes that are slow-moving bottom grubbers. They once grew to great size (20 feet) on the western North American coast but overfishing, pollution, and dams have taken a heavy toll. Today the fishery is so decimated that a $10,000 fine and a one-year jail sentence are imposed for selling any sturgeon taken in California. ◆

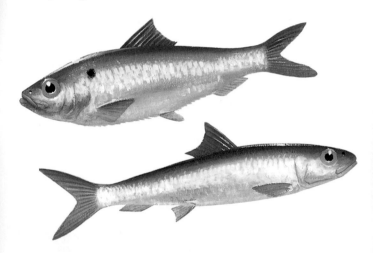

Flatiron herring (sardina) *Harengula thrissina* To 7¼ inches. Distinctive for the black spot just behind the gill cover, and the large eye. There are strong scutes on the belly. A small, compressed, pelagic herring found in large schools inshore; abundant in the central and lower Gulf of California, where it is preyed upon by the machete, leopard grouper, and other fish. **Range:** La Jolla Cove (southern California) to Peru, including the Gulf of California. **Edibility:** fair—used as a bait fish.

Pacific round herring (sardina) *Etrumeus teres* To 1 foot. As the name implies, a cigar-shaped herring with a rounded, smooth belly (compared with the sawlike-scuted bellies of other herrings). The dorsal fin is at midback; the pelvic fin begins behind the dorsal fin. There is one, slight W-shaped scute at the base of the pelvic fin. Swims in large schools inshore. **Range:** Monterey Bay (central California) to Chile. **Edibility:** fair.

Northern anchovy (anchoa) *Engraulis mordax* To 9¾ inches but rarely over 7 inches. A splendid fish, always found in schools. The long snout overhangs the large, sharklike mouth. The northern anchovy has increased prodigiously in California over the past 30 years, probably by filling the gap left by the the Pacific sardine. It is vital as food for larger fishes, as well as for sea birds and marine mammals. Also important as a bait fish. Commercial fishermen take large quantities of these anchovies for processing into fish meal and oil. A round, not compressed anchovy with an anal fin beginning below the rear of the dorsal fin. Also note the silvery stripe on the side. **Range:** Queen Charlotte Island (British Columbia) to Cabo San Lucas (Baja California). **Edibility:** good.

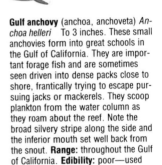

Gulf anchovy (anchoa, anchoveta) *Anchoa helleri* To 3 inches. These small anchovies form into great schools in the Gulf of California. They are important forage fish and are sometimes seen driven into dense packs close to shore, frantically trying to escape pursuing jacks or mackerels. They scoop plankton from the water column as they roam about the reef. Note the broad silvery stripe along the side and the inferior mouth set well back from the snout. **Range:** throughout the Gulf of California. **Edibility:** poor—used for bait.

Milkfish (sabalo, abuela) *Chanos chanos* To 5 feet. In spite of its many fine bones, the milkfish is a valuable food fish throughout most of its range. The body is brilliantly metallic, like the tarpon, as though it had been silver-plated. Scales, hard and silvery, are used for ornamentation. The milkfish spawns in shallow, brackish water. A single fish may produce nine million eggs. In Hawaii and the Philippines, the fry are collected, carried to freshwater ponds, and cultivated for food. Identified by the small, toothless mouth, single spineless dorsal fin, and large, forked tail fin. **Range:** San Francisco Bay to Panama; also widespread in the western Pacific and the Indian Ocean. **Edibility:** good.

Bonefish (macabi, sanducha, quijo) *Albula vulpes* To 1½ feet. Prefers wide stretches of shallow-water flats, from white ocean sand and shallow creek beds to thick turtle grass and mangrove-choked estuaries, bays, and sounds. On the Atlantic Coast, bone-fish will put up a spectacular fight when hooked, tearing off hundreds of feet of line at lightning speed, but the Pacific populations do not have this fighting spirit—to the chagrin of anglers. In the Atlantic, the bonefish grows to 3½ feet; the Pacific fish—same species—is much smaller, which may also explain why it is not fervently fished in the Pacific. Note the silvery body and the conical snout, which projects beyond the lower jaw; the mouth is small. There is one dorsal fin at midbody over the pelvic fins. **Range:** circumtropical; from San Francisco (California) to Peru; uncommon north of Baja California. **Edibility:** poor food because the meat has many small bones.

Machete (chiro) *Elops affinis* To 3 feet. This long, slim fish is related to the tarpon and is also called ladyfish and ten-pounder in other parts of the world; but it is doubtful if it ever attains 10 pounds in weight. Some fishermen say that when hooked it will "fight like a ten pounder"—hence the name. It will not strike and run like the bonefish, but leaps and shakes like the tarpon—often working loose from the hook; thus it is an attractive game fish. Like the bonefish, the machete is a denizen of shallow water, especially brackish lagoons and estuaries. It is abundant in the Gulf of California and often swims in schools. Distinctive for the slightly projecting lower jaw, deeply forked tail, and bony plate on the throat between the branches of the lower jaw. **Range:** Mandalay Beach (southern California) and throughout the Gulf of California to Peru. **Edibility:** poor, owing to oily flesh.

White sturgeon *Acipenser transmontanus*   In earlier times to 20 feet, but today to about 10 feet. In various European tongues, sturgeon means "the stirrer," a reflection of the way these large, slow-moving bottom grubbers poke and probe into the sand and mud for mollusks, crustaceans, and worms. They once grew to enormous size; one hooked in the Columbia River years ago weighed 1,285 pounds. The Russian beluga sturgeon, which supplies half of the world's finest caviar—the food of kings—is the largest, reaching 28 feet and 3,210 pounds. In the 1880's and 1890's the sturgeon fishery in California and Canada was a booming and profitable business. Waste, overfishing, and greed soon brought it to a halt and nearly eliminated the Pacific Coast sturgeons. Hart (1973) reports that the Canadian sturgeon fishery peaked in 1897 with a landing of 1,137,700 pounds; yet by 1901 the fishery was, according to the Fisheries Inspector, "practically extinct commercially." Today's caviar prices—from $50 to $60 an ounce—have made fishery experts desperate to revive the almost extinct sturgeon stocks. Sturgeons have primitive skeletons partly of bone and partly of cartilage. The backbone curves upward into the tail fin much like the shark's. The mouth, toothless, is under the head, with a row of four barbels in front of the mouth. There are five rows of scutes on the body: one on the back, one along each mid-side, and one along each side of the belly. The white sturgeon has 38 to 48 bony scutes in each mid-side row and the four barbels are closer to the end of the snout than to the mouth. A similar species, the green sturgeon (*Acipenser medirostris*) has 23 to 30 scutes in each mid-side row and the four barbels are usually closer to the mouth than to the end of the snout. The white sturgeon is grayish white and the green sturgeon is usually olive-green above dorsally and gray-white below. **Range:** anadromous; white sturgeon, Alaska to northern Baja California; green sturgeon, Japan to northern Baja California. **Edibility:** excellent; the eggs are prized as caviar.

CODS, HAKES, WHITEFISHES, TILEFISHES, BUTTERFISHES, AND REMORAS

Almost all of North America's 24 species of cods (family Gadidae) and hakes (family Merlucciidae), are cold- and temperate-water bottom fishes. Omnivorous, they roam sand and rock bottoms 100 to 3,000 feet down, preying in voracious packs upon crustaceans, mollusks, fishes, worms, and vegetation. They are vitally important to the world's food supply, and support huge fisheries on both sides of the Atlantic and on the American Pacific Coast. The profitable codfish pulled Europeans across the North Atlantic by the shipload to settle New World shores. It was paramount to the settlers of New England, who placed its image on the colonial seal of Massachusetts. It is still a basic food. The Grand Banks off Newfoundland and the coastal shelves of Greenland still attract the fishing fleets of the world in search of succulent nutritious cods and hakes. On the Pacific Coast the cod fishery is smaller, but 20 million pounds of the Pacific cod, *Gadus macrocephalus*,

Pacific cod, gray cod (bacalao) *Gadus macrocephalus* To 3 feet, 9 inches. The Pacific Coast counterpart to the famous Atlantic cod (*Gadus morhua*), which it resembles closely in appearance and habits. It is fished as far south as Oregon but the main fishery ranges from Washington to Vancouver Island, Queen Charlotte Sound, and northern Hecate Strait. It is the most important of the trawl-caught bottom fishes of British Columbia. Hart (1973) reports that 20 million pounds were landed in British Columbia in 1966; this had dropped to 5 million pounds by 1970. The chief market is for fillets and "fish sticks"; a small quantity is sold fresh or smoked. Cod migrate from deep to shallow water in the spring of the year, ranging over depths from 40 to 3,000 feet. Spawning occurs in late winter; some large females produce from 1 million to 15 million eggs. Note the three dorsal fins, the chin barbel, and two anal fins. The first anal fin begins below the front of the second dorsal fin. **Range:** Japan to the Bering Sea and south to Santa Monica (southern California). **Edibility:** excellent.

146

are taken annually from Oregon to British Columbia. Commercial fishermen use large trawling nets, set lines, seines, and gill nets. Because the flesh keeps so well, dried and salted cod can be shipped to any part of the world. Codfishes and their relatives have a distinctive "cod look," owing partly to the position of the ventral fins ahead of the pectoral fins, often under the throat. All possess soft-rayed fins, usually without spines.

The ocean whitefish is a tilefish of the family Malacanthidae; a popular sport fish found in deep rocky off-

Pacific tomcod (bacalao) *Microgadus proximus*   To 1 foot. Not large enough or abundant enough to interest commercial fisheries, but highly valued by many fishermen for its taste. It is a minor game fish in central California and often caught in trawls while fishing for other species. A bottom feeder, ranging over depths from 90 to 720 feet. Young tomcod are often taken in shallow water. Note the three dorsal fins, two anal fins, and the short chin barbel. The first anal fin of this fish is farther forward than that of the Pacific cod—beginning below the rear of the first dorsal fin. **Range:** Bering Sea to Point Sal (central California). **Edibility:** excellent.

Walleye pollock, whiting, Pacific pollock, bigeye pollock *Theragra chalcogramma*   To 3 feet. Occurs in abundance along the coast from the Bering Sea to northern California. It is taken in waters of moderate depth from the surface to 1,200 feet, where it feeds on crustaceans, herring, and sand lance. Large quantities are caught in trawls in the Strait of Georgia (British Columbia) and marketed as mink food. The flesh is soft and pasty; not a popular food fish. Hotly pursued by seals, porpoises, and numerous predatory fishes. Note the three dorsal fins, two anal fins, and the projecting lower jaw. **Range:** Japan to the Bering Sea and south to Carmel (central California). **Edibility:** poor.

147

shore banks, it is also fine food, for which there is a minor market in southern California. The Pacific golden-eyed tilefish, another malacanthid, is an abundant deep-water species and a fishermen's favorite around Guaymas in the Gulf of California, and it is also good food. It is distinctive for the gold stripe between the eyes.

The Pacific butterfish, belonging to the family Stromateidae, is a gourmet item in many southern California fish markets because of its fine texture and flavor. It is often called the "Pacific pompano," but is not related to the jacks and pompanos.

The remora or sharksucker (family Echeneididae) is the hitchhiker of the sea. By means of a disc (consisting of a number of ridges or laminae) on the top of its head, the remora clamps itself firmly to almost any floating or swimming host and takes a free ride. Sharks are popular hosts, but remoras are also found attached to whales, marlin, groupers, rays, boats, and timbers. Various species of remoras appear to be always associated with the same kind of host. Some species are found only on billfishes, and others only on barracudas. Ingeniously, remoras have been used as "living fishhooks" by the Arawak Indians of southern Cuba, Venezuelan Indians, Australian aborigines, and numerous other tribes. A line is tied to the tail of the remora and it is thrown overboard in the vicinity of a large turtle or other prey. When it attaches itself to the turtle, fishermen play the turtle near to the boat, and it is captured. ◆

Pacific hake (merluza) *Merluccius productus*   To 3 feet. Hakes are closely related to cods; the Pacific hake resembles some cods in most respects but has a V-shaped ridge on top of the head, two dorsal fins instead of the usual three, and only one deeply notched anal fin, almost a mirror image of the second dorsal fin. These fishes swim in great schools at substantial depths—from 450 to 3,000 feet. The flesh, soft and pasty, is not a target of U.S. and Canadian fishermen, but fleets in other countries harvest this hake for fresh-freezing or processing into fish meal. Often marketed as "Pacific whitefish." Sea lions, small whales, and porpoises feed voraciously on hake. **Range:** Japan and Alaska to Bahía Magdalena (Baja California) and the Gulf of California. **Edibility:** poor.

Pacific butterfish *Peprilus simillimus* To 11 inches. Renowned for its fine flavor, and a gourmet item in southern California. It seems to be common one year, uncommon the next. A member of the stromateid or harvest fish family, it is distinguished by a mouth with a modified pharynx (with an esophageal pouch on either side) lined with unique teeth. Also note the small mouth, long dorsal and anal fins, absence of pelvic fins, and deeply forked tail. **Range:** Queen Charlotte Sound (British Columbia) to central Baja California and the Gulf of California. **Edibility:** excellent.

Ocean whitefish (blanquillo) *Caulolatilus princeps* To 3 feet, 4 inches. The ocean whitefishes are found in fairly deep, rocky offshore banks ranging from 33 to 300 feet—usually at about 165-foot depths, and often found around islands. They are fine food, for which a minor market exists in southern California. Sport fishermen take them along the Santa Barbara and Ventura county coasts and in the Channel Islands. Note the small mouth and long blue-and-yellow-striped dorsal and anal fins, and the yellow-tinged pectoral and caudal fins. **Range:** Vancouver Island to Peru and the Galapagos Islands.

149

Pacific golden-eyed tilefish (blanquillo) *Caulolatilus affinis* To 19½ inches. Like the ocean whitefish, this tilefish is recognized by its long dorsal and anal fins. The yellow patch or stripe between the eyes is distinctive, as is the dark blotch at the top edge of the pectoral fin. Favors deep water and is abundant and frequently fished at 100- to 300-foot depths over rocky and sandy bottoms and around patch reefs. **Range:** throughout the Gulf of California to Peru.

Remora (pegador) *Remora remora* To 34 inches. One of the well-known sea hitchhikers. By means of laminae in a disc on its head, it clamps itself firmly to a host and rides. Sharks are favorite hosts, but remoras are also found attached to marlins, whales, turtles, boats, timbers, or other floating objects. Recent investigations have shown that this remora feeds on parasitic copepods found on host shark bodies and gill chambers. Thus it appears that some remoras function somewhat like cleaner fishes. The color of the remora is black or dark brown. **Range:** circumtropical; San Francisco (California) to Chile.

Sharksucker (pegador) *Echeneis naucrates* To 38 inches. The largest remora and an effective sea hitchhiker, distinctive for the dark side stripe with a white border. It seems to prefer sharks and rays as hosts but will attach to a large number of fishes and even bathers and divers when so inclined. It often enters shallow beach and coastal waters. **Range:** circumtropical; southern California to Chile.

150

SNOOKS, SABLEFISHES, SKILFISHES, SEA CATFISHES, AND HAWKFISHES

Snooks or robalos of the family Centropomidae are shovel-nosed fishes frequently found inshore in mangrove sloughs and river mouths. Six species of snook are known in the eastern Pacific. The black snook shown here, the largest in the Americas, ranges from the Gulf of California to Panama. In his book *The Sea of Cortez* (1966), Ray Cannon tells of a memorable landing of a 5-foot-7-inch black snook near a river mouth. He marveled that the river literally churned with the giant fishes. Today there are probably few such giants to be found in the Gulf of California, owing to the heavy fishing of the past 10 to 20 years. The black snook is an excellent food fish with delicate, white, flaky flesh, not unlike that of the striped bass.

The sablefish and skilfish, found in the cold, deep waters of the North Pacific, are the only members of the family Anoplopomatidae. The sablefish reaches 3 feet, is fished commercially, and is esteemed in Canada as a table fish, especially when smoked. Although it grows to 6 feet and 200 pounds, the skilfish has limited commercial value. Both frequent deep water offshore to 1,440 feet.

Black snook, robalo (róbalo prieto) *Centropomus nigrescens*   To 5 feet. The largest American snook. Snooks inhabit salt and brackish water and are found in sloughs, estuaries, rivers, and streams. Some swim upstream many miles from the sea. They have an unmistakable shovel-shaped head, a very prominent dark lateral line running out onto the tail, and the lower jaw projecting well beyond the upper jaw. The jaws and the roof of the mouth are lined with bands of very fine, small teeth. Also note the well-separated dorsal fins and the prominent anal fin spine.
Range: Gulf of California to Panama.

151

Sablefish, black cod *Anoplopoma fimbria* To 3 feet, 4 inches. Highly regarded in Canada as a table fish, especially when smoked; termed black cod there and by commercial fishermen. Great quantities are taken by the commercial fishermen of Canada, the U.S., Japan, and the Soviet Union in trawls and traps and on longlines. Many are quick-frozen and marketed worldwide. They are wide-ranging, migratory fishes; adults swim over mud bottoms at depths from 1,000 to 6,000 feet or deeper. The preferred habitat is at the edge of the continental shelf. Note the two dorsal fins with the anal fin opposite the second dorsal fin. **Range:** Japan and the Bering Sea to central Baja California.

Skilfish *Erilepis zonifer* To 6 feet. A large, basslike fish with two almost-joined dorsal fins and 12 to 14 spines in the first dorsal fin. The large pale blotches on the body are typical of young adults. Older fish grow almost completely black dorsally. They inhabit deep water offshore to 1,440 feet. In spite of their large size, they have a very limited commercial value, though some are taken by trawl and longlines. **Range:** Japan and the Bering Sea to Monterey Bay (central California).

Chihuil, sea catfish *Bagre panamensis* To 20 inches. Resembles the freshwater channel catfish that anglers know and love. However, the spines at the front of the dorsal and pectoral fins are venomous and fishermen should beware—they can cause a painful wound if handled carelessly. Note the familiar catfish shape, with long barbels at the rear corners of the mouth, another pair on the chin, and strong dorsal and pectoral fin spines. There is an adipose fin near the tail. Found in coastal shallows, usually over mud bottoms. **Range:** Santa Ana River (southern California) to Peru; rare north of Baja California.

152

The sea catfish, or chihuil, which ranges from southern California to Peru, closely resembles the familiar freshwater channel catfish. The sea catfishes, of the family Ariidae, are mouthbrooders, like the cardinalfishes. The male fish may carry from 50 to 60 large eggs in his mouth until they hatch some nine weeks after spawning. Even after they hatch, he nurtures them in his mouth for an additional two to four weeks, until they are about 3 inches long and ready for independence. During the entire brooding period, the male catfish goes without food.

Hawkfishes of the family Cirrhitidae take their avian name from their manner of perching in the branches of coral heads or in rocky crevices and swooping on smaller fishes and crustaceans. Hours of motionless vigil are punctuated by sudden dashes for food. Although many species are common in the Indo-Pacific, only three are known from the tropical eastern Pacific—the giant hawkfish, the coral hawkfish, and the longnose hawkfish. ◆

Coral hawkfish (halcón de coral) *Cirrhitichthys oxycephalus* To about 3 inches. Usually found in the branches of coral growths. Not unlike a hawk, it sits and watches the reef closely, and swoops down for the kill when a potential meal approaches in the form of a crustacean or small fish. Red spots on the body are changeable and can flash to orange or pink to match the coral head where the fish takes cover. Where coral heads are rare, as in the central Gulf of California, it seeks shelter in rocky reef cracks and crevices. Distinctive for the large scales on the cheeks and serrated edges on the preopercle. The first dorsal soft ray is filamentous. **Range:** throughout the tropical Indo-West Pacific; here, from the central Gulf of California to Colombia and the Galapagos Islands.

153

Longnose hawkfish *Oxycirrhites typus* To about 3 inches. The first two Hawaiian specimens were found off the island of Oahu in 120 feet of water, perched on the branches of a black coral growth. In the Gulf of California, they are usually found in or around yellow-polyped coral at depths from 90 to 150 feet, but occasionally in just 15 feet of water. Easily recognized by the long, pointed snout and the red checkerboard pattern on a white body. **Range:** throughout the tropical Pacific; here, from the central Gulf of California (Bahía San Carlos) to Cabo San Lucas.

Giant hawkfish (chino mero) *Cirrhitus rivulatus* To 20½ inches. A beautiful animal covered with greenish markings lined with light blue borders, somewhat resembling oriental script; these and the basslike shape produced the Spanish name "chino mero" or "Chinese bass." The fish is also basslike in sitting patiently in or near a cave, crevice, or reef hole waiting for a meal to swim by. It feeds voraciously on small fishes and crustaceans; and will leave the shelter of its rocky home, like a large bass does, to investigate divers in the area. As a result of their curiosity they are often speargunned to extinction in many areas frequented by divers. Note the heavy, thickened lower pectoral fin rays that support the fish while at rest. Also distinctive are fringes or cirri projecting from the membranes near the tips of the dorsal spines, and the cirri on the rear edge of the nostrils. Juveniles have four or five dark bars crossing the body and a bright red spiny dorsal fin. **Range:** throughout the Gulf of California to Colombia and the Galapagos Islands.

FLATFISHES

If you see what appears to be a flying carpet with fins and a white underside rippling about the reef, gliding to the bottom to disappear into the sand, you are watching a flatfish. The flatfishes include many of the world's tastiest and most valuable food fishes, such as the sole, flounder, halibut, sanddab, turbot, and plaice.

All flatfishes begin life much like any other symmetrical fish, with an eye on either side of the head. Within a few days, however, one eye starts migrating toward the other, and soon both eyes are close together on the upper side of the animal's body. The mouth becomes strangely twisted, and the dorsal fin grows forward on the fish, almost reaching the mouth. This metamorphosis prepares the fish for its bottom-dwelling existence. Within a few more days, the young flatfish sinks to the ocean bottom, where it spends the rest of its life lying on its eyeless side (which is usually white), with the eyed side up.

Most flatfishes can change colors to match the ocean bottom. Their ability to match a background so exactly seems to be dependent on their sight. If a flatfish becomes blinded by injury, it no longer can adapt its coloration to its surroundings. The excellent flatfish camouflage is enhanced by an ability to quickly bury itself in the bottom sand, and flatfishes are extremely difficult to locate with an untrained eye. Most flatfishes are carnivorous, and dash out of hiding to gobble down smaller fishes and crustaceans. They range in size from only a few inches to great, flat 9-foot giants weighing 800 pounds.

American flatfishes are separated into two broad categories. One includes the families Bothidae and Pleuronectidae (flounders, halibuts, turbots, sanddabs, and soles); the other includes the families Soleidae and Cynoglossidae (broadsoles and tonguefishes). The Bothidae are lefteye flatfishes (so called because both eyes are usually positioned on the left side of the head), and the Pleuronectidae are usually righteye flatfishes.

The use of the name "sole" when referring to some members of the families Pleuronectidae and Bothidae is a source of confusion, since the only true soles are those belonging to another family, the Soleidae. Because the name "sole" has been in use for years, has become standard in the literature, and is used by fishermen to describe pe-

Starry flounder, rough jacket *Platichthys stellatus*   To 3 feet and 20 pounds. A popular sport fish and a good food fish. It is found over sand, mud, and gravel bottoms, but not rocky areas, from shore to 900 feet; it can tolerate fresh water and is often found in coastal rivers, especially as juvenile. Note the black-banded dorsal and anal fins, and the black-striped tail fin. The eyed side is rough and covered with scattered tubercles or starlike scales, hence the name starry flounder. Even though they belong to the righteye flounder family, the majority of starry flounders on the Pacific Coast are left-eyed; in Japan, almost all are left-eyed. **Range:** Korea and Japan to Alaska and the Bering Sea, and south to Santa Barbara (southern California). **Edibility:** good.

Pacific halibut *Hippoglossus stenolepis*   To 8 feet, 9 inches and 800 pounds (average: 5 to 10 pounds). This giant, the largest flatfish on the Pacific Coast, was at one time badly depleted due to overfishing. The International Halibut Commission mandated a reduction in fishing for both American and Canadian fishermen, and gradually populations regenerated. It is now one of the most important commercial and sport fishes in northern Pacific waters, taken at depths from 20 to 3,600 feet. Almost always right-eyed, it can be identified by the slightly indented tail fin, the stout body, lateral line arched over the pectoral fin, and the jaw reaching only to the middle of the eye. After 35 years a female may reach 470 pounds, while after 25 years a puny male will weigh only 40 pounds. A 140-pound female may lay as many as 2,700,000 eggs. **Range:** Sea of Japan to Bering Sea and to Santa Rosa Island (southern California). **Edibility:** excellent.

trale, fantail, rex, and butter flatfishes, it seems practical to accept its use. The phrase "fillet of sole" was once reserved for the prized common European sole *Solea solea*, but is now used for almost any filleted flatfish.

Because bottomfishes are particularly susceptible to contamination and pollutants, a disturbing development in southern California was the posting of warning signs by the Los Angeles County Department of Health Services in 1985 regarding flatfishes. Every fishing pier from Santa Monica Bay to Long Beach was posted to warn of the dangers of eating the California halibut (see page 161) and the white croaker (see page 59), owing to contamination by toxic DDT and PCB. ♦

Petrale sole, brill (lenguado) *Eopsetta jordani* To 27½ inches. Because this deep-bodied fish is large and is such fine food, it is pursued by both American and Canadian commercial trawlers. At its peak in 1948, the Canadian fishery alone took 6.7 million pounds. For identification, note that this right-eyed flatfish has a large mouth extending to the middle of the eye, teeth that are in two rows in the upper jaw, and scales that are very small. Named for David Starr Jordan, the first president of Stanford University and a pioneering ichthyologist. **Range:** Bering Sea to northern Baja California. **Edibility:** excellent.

Rex sole, longfin sole, witch sole (lenguado) *Glyptocephalus zachirus* To 23¼ inches. Though a superior table delicacy, this flounder is not taken in great quantity by commercial fishermen because of generally small size, delicate body, and need for special handling. Even so, it is an important and esteemed food fish, taken over soft bottoms from 60 to 2,100 feet. Look for the slender body, long dark pectoral fin, large eyes, and straight lateral line. **Range:** Bering Sea to northern Baja California. **Edibility:** excellent.

Dover sole, slime sole, slippery sole (lenguado) *Microstomus pacificus*   To 2½ feet.
In the early 19th century an enterprising London merchant arranged fast, horse-drawn gigs to bring shipments of the European common sole (*Solea solea*)—a fine food fish—post-haste to the city from Dover; hence the name Dover sole. The name has somehow become attached to a Pacific Coast flatfish that is not from Dover or even a sole but a flounder in the family Pleuronectidae. Clemens and Wilby (1961) report that the Dover sole produces a distinctively large amount of slime that covers fishermen's trawls and catches with an undesirable white mucilaginous coating, which reduces the value of this flatfish and makes filleting difficult. But the flesh is quite palatable. Marketed as fillet of sole and as mink food. Easily recognized by the small mouth, straight lateral line, and soft flaccid body, slippery to the touch. **Range:** Bering Sea to central Baja California. **Edibility:** good.

Diamond turbot (lenguado) *Hypsopsetta guttulata*   To 1½ feet. The name turbot describes certain deep-bodied flatfish species highly regarded as food owing to the thickness, weight, and fine flavor of the flesh. The five Pacific Coast turbots are the diamond, curlfin, spotted, C-O, and horneyhead. The diamond turbot has a distinctive diamond shape due to the long, high, pointed dorsal and anal fins. It has a small mouth and branched lateral line. The underside is a bright, porcelain white; around the mouth is a lemon-yellow patch. Prefers mud and sand bottoms around reefs, piers, or other solid objects, from inshore to 150 feet and in bays, and sloughs. Considered excellent eating, but the skin is tough and some fish have a slight iodine taste. **Range:** Cape Mendocino (northern California) to Bahía Magdalena (Baja California), and the Gulf of California. **Edibility:** good.

Rock sole, roughback sole *Lepidopsetta bilineata*   To 23½ inches. This flounder is a master color changer adept at switching its colors to exactly match its background—as it moves from rocky bottom to pebbly gravel, or sandy bottom—thus becoming almost invisible. A very tasty food fish taken by sport and commercial fishermen from shore to 1,200 feet. Feeds on clam siphons, shrimps, crabs, worms, brittle stars, and sand lances. Female lays from 400,000 to a million bright, yellow-orange eggs from February to April. Notable for the deeply ovate body, rough tuberculated scales on the eyed side, the high arch in the lateral line, and short accessory dorsal branch. **Range:** Sea of Japan and Bering Sea to Tanner Bank (southern California). **Edibility:** excellent.

Butter sole *Isopsetta isolepis*   To 21¾ inches. Reputed to have the finest, most delicate taste of all Pacific Coast flounders. Since it is rather small, thin, and covered with rough scales, however, commercial fishermen do not waste much time on it. Most of the many tons caught each year go for mink food; only a small part is filleted for the fish markets. Distinctive for the yellow margins on the dorsal and anal fins and the yellow blotches on the gray or brown body. Lateral line slightly curved over pectoral fin with small dorsal branch. **Range:** Bering Sea to Ventura (southern California). **Edibility:** excellent.

Curlfin turbot, curlfin sole (lenguado) *Pleuronichthys decurrens*   To 14½ inches. The curlfin, the most desirable table fish of the Pacific Coast turbots, is fished commercially and by some sport fishermen—especially in the San Francisco area. Large quantities are processed for mink food. Like other turbots, it is an oval-shaped, deep-bodied fish. The dorsal and anal fins are quite high in the middle, giving the fish a diamond shape not as pronounced as in the diamond turbot. The first 9 to 12 rays of the dorsal fin are on the blind side. Note the very slight arch in the lateral line with a long dorsal branch. Occurs over soft bottoms from 25 to 1,700 feet. **Range:** Prince William Sound (Alaska) to Bahía San Quintín (northern Baja California). **Edibility:** excellent.

C-O turbot, C-O sole (lenguado)
Pleuronichthys coenosus To 14½
inches. The large, protruding eyes of
this flatfish earn it the name popeye
from some fishermen. Others see the
dark, curved bar and round spot on
the tail fin as reading C-O. Also note
the deep body and large round spot
in the middle of the eyed side of this
turbot. Taken in small quantities by
commercial trawlers, but tough hide
makes filleting difficult. Occurs over
hard and soft bottoms from shore to
1,150 feet. **Range:** southeast Alaska
to Cabo Colnett (northern Baja California). **Edibility:** good.

Horneyhead turbot (lenguado)
Pleuronichthys verticalis To 14½
inches. The horneyhead ranks third in
quality among the turbots; though a
fine food fish, it has little commercial
importance. Like the curlfin turbot it
has a bony ridge between the eyes;
a prominent backward-directed spine
at the rear of the ridge is sharp and
hornlike, hence the name horneyhead.
The first four to six rays of the dorsal
fin are on the blind side. Found over
soft bottoms from 30 to 660 feet.
Range: Point Reyes (central California) to Bahía Magdalena (southern
Baja California) and throughout the
Gulf of California. **Edibility:** good.

Sand sole *Psettichthys melanostic-
tus* To 24¾ inches. As the name implies, this flounder likes shallow,
sandy areas and is frequently caught
by anglers quite close to shore. It is a
fine food fish. The back or eyed side
varies in coloration to match its background but is usually a light tan or
brown with tiny black speckles—
much like a sandy ocean bottom. Also
distinctive for the elongated rays at the
front of the dorsal fin, the large
mouth, and the slightly curved lateral
line with a dorsal branch. Found from
near shore to 600 feet. **Range:** Bering
Sea to Redondo Beach (southern California). **Edibility:** good.

Spotted turbot (lenguado) *Pleuronichthys ritteri* To 11½ inches. Lowest-
ranked in quality of the Pacific Coast
turbots but still very good food. Quite
similar to the C-O turbot, but this fish
has four distinct spots on its back that
aid in identification: two small spots
along the lateral line, and two larger
spots located farther back near the
tail—one above and one below the
lateral line. Note the straight lateral
line with long dorsal branch. Habitat
ranges from 4- to 150-foot depths.
Range: Point Conception (southern
California) to Bahía Magdalena (southern Baja California). **Edibility:** good.

California halibut (lenguado de California) *Paralichthys californicus* To 5 feet and 60 pounds. A large, tasty, very popular flatfish sought by both sport and commercial fishermen. At one time, annual commercial catches ranged from 500 to 1,000 tons and sport fishermen reeled in 300,000 halibut each year. Overfishing and reduction of natural habitat have caused stocks to dwindle in recent years and fishermen have given up trying to hook these fishes. All California halibut must now be over 22 inches in length to keep, a regulation designed to replenish this fish. Although a member of the lefteye flatfish family, 40 percent of all fishes taken are right-eyed. Found over soft bottoms from shore to 600 feet, along surf lines, and even in bays and estuaries. Note the unbranched lateral line arching over the pectoral fin, the large mouth reaching beyond the eye, and the indented tail fin. **Range:** Quillayute River (British Columbia) to Bahía Magdalena (Baja California) and throughout the Gulf of California. **Edibility:** excellent, except in Santa Monica and San Pedro bays off Los Angeles, where California halibut are contaminated with trace amounts of toxic DDT and PCB.

Pacific sanddab, mottled sanddab (lenguado) *Citharichthys sordidus* To 16 inches. A very popular fish pursued by both sport and commercial fishermen and, because it is excellent eating, often listed on the menus of seafood restaurants, especially in California. A left-eyed flatfish with a short pectoral fin. The similar longfin sanddab (*C. xanthostigma*) grows to just 10 inches and has a long, blackish pectoral fin on the eyed side. Both fishes have straight lateral lines and brownish coloration on the back, with orange speckles. Found over soft bottoms from 30 to 1,800 feet (longfin ranges from 8 to 660 feet). Pacific sanddab females spawn in the summer; in three years young are 8 inches long. **Range:** Pacific sanddab, Bering Sea to Cabo San Lucas (Baja California); longfin sanddab, Monterey Bay (central California) to Costa Rica. **Edibility:** good, both species.

161

Cortez halibut (alabato, lenguado) *Paralichthys aestuarius* To 3 feet and 50 pounds. The largest flatfish in the Gulf of California and common there near shore during the winter cold-water months. During the summer it retreats to deeper, cooler water. Very tasty and important as a food fish. Similar to the California halibut but with a broader body and more numerous fin rays (84 dorsal and 63 anal rays, compared with just 70 dorsal and 55 anal rays for the California halibut). The eyes are found on the right side almost as often as on the left. **Range:** throughout the Gulf of California. **Edibility:** excellent.

Threespot flounder (lenguado) *Ancylopsetta dendritica* To 1 foot. A striking member of the ocellated flounders, three species of which are found on the American Atlantic Coast. All are assigned to the genus *Ancylopsetta*; and two species have three large ocelli or "eye" spots on the eyed side, as does this flounder. Note the platter-like shape and the very long pelvic fin. **Range:** Bahía Magdalena (Baja California) to Ecuador, including the Gulf of California. **Edibility:** good.

Fourspot sole (lenguado) *Hippoglossina tetrophthalmus* To 1 foot. A handsome Gulf of California flatfish with four spots on its back. Note the large mouth, lateral line arched over the pectoral fin, and the fan-shaped tail. Divers unfamiliar with flatfishes have difficulty finding and identifying these quick color change artists. If threatened, fourspot soles dive to the bottom and bury themselves in the sand or mud, or simply lie flat and change colors to match the sediment. **Range:** Puerto Peñasco (northern Gulf of California) to Cabo San Lucas. **Edibility:** good.

Fantail sole (lenguado) *Xystreurys liolepis* To 21 inches. This flatfish spends most of the time buried beneath sand or mud on soft bottoms from 15- to 260-foot depths. Consequently, it is rarely caught by sport or commercial fishermen. Note the two large "eye" spots on the back, the small mouth, the lateral line arched over the pectoral, and the indented tail. Although a left-eyed flatfish, those taken are often right-eyed. **Range:** Monterey Bay (California) to the Gulf of California. **Edibility:** good.

Broadsoles

Mazatlan sole (sol Mexicano, tepalcate) *Achirus mazatlanus* To 9 inches (usually under 6 inches). The broadsole is a true sole of the family Soleidae, quite similar and closely related to the Atlantic Coast hogchoker sole, *Trinectes maculatus*. As the name "hogchoker" implies, the rough, bristly scales of these soles make them inedible. Note the oval body, straight lateral line, small eyes and mouth, and tiny pectoral fin. Often enters freshwater rivers and streams. **Range:** abundant on the Pacific Coast of Mexico and common throughout the Gulf of California; south to Panama. **Edibility:** poor.

Tonguefishes

California tonguefish (lengua) *Symphurus atricauda* To 8¼ inches. Members of the family Cynoglossidae, the tonguefishes are for the most part too small to be of much interest as food fishes. Tongue shaped, they taper like an arrow to a narrow point at the tail. The eyes are on the left side of the body; eyes and mouth are very small. There are no pectoral fins or lateral line. Dorsal and anal fins are joined and continuous with the tail fin. The blind side is white. These fishes like to bury themselves in sand or mud-sand bottom sediment from about 5- to 600-foot depths. Consequently, though abundant in southern waters, they are rarely seen. **Range:** Humboldt County (California) to Panama. **Edibility:** poor.

163

SURGEONFISHES, TANGS, AND MOORISH IDOLS

If, while diving around coral heads, you are suddenly engulfed in a vast cloud of spotted, yellow-tailed fishes, you have met the magnificent yellowtail surgeonfishes of the eastern Pacific. Large schools of these fishes are common around reefs in the lower Gulf of California and range from the Gulf to Panama and El Salvador. To see one or two hundred of these fishes rising from a reef head is a feast for the eyes. The surgeonfishes (family Acanthuridae), frequently also called tangs or doctorfishes, are named for the scalpel-like spine on either side of the body just in front of the tail. The spine in most surgeonfishes and tangs may be aptly compared with a switchblade knife, because it is hinged and lies flat along the body in a sheath. The fish can flick the blade out, point it forward, and, by repeatedly sideswiping another fish, cause serious injury. Careless or unaware fishermen can receive nasty cuts when handling these spined fishes. A few genera, including the yellowtail

ADULT

JUVENILE

Yellowtail surgeonfish (cochinito) *Prionurus punctatus* To 2 feet. A handsome fish, abundant along the rocky reefs and shores of the central and lower Gulf of California. They cluster in small aggregations of 10 or 12 fishes and sometimes into large schools that roam the rock and coral reefs grazing the algae at depths from 20 to 40 feet. Juveniles have two color phases: a brilliant yellow phase, shown here, and another that is spotted overall like the mature fish. Males and females are colored alike. Note the three whitish spine-tipped knobs near the tail, which can be quite effective weapons when used against other fishes and unwary fishermen. An almost identical fish, the Galapagos surgeonfish (*P. laticlavius*), found around the Galapagos Islands and Islas Revillagigedo, lacks the spots over the body. **Range:** upper Gulf of California to El Salvador and Islas Revillagigedo.

surgeonfish, have fixed, unhinged spines on either side of the tail. A beginning diver need not fear an attack by hordes of surgeonfishes. The usual object of attack is another fish, often of the same size and species, that acts as if it may threaten the first fish's hold on its section of reef or "territory." In its natural reef habitat, the surgeonfish has but to give a warning flick of its tail toward an intruder fish, which invariably withdraws. In an aquarium, however, where there is no place to hide, an aggressive surgeonfish can do considerable damage to its tankmates.

Like parrotfishes, tangs are herbivorous grazers, continually searching out and cropping the reef algae. A large school of tangs may swoop down on a small coral head and leave it practically bare of algae. They are not much esteemed by gourmets because of the strong odor and savor of the flesh. But in Hawaii both the convict tang and the kole are relished as food fishes. In certain areas of the Indo-Pacific, the flesh of some surgeonfishes is extremely poisonous for humans to eat; they are suspected of being key links in the uptake of ciguatera toxin into the food chain. ◆

Purple surgeonfish, yellowfin surgeon (lancero) *Acanthurus xanthopterus* To 20 inches. One of the largest fishes of the genus *Acanthurus* and probably the most wide-ranging—from Africa through the Indian Ocean to the Indo-Pacific, Hawaii, and Mexico. Noteworthy for its size, the yellow-and-blue-striped dorsal and anal fins, the yellow pectoral fins, and the pale white bar or blotch on the tail. The body color is extremely variable from blue to purple to gray to green. Common in turbid lagoons, channels, and seaward reefs to depths of 100 feet or more. Referred to as *Hepatus crestonis* in early literature. **Range:** central Gulf of California to Panama, Isla del Coco, and the Galapagos Islands.

Achilles tang (lancero) *Acanthurus achilles*   To 10 inches. Its colors glow like neon under water. The bright red spot on the tail suggests the vulnerable heel of Achilles. Juveniles begin to acquire this spot at about 2½ inches. Like the goldrimmed surgeonfish, to which it is closely related, this fish prefers exposed inshore reef areas where surge and surf are turbulent. **Range:** quite rare in the eastern Pacific, but sighted around Cabo San Lucas; common in Hawaii and the Indo-West Pacific.

Kole, bristle-toothed tang (lancero) *Ctenochaetus strigosus*   To 7 inches. A beautiful little fish, abundant throughout the Hawaiian Islands but so far found in the eastern Pacific only at Isla del Coco off Costa Rica. Investigation may reveal that it occurs elsewhere on our coast. Look for it around both protected and exposed rock and coral reefs. Note the gold ring around the eye. Feeds on detritus from bottom sands and microorganisms with its delicate, fine, bristlelike teeth. **Range:** see above.

Moorish idol (idolo moro) *Zanclus cornutus*   To about 9 inches. The beauty and fragility of this fish put it in a class by itself; it is the only member of the family Zanclidae. It is closely related to the surgeonfishes, but lacks a spine at the tail base. Usually found in hard substrate, rock, or coral reef areas from near shore out to 150 feet, in pairs or small groups of three to six or more, probing into crevices with their long snouts for sponges, coralline algae, and small invertebrates. It is widespread throughout the Indo-Pan-Pacific, including all tropical and subtropical island groups except Easter Island. **Range:** in the eastern Pacific, from the lower Gulf of California to El Salvador, including offshore islands.

Goldrimmed surgeonfish, whitecheek surgeonfish (lancero) *Acanthurus glaucopareius*   To 8 inches. A beautiful fish, usually found in exposed inshore reef areas where the water is turbulent. It is easily recognized by the gold rims or stripes along the bases of the dorsal and anal fins. The white blotch or ''whitecheek'' below the eye is also a good identifier. A very similar surgeonfish found in Japan (*A. japonicus*) is virtually identical but has a larger white patch on the cheek extending down to the mouth. The goldrimmed surgeon is common in the Indo-Pacific but seems to be rare in the eastern Pacific. It is seen occasionally in the Cabo San Lucas region of the Gulf of California. **Range:** Isla Santa Cruz and La Paz (Gulf of California) to Panama, including Islas Revillagigedo and Isla del Coco.

Convict tang (lancero) *Acanthurus triostegus*   To about 9 inches. Sometimes seen in great schools roving like silvery-green, brown-striped clouds over coral and rock reefs, especially on outer reef flats and shallow seaward reefs. A large school can descend on a small reef and leave it practically bare of algae. Fortunately the algae recovers quickly. Note the six dark bars on the silvery green-gray body. The Spanish name *lancero* (lance) refers to the razorlike spine at the tail base. This tang is very wide-ranging in the Indo-Pacific. In Hawaii, where it is called the *manini*, it is abundant over coral and lava reefs. **Range:** Bahía Los Frailes (near Cabo San Lucas, Gulf of California) to Panama; also abundant around Islas Revillagigedo.

The triggerfish of the family Balistidae is an intelligent, fascinating animal, and a fearless, aggressive carnivore. Probably because they are such slow swimmers, triggerfishes have developed a number of protective devices, the one for which they are named being a peculiar locking-spine mechanism. When attacked or threatened by a larger fish, the fish erects an imposing first dorsal spine and immediately becomes less attractive as a meal. When the first dorsal spine is erected, the smaller second dorsal spine or "trigger" moves forward and locks the first into an upright position. Many a predator attempting to dine on a triggerfish has spent some very uncomfortable moments trying to dislodge the creature from its throat. If all else fails, the resourceful triggerfish may dive for a reef hole or crevice, where it erects its locking dorsal spine. Thus wedged into its hole, there is no way a predator, or even a human fish collector, can remove the fish, and it is usually left alone.

Triggerfishes swim by undulating the soft dorsal and anal fins languidly, bringing their tail into action only when speed is required. Although seemingly grotesquely configured, with their eyes set far back on their bodies, they are well designed to prey upon prickly crustaceans, mollusks, echinoderms, and even venomous fireworms and starfish. They are one of the few fishes that can attack a spiny sea urchin with impunity. Since their eyes are well out of danger, they can bite the urchin's spines off with their sharp teeth and feast on the soft underbelly. A surprising technique used by the triggerfish against a strolling sea urchin is blowing jets of water at the base until the urchin is bowled over by the force of the jets. Once on its side, the urchin becomes a meal for the hungry trigger. Triggerfishes are also adept at uncovering crustaceans and worms hidden in the sand by blowing jets of water into the bottom. The intelligence of the trigger has been demonstrated by a scientist who assembled a large clump of rocks and coral fragments over a sandy patch, then placed a sea urchin in the rocks. The triggerfish reconnoitered briefly, then began plucking the rocks and coral fragments away, one by one. The hapless sea urchin, uncovered, was quickly overturned and devoured. Recent studies reveal that large triggerfishes hollow out nests on the reef bottom—some 6 feet in diameter—to receive eggs. The eggs, often numbering over 10,000, are deposited in a cup in the center and vigorously defended, sometimes by the male, sometimes by the female, depending on the species.

Filefishes, also of the balistid family, are closely related to the triggers but have the first dorsal spine located far forward, usually over the eye; on the triggerfish the first dorsal spine is in back of the eye. Filefishes usually have two dorsal spines, triggerfishes three. All have a first dorsal spine that locks when erect. Filefishes also have narrower bodies than triggerfishes and a skin that is almost filelike (hence the name) and sometimes prickly-velvet to the touch. Like the triggerfishes, filefishes have jaw teeth much like human incisors, and strong jaws, which they use to pierce and crush mollusks, crustaceans, sea urchins, and

Orangeside triggerfish (cochino) *Sufflamen verres*　To 15 inches. Roams the reef bottom searching out crustaceans, worms, and other invertebrates from sandy-bottom hiding places (sometimes by blowing them out with jets of water). Also adept at blowing to overturn sea urchins, to feast on the underbellies. Unmistakable with the large orange blotch on the side and the orange line that runs from the mouth back toward the pectoral fin base. Males are distinctly and brightly colored. Females are less so. At night they wedge themselves into small reef caves or rock crevices, by erecting the first dorsal spine and locking it in place. **Range:** Isla Cedros (central Baja California), the Gulf of California, and south to Ecuador.

Finescale triggerfish (pez puerco, cochi) *Balistes polylepis*　To 2½ feet. A wide-ranging trigger found from northern California to Chile, but rare north of Baja California. Recognized by the very fine scales on the round, deep body, and the deeply notched teeth, almost like small human incisors. They cluster by day in small groups that graze rocky areas and sandy bottoms feeding on mollusks, crustaceans, and sea urchins. In July and August, adults hollow out large nests to receive eggs that are laid in clusters. The nest is vigorously defended by the female. **Range:** Crescent City (northern California) to Chile, and throughout the Gulf of California.

Redtail triggerfish, sargassum triggerfish, crosshatch triggerfish (pez puerco) *Xanthichthys mento* To 10 inches. The crosshatch coloration on this fish shows the plate-like, armor-like scales that cover most triggerfishes. Males have five to eight blue-streaked grooves on the cheek, as illustrated here. Males also sport the bright red tail. Females have a yellowish tail, a bluish-green body, and a bluish head. Sometimes found near the surface around reefs, other times in fairly deep water, and seen on occasion in large schools hovering 20 to 30 feet off the bottom. They are frequently found around oceanic islands, including Hawaii, Japan, and Easter Island. **Range:** Ventura (southern California) to Acapulco (Mexico) and Clipperton Island; also common around Islas Revillagigedo and most other offshore tropical islands.

Black durgon, black triggerfish (cochi negro) *Melichthys niger* To 20 inches. Striking and distinctive, and the only black triggerfish found on the coasts of America. On the Pacific Coast, it is found in the southern Gulf of California and around the Islas Revillagigedo, Clipperton Island, Isla del Coco, and Isla de Malpelo. Seems to prefer clear-water outer reefs at depths of 50 feet or more. Note the whitish line along the base of the dorsal and anal fins, and a distinct groove just below the eyes. **Range:** circumtropical; here, San Diego (California) to Colombia, including the southern Gulf of California and offshore islands.

Vagabond filefish, gray filefish *Cantherhines dumerili* To 12 inches. Compressed, flat fishes probably called vagabond because they are found in a variety of habitats—over seagrass, patch reefs, rocks, and sand bottoms—feeding on algae, seaweed, and such unlikely fare as hydroids, sponges, and gorgonians. Note the white tail with the yellow rays, the two recurved spines on the tail base, and the 10 to 12 vague lines on the side. A dorsal spine can be locked into place when another fish threatens. **Range:** almost circumtropical; here, La Paz (southern Gulf of California) to Islas Revillagigedo.

various other prey. Many balistids, especially the larger triggerfishes, are esteemed as food fishes, called "turbot" in the West Indies, because they resemble the flatfish when skinned. ◆

Blunthead triggerfish (pez puerco de piedra) *Pseudobalistes naufragium*   To 3 feet. The largest triggerfish in the Gulf of California, but it is uncommon there. It occurs around reefs and over sandy patches, searching out sea urchins, mollusks, and various crustaceans. It ranges out to 100-foot depths. Recognized by the blunt head, prominent forehead, and the vague dark bars on the bluish-gray body. Note the three prominent dorsal spines. **Range:** Bahía de San Quintín (northern Baja California) and the central and lower Gulf of California to Ecuador.

Scrawled filefish (lija, lija trompa) *Alutera scripta*   To 35 inches. Distinctive for its large size, brilliant blue scrawls and markings on the olive-brown to yellowish body, and its broomlike tail. The dorsal spine is reduced to a long needlelike organ, quite fragile. Often seen drifting along, head downward, surveying the reef bottom for food. Known to eat stinging coral, algae, worms, sea anemones, coral polyps, gorgonians, and tunicates. Like most filefishes, the body is wafer thin and the skin has a rough-velvety filelike texture. **Range:** circumtropical; here, central Gulf of California to Islas Revillagigedo.

PUFFERS, PORCUPINEFISHES, AND TRUNKFISHES

When threatened by a predator, a puffer fish sucks in a bellyful of water and almost instantly becomes three times larger. The hungry predator, realizing that the fat little puffer is now too big to fit in its mouth, looks elsewhere for a meal. When removed from the water by curious humans, puffers use the same defense, gulping air instead of water and producing angry grunting noises. As a result, they frequently become lampshades or mantelpieces in seaside restaurants and the homes of marine collectors.

The organs and sometimes the flesh of certain puffers contain a deadly poison, tetrodotoxin. Although it has wide medical application, the poison can kill quickly if eaten, and 60 percent of the puffer food-poisoning cases are fatal. Even so, puffers are eaten with great relish in Japan, in a dish called *fugu*. Fortunately, the dish is prepared by certified *fugu* cooks. Even with great precautions, however, for many Japanese the puffer has been their last supper. From 1893 to 1963 there were 10,745 cases of puffer poisoning reported in Japan. Of these, 6,386 were fatal.

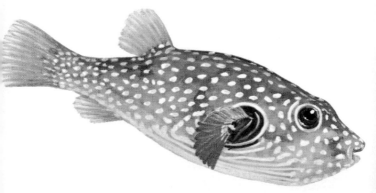

Spotted green puffer, striped-belly puffer (botete verde) *Arothron hispidus*   To 10 inches. Ranges throughout the Indo-West Pacific, including Hawaii, where some maintain it is the most poisonous of all puffers (called *make make*, or deadly death in corrupted Hawaiian), and some old warriors claim that war arrows were once dipped in the entrails of this puffer to ensure a kill. This has not been verified, but the green puffer is not recommended for the table. Recognized by the white spots on a greenish-gray body, stripes on the belly, and the black circles around the pectoral fin base. **Range:** Cabo San Lucas (Baja California) to Panama, including most off-shore islands. **Not edible;** the flesh and viscera are toxic and can be fatal to humans.

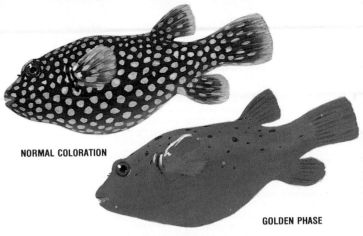

NORMAL COLORATION

GOLDEN PHASE

Guineafowl puffer, spotted puffer, golden puffer (botete negro, botete de oro)
Arothron meleagris   To 12 inches. A strikingly handsome fish in clear, sunlit water
on the reef. The white spots over the purple-black body are distinctive and probably
serve to warn hungry predators that this fish will make an unpleasant meal; the
potent poison tetrodotoxin is concentrated in the liver, gonads, ovaries, intestines,
and skin, and a predator attempting to bite or swallow the guineafowl puffer will
find the mucous skin coating heavily charged with poison. The puffer will inflate
itself when under attack; its body is covered with short spines that become erect,
and it makes a loud rasping sound as it inflates, by rubbing its two rows of fused
teeth together. This fish has a golden color phase that is also very striking when
seen on the reef. It is not known just why the puffer changes color or what ecological purpose change serves. The fish feeds on live coral polyps and tunicates.
Range: very common throughout the tropical Pacific; here, Guaymas (central Gulf
of California) to Ecuador, including all of the offshore islands. **Not edible;** the flesh
and viscera are toxic and can be fatal to humans.

The sharp-nosed puffers of the family Canthigasteridae
have distinctive long, pointed snouts. They are dainty
fishes, rarely exceeding $4\frac{1}{2}$ inches in length. The common
puffers, family Tetraodontidae, differ from the sharp-
nosed puffers in having short, rounded snouts and
rounder, more uniform bodies. The common puffers also
grow to be considerably larger than sharp-nosed puffers.
The oceanic puffer shown here reaches 2 feet, the bullseye
puffer 15 inches. The common puffers are most often implicated in cases of tetraodon poisoning. They feed on
sponges, algae, corals, mollusks, and fishes.

The porcupinefishes and burrfishes of the family Dio-
dontidae are also adept at puffing themselves up when
disturbed. They reach lengths of 3 feet. Of the three spiny
puffer species shown, the species of *Diodon* have the long-   173

Bullseye puffer (botete diana) *Sphoeroides annulatus* To 15 inches. A diver viewing this abundant puffer from above sees a "bullseye" pattern of rings quite clearly in the middle of the back, radiating out to the sides. Usually found over sandy bottoms near shore but also ranging out to patch reefs where sand and rock meet. At night it burrows into the sand for protection. It grows quite large and can puff itself up to near basketball size when threatened. The body is smooth, with tiny buried spines on the throat and belly. Although poisonous, it is often sold as food in Guaymas fish markets and reputed to be good eating, but only after careful preparation by an experienced cook. Unsuspecting southern California fishermen occasionally hook strays that wander up from southern waters. **Range:** San Diego (California) and the Gulf of California to Peru and the Galapagos Islands. **Not edible**; the flesh and viscera are toxic and can be fatal to humans.

Longnose puffer, lobeskin puffer (tambor, botete) *Sphoeroides lobatus* To 10 inches. A common inshore puffer similar to the bullseye puffer but with a longer snout, short spines behind the eyes, and lack of concentric circles on the back. Ordinarily rare north of Baja California, these puffers were taken at Redondo Pier, in southern California, in 1972, 1978, and again in 1984 when four were hooked by startled fishermen. California Department of Fish and Game spokesmen take pains to see that local anglers are advised not to take these home for dinner. Stories in coastal newspapers headlined "Local Angler Has Death on the Line" get the message across. **Range:** Redondo Beach (southern California) and the central and southern Gulf of California to Peru. **Not edible**; the flesh and viscera are toxic and can be fatal to humans.

est spines, which fold back against the body when not inflated. The *Chilomycterus* species possess three-rooted spines that are always rigidly erect.

The trunkfishes include the boxfishes and cowfishes of the family Ostraciidae. For protection against predators, these odd, fascinating fishes are enclosed in a solid, bony box with holes for the eyes, mouth, fins, and vent. Their 174 movements on the reef are curious, almost like miniature

Oceanic puffer (tambor, conejo) *Lagocephalus lagocephalus*   To 2 feet. Grows very large and is found in all warm seas offshore near the surface. It is the most oceanic of all puffers; when it occurs near shore, it is usually found cast up on the beach. Note the blue back, white belly, and the spots along the silvery sides. There are tiny buried spines on the throat and belly. The mouth is small with a projecting beak of four teeth—two upper and two lower. **Range:** Mendocino County (northern California) to Peru, including the central and southern Gulf of California. **Not edible;** the viscera may be poisonous.

Spotted sharpnose puffer (botete bonito) *Canthigaster punctatissima*   To 3½ inches. A striking, dainty fish common in the central and lower Gulf of California, especially on the Baja coast. It is slow-moving and can easily be approached by divers as it flutters and pokes around the reef where coral growth is rich. Like its similar Hawaiian cousin, the whitespotted puffer (*C. jactator*), it probably feeds on coralline algae and invertebrates. It would seem to be attractive to large predators, but is protected by extremely toxic skin secretions. Easily recognized by the white spots covering its body, which probably serve to warn off attackers. The long, sharp snout is distinctive and helps to separate the Canthigasteridae puffers from most other puffers with short, rounded snouts. It has a sharp ridge on its back in front of the dorsal fin. **Range:** Guaymas (central Gulf of California) to Panama and the Galapagos Islands. **Not edible;** the viscera may be poisonous.

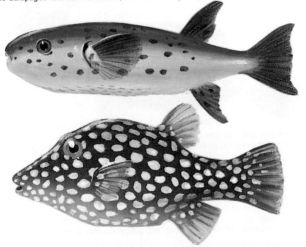

helicopters as they manuever their rigid bodies with the aid of tiny, fluttering fins and tail. They are such slow swimmers that they can easily be approached and studied by divers. Some trunkfish species can discharge a toxin into the water when under stress. This poison, named ostracitoxin, will kill other fishes in aquaria and bait tanks, even after the trunkfish is removed. Although frequently poisonous, trunkfishes are roasted in their shells and eaten like chestnuts by some Pacific islanders. ◆

Spotted porcupinefish (pez erizo) *Diodon hystrix*   To about 3 feet. The illustration shows an inflated porcupinefish, ready to repel an attacker. The spotted porcupinefish can be distinguished from the very similar barred porcupinefish by the numerous small spots on the body, with no bars or blotches. Found around shallow reefs, sand, and grassy areas, it is worldwide in distribution and common on both the Atlantic and Pacific coasts of America. Bohlke and Chaplin (1968) report spearing a large female porcupinefish, which was swimming with a smaller male, in the Bahamas. The male refused to leave his mate and swam close by while she was on the spear. **Range:** circumtropical; here, San Diego (California) to Chile, including the central and southern Gulf of California. **Not edible;** the viscera may be poisonous.

Balloonfish, barred porcupinefish (pez erizo) *Diodon holocanthus*   To about 1½ feet. Porcupinefishes grow quite large and are sometimes seen on shallow reefs taking cover in grassy areas, behind rocks or vegetation. They are adept at inflating and erecting long sharp spines when distressed, thus presenting the predator with a formidable spiny ball to swallow. Because they are slow-moving, they are often taken by divers as prickly "souvenirs." Like puffers, their skin and viscera can be very poisonous and should not be eaten. They are similar to the spotted porcupinefish but have large dark bars passing through the eyes and four large dark blotches or saddles on the back. The illustration shows a porcupinefish in a relaxed cruising mode, with the spines tucked away. **Range:** worldwide in tropical seas; recently recorded from La Jolla (southern California) and very common in the central and lower Gulf of California. **Not edible;** the viscera may be poisonous.

Pacific burrfish (pez erizo) *Chilomycterus affinis* To about 20 inches. The short, fixed, three-based spines of the burrfish are always erect on its body, unlike the movable, two-based, much longer spines of the barred and the spotted porcupinefishes. A common inhabitant of coral and rocky reefs in shallow water, and of patch reef and sandy bottom areas. Often found washed up on beaches. Similar to the spotted porcupinefish in having numerous dark spots on its body. Note the bluish back and white belly. **Range:** tropical Pacific; here, San Pedro (southern California) to Peru and the Galapagos Islands. **Not edible;** the viscera may be poisonous.

Spiny boxfish, brown cowfish (torito, pez cofre) *Lactoria diaphanus* To 10 inches. In Spanish, *torito* means little bull; this fish earns that name and the term cowfish because of the "horn" over each eye, the bovine expression on the boxed-in face, and the large, expressive eyes. A wide-ranging pelagic fish found at or near the surface in the tropical waters of the Pacific and Indian oceans. Seen occasionally around San Felipe and Cabo San Lucas in the Gulf of California. Note the spine in the middle of the back, the small paired spines on the dorsal and ventral ridges, and the long tail. **Range:** Santa Barbara (southern California) to Peru. **Not edible;** the skin and viscera may be toxic.

JUVENILE AND ADULT FEMALE

MALE

Pacific boxfish, spotted trunkfish, blue boxfish (pez caja) *Ostracion meleagris* To about 7 inches. The male trunkfish is brilliant and gaudy, and quite splendid to see on the reef, especially in bright, sunlit waters. The female and juvenile are also handsome in their white-spotted jackets—a striking example of sexual dimorphism. So different are the male and female in coloration that for years the male was described as a separate species. These slow movers float and hover over shallow rock and coral reefs grazing on algae and invertebrates. As a defense they exude a poison—ostracitoxin—from their skin. It is toxic to other fishes. **Range:** La Paz and Cabo San Lucas (Baja California) to Panama; also widespread in the Indo-West Pacific. **Not edible;** the skin and viscera may be poisonous. 177

ANGLERFISHES, TOADFISHES, SANDFISHES, SEAROBINS, AND LIZARDFISHES

The anglerfishes of the order Lophiiformes spend most of their time sitting motionless on the bottom, trying to appear as rocklike and inconspicuous as possible. Most of them are formless, lumplike fishes endowed with warty, prickly skin and an expert talent for catching their food with the aid of an appendage like a fishing rod, which is raised over the mouth when hungry. A curious smaller fish unwise enough to investigate this strange baited fishpole is sucked into the mouth of the anglerfish with such speed that the human eye cannot follow its movement.

The frogfishes of the family Antennariidae are excellent anglers and very adept at camouflage. They are voracious and, when angling is poor, they have been known to stalk other fishes, commonly swallowing fishes longer than

Roughjaw frogfish (pez antenado) *Antennarius avalonis*   To 13½ inches. Although seemingly an ill-adapted fish, it is in fact a well-designed underwater angler. After finding a good location under a ledge or in a reef crevice, it precisely matches its color and contour to blend into the reef; it can phase from lemon-yellow to orange and red, or to green, brown, and black. It attracts smaller fish by waving and wriggling an esca (lure) on the tip of its illicium (fishing pole). When a curious fish comes close to investigate, the frogfish engulfs it in a flash. Juveniles are found inshore hiding around shallow reefs and tidepools. Adults also occur inshore, and move out to deeper rocky areas, to 360 feet. **Range:** Santa Catalina Island and Orange County (southern California) to Peru and throughout the Gulf of California.

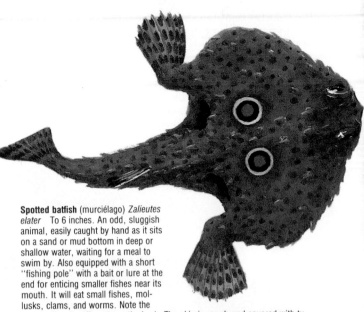

Spotted batfish (murciélago) *Zalieutes elater*   To 6 inches. An odd, sluggish animal, easily caught by hand as it sits on a sand or mud bottom in deep or shallow water, waiting for a meal to swim by. Also equipped with a short "fishing pole" with a bait or lure at the end for enticing smaller fishes near its mouth. It will eat small fishes, mollusks, clams, and worms. Note the two ocelli or "eye" spots on the back. The skin is rough and covered with tubercles. **Range:** Point Conception (southern California) to the Gulf of California and Peru; rare north of Baja California.

their own bodies. Batfishes (family Ogcocephalidae) are bat-shaped anglers often seen sitting quietly on sandy bottoms blending nicely with their surroundings. If prodded, they lurch awkwardly for a few feet and return quickly to their motionless position. They eat small mollusks and crustaceans as well as small fishes, and their lure apparently is not always used when feeding.

Lizardfishes of the family Synodontidae are also voracious carnivores, and also motionless bottomsitters. They may even bury themselves in the sand until only their eyes protrude. When a smaller fish draws near, they dart upward, lizardlike, to engulf their prey in a cavernous mouth lined with fine, sharp teeth.

Toadfishes of the family Batrachoididae include the plainfin midshipman. This unique fish has over 600 photophores on its side that can gleam so brightly that one may read a newspaper 10 inches away. Amorous males called "singing" fish signal females at mating time by vibrating swim bladders.

179

The colorful searobin (family Triglidae) "walks" across the bottom on three or more pairs of detached lower pectoral rays, feeding chiefly on small crustaceans and mollusks. The largest members of the searobin family reach 3 feet and are considered excellent eating in some areas.

The sandfishes, Trichodontidae, are a small family of northern Pacific fishes with an upturned mouth lined with brushlike teeth. They live on bottom mud or sand, or bury themselves with only the mouth protruding. ◆

Plainfin midshipman (pez sapo) *Porichthys notatus*   To 15 inches. The midshipman is a toadfish named for the 600 or more photophores along its side. They gleam in the dark like a navy midshipman's buttons and can give such bright light that one may read a newspaper ten inches away. Each luminous organ is covered by a tiny lens. In the spring, humming or "singing" males call to females for mating by vibrating air bladders. Females attach amber eggs to rocks or shells. In the summer of 1985, houseboat residents in a shallow bay north of San Francisco were tormented night after night by a mysterious buzzing sound. Suspicions ranged from "a secret military device" to "an obscure sewer pump." But underwater acoustical detectives soon matched the humming sound exactly to the jolly "singing fishes"— the plainfin midshipmen. Nothing could be done for the houseboat owners, but at least they knew where the sound was coming from. **Range:** Alaska to Cabo San Lucas (Baja California) and throughout the Gulf of California.

Southern midshipman (pez sapo) *Porichthys margaritatus*   To about 1 foot. Like the plainfin midshipman, this toadfish has hundreds of photophores running the length of its body. It differs in having a deeper body and a large superior mouth with many sharp teeth. Although usually found in moderately deep water (to 400 feet), they migrate to shallow water to spawn and often lay their eggs in tidepools under rocks. Also noted for the humming and croaking sounds they make. **Range:** upper Gulf of California to Colombia.

California lizardfish (pez lagarto) *Synodus lucioceps*   To about 25 inches. Named for its alert, lizardlike head, this fish is a master of camouflage. It sits on sand or mud bottoms, from 5 to 750 feet, sometimes buried with only the eyes exposed, waiting to capture a meal. Note the large, needlelike teeth and adipose fin near the deeply forked tail. Young less than 3 inches long are nearly transparent, with a row of black spots on the belly. **Range:** San Francisco (California) to Guaymas (central Gulf of California).

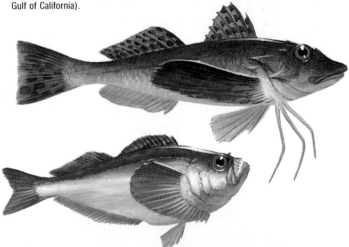

Lumptail searobin (rubio, lapón) *Prionotus stephanophrys*   To 15½ inches. Occasionally seen by sharp-eyed divers lying half-buried in the sand or mud bottom. It ranges over 48- to 360-foot depths. Its three lower pectoral rays have developed into distinctive fingerlike tactile organs. The searobin creeps over the bottom on these rays, picking, probing, and overturning stones in search of food. When threatened, it will unfurl and spread its colorful pectoral fins, long and winglike, in an impressive display. Note the purplish-brown dorsal coloration, and pale belly. **Range:** Columbia River (Washington) to Chile, including the Gulf of California; rare north of Baja California.

Pacific sandfish *Trichodon trichodon*   To 1 foot. Easily recognized by the nearly vertical mouth with peculiar brushlike or hairlike teeth. The preopercle has five sharp spines, the middle being the longest. In its normal habitat buried in the sand or mud bottom with only the mouth and eyes showing, it is a very effective predator. It ranges from Alaska to northern California. A second species, the sailfin sandfish, *Arctoscopus japonicus*, is found from Korea to Alaska and is an important food fish in Japan. The two similar sandfishes can be separated by counting 14 or 15 dorsal spines for *T. trichodon* and 10 or 11 for *A. japonicus*. **Range:** see above.   181

BIGEYES, SQUIRRELFISHES, AND CARDINALFISHES

As dusk descends over the reef, and all the daylight-active fishes have retired to their reef holes and crevices, there is a short period of calm and inactivity. One by one, like sentries on guard duty, the nocturnal fishes appear. The bigeyes, squirrelfishes, and cardinalfishes are among these nighttime-active fishes that, because they are so numerous, are virtually the masters of the night reef. Many of these fishes occupy the same stations around the reef that have been vacated by various fishes active only during the day. Many of them feed on small fishes, crustaceans, and zooplankton in the tides that sweep the reef, and their shiftlike day-night activity assures that each fish species has its turn to feed, without overcrowding.

The bigeyes, also known as catalufas, of the family Priacanthidae, are compressed fishes with small, rough scales, usually found in deep water, preferring rocky areas from 30 to 200 feet. Their huge eyes and red color make them effective, almost invisible night predators. During the day

Glasseye, glasseye snapper (semáforo) *Priacanthus cruentatus*   To 1 foot. The glasseye is not really a snapper. It is a bigeye like the popeye catalufa with the same characteristics and nocturnal activity. It is very changeable in color and can flash from silvery with red patches to all-red like the popeye catalufa. When stressed, it shows the blotchy coloration. The glasseye seems to prefer offshore islands both on the Atlantic Coast, where it is found from Bermuda through the Caribbean to Chile, and on the Pacific Coast. **Range:** circumtropical; here, the lower Gulf of California to Islas Revillagigedo.

Barspot cardinalfish (cardenal) *Apogon retrosella*　To 4 inches. One of the commonest of the Gulf of California cardinalfishes. Recognized by the prominent subdorsal bar and the bold spot near the tail fin. Two other cardinalfishes in or near the Gulf have a distinctive tail spot but no bar (the tailspot cardinalfish) and a bar but no tail spot (the pink cardinalfish). Barspot cardinalfishes are nocturnal; they cluster in reef caves during the day, and at night, often near the surface, feed on plankton and small crustaceans. They are mouth brooders and carry bright orange egg masses in their large mouths for incubation. The eggs may number in the tens of thousands and are glued together by fibrous tissue into a compact ball. **Range:** northern Gulf of California to Cabo San Lucas and south to Mazatlán (Mexico).

Panamic soldierfish (soldado) *Myripristis leiognathos*　To 7 inches. Although quite shy during daytime hours, these squirrelfishes are not difficult for the sharp-eyed diver to locate. They cluster in reef grottoes and crevices, which they often share with tinsel squirrelfishes or cardinalfishes, and emerge at night to cruise the reef in small aggregations, feeding on shrimps, crabs, and other crustaceans. It is thought the name soldierfish comes from their habit of always swimming in schooling formations. Recognized by their bright red coloration, large eyes, and rough, prickly scales. **Range:** Bahía Magdalena (southern Baja California) to Ecuador, including the Gulf of California.

they are often found sharing a reef cave or grotto with cardinalfishes or squirrelfishes.

The holocentrids, commonly known as squirrelfishes or soldierfishes, are nocturnal animals with large squirrel-like eyes and, usually, red coloration. During the day they hide in or near their caves and crevices on the bottom. At night their keen eyes enable them to forage across the reef for shrimps, crabs, and other crustaceans. They are rough, spiny, prickly fishes, not attractive meals to bigger fishes, and certain squirrelfishes can inflict painful wounds with a sharp spine at the base of the gill cover. Some squirrelfishes seem to be quite noisy, much like the croakers, and scientists have recorded a surprising array of squirrelfish sounds, ranging from staccatos and chirps to quacks and a "squeaking door" sound. The reasons for these sounds are not clear, but they may be a component of courtship, aggression, or flight activity.

Like the bigeyes and the squirrelfishes, the cardinalfishes (family Apogonidae) can be seen by the daylight

Popeye catalufa (catalufa, ojotón) *Pseudopriacanthus serrula*   To 13 inches. Bigeyes, also known as catalufas and popeyes, are shy, secretive nocturnal fishes. Their bright red color makes them all but invisible on the night reef as they stalk small fishes, crustaceans, plankton, and polychaete worms. Their large popeyes make them effective predators even in darkness. Unmistakable with the large eyes, bright red color, and compressed saucerlike shape. Also note the black-edged fins and upturned mouth. **Range:** Monterey Bay (California) to Peru, including the central and lower Gulf of California.

diver only in the darker areas of the reef. An alert diver in the Gulf of California may discover the barspot or the pink cardinalfish skulking under rocky ledges, sometimes with squirrelfishes or bigeyes. The barspot cardinalfishes emerge at night and rise to the surface to feed on plankton and small crustaceans in the shifting tides. Clusters of plain cardinalfishes are sometimes seen by day sheltering among the spines of sea urchins. Like most night-roaming fishes, cardinalfishes are handsomely colored in tones of bright red or bronze. Many incubate their eggs in their mouths. In most species, it is the male who takes this responsibility. This nurturing of the eggs, compared with other fishes that allow the eggs to drift with the tides, assures that cardinalfishes will hatch and grow to maturity. ◆

Tinsel squirrelfish (candil) *Sargocentron suborbitalis* To 10 inches. These often swim in large aggregations like the Panamic soldierfishes. They frequent the rocky surge zone in 5- to 10-foot depths where the waves break, usually staying hidden in rocky crevices. At night they come out to feed on small crustaceans. Previously known as *Adioryx suborbitalis*. Note the silvery body color, the very large second anal fin spine, and the prominent spines on the gill cover. **Range:** central Gulf of California to Ecuador, including most offshore islands.

Tailspot cardinalfish (cardenal) *Apogon dovii* To 4 inches. Its brilliant red color is quite handsome when lit by lights in the obscure caves and crevices where it shelters by day. It has a bold tail spot but lacks the subdorsal bar of the pink and barspot cardinalfishes. It feeds exclusively at night, preying on small crustaceans and plankton in the night tides. **Range:** Mazatlán (Mexico) to Peru.

185

Plain cardinalfish (cardenal) *Apogon atricaudus* To 3 inches. Hardly a plain fish, this beauty is lavender-blue dorsally and reddish-orange below—a splendid little fish—but it is "plain" in that it lacks a bar or a tail spot, and so is easily separated from most other cardinalfishes described here. It is often seen taking shelter among the spines of sea urchins by day, as well as under ledges and in caves. It emerges at night to feed on zooplankton. Usually found in rocky areas from 30- to 60-foot depths. Note the dark blotch on the first dorsal fin. The Guadalupe cardinalfish (*A. guadalupensis*) is almost indistinguishable from the plain cardinalfish but lacks the dark blotch on the first dorsal fin. **Range:** plain cardinalfish, Cabo San Lucas and Islas Revillagigedo; Guadalupe cardinalfish, San Clemente Island (southern California) to Cabo San Lucas.

Pink cardinalfish (cardenal) *Apogon pacifici* To about 2 inches. The smallest of the cardinalfishes described here; quite common skulking in rocky reef caves by day along the peninsula side of the lower Gulf. It has no tail spot but does have a bar under the soft dorsal, though a much less conspicuous bar than that of the barspot cardinalfish. From tidepools out to 100 feet. **Range:** lower Gulf of California to Peru.

TUBEMOUTHED FISHES: SEAHORSES, PIPEFISHES, TRUMPETFISHES, CORNETFISHES, AND STICKLEBACKS

If you should glance back while diving and see a 2-foot length of blue-striped "garden hose" peering over your shoulder, don't panic. It is merely one of the curious and friendly cornetfishes that are found off eastern Pacific reefs. They are astonishing fish to see, as they stare back at you with their large, independently movable eyes set at the front of slender, luminous bodies. Cornetfishes are specialists at following larger fishes (and even divers) about the reefs, using them as stalking horses to prey on unsuspecting smaller fishes. A curious fish is sucked up, in one quick intake of water, by the vacuumlike snout.

The tubemouthed fishes (order Gasterosteiformes) consist of two suborders: one includes the seahorses, pipefishes, and snipefishes; the other is the trumpetfishes and the cornetfishes. The tubelike snout is common to all tubemouths. They are masters at vacuuming up their food by rapid intakes of water. Most possess a partial or complete armor of bony plates, and most demonstrate curious spawning behavior where the female deposits her eggs in a brood pouch or patch near the tail of the male. The

Pacific seahorse (caballito de mar) *Hippocampus ingens* To 1 foot. This is the only seahorse in the entire eastern Pacific. In order to match its background, whether seaweed, coral, or reef, it can phase gradually to shades of red, tan, black, green, or yellow. Not easily found, it is captured offshore in the Gulf of California by shrimp trawlers at 33 feet or deeper. Also found occasionally in seaweed and around beds of sea whip corals in offshore patch reefs. The male seahorse has a brood pouch under the tail. The female courts the male, sometimes for several days, until finally she transfers her eggs to his brood pouch. In certain species, as many as 200 eggs can be released into the pouch within ten seconds. **Range:** San Diego (California) to Peru, including the Gulf of California and the Galapagos Islands.

187

gravid father then incubates the eggs and ejects tiny live hatchlings into the sea some eight to ten days later. Eastern Pacific tubemouthed fishes range in size from tiny adult pipefishes of 3 inches to huge adult cornetfishes reaching 4 feet.

Cornetfishes and trumpetfishes are similar except that trumpetfishes lack the long filament extending from the tail, which is characteristic of the cornetfish. The cornetfish is round, the trumpetfish compressed and flattened from side to side. Trumpetfishes have a barbel on the chin and a set of dorsal spines in front of the soft dorsal fin.

Most pipefishes and seahorses are sargassum and seagrass dwellers, usually so well camouflaged in their weedy environment that they are rarely seen by divers. Although quite different in appearance, seahorses and pipefishes are very closely related; in fact, seahorses are pipefishes with curled-up tails and horselike tilted heads. Unlike pipefishes, seahorses lack a caudal fin.

The snipefish, sometimes called the bellows fish, is also a tubemouthed fish. It is a member of the family Macroramphosidae, compressed, silvery fishes with a small mouth at the end of a long, tubular snout. They have bony

Bay pipefish (pez pipa) *Syngnathus leptorhynchus*   To 13 inches. This fish is often found in bays and sloughs where it seeks cover in eelgrass beds. In its green coloration it quickly disappears among the eelgrass blades. It can easily change color to match virtually any seaweed background. Like the seahorses, the pipefishes swim in a more or less upright position, sculling themselves along partly by the dorsal and pectoral fins and partly by wriggling movements of the head, tail, and body. There is a marsupium-like brood pouch on the underside of either the abdomen of the male pipefish or the tail, depending on the species. The eggs are transferred by the female to the male's brood pouch where they are incubated for eight to ten days. Recognition and identification among the various species of pipefishes is difficult because of their close similarity. Counting the rings around the body and tail is the only certain way to separate species. The bay pipefish has 16 to 21 trunk rings and from 36 to 46 tail rings and a long snout. **Range:** Sitka (Alaska) to southern Baja California.

Fantail pipefish (pez pipa chica) *Doryrhamphus excisus excisus*   To 3 inches.
A beautiful little animal, usually found hiding in rocky holes, crevices, and under
dark ledges, often swimming upside down. These pipefishes mate early and are
frequently found in male-female pairs, invariably staying in or near their shelter.
They are unaggressive except at courting and spawning time, when competing
males are very territorial and peevish with competing male pipefishes. Easily identified by the yellow-spotted fanlike tail and short, stubby shape. Total body rings are
35—the lowest ring count of all the eastern Pacific pipefishes. **Range:** widely distributed in the Indo-Pacific; here, Bahía Magdalena (Baja California) to Ecuador,
including the Gulf of California, Clipperton Island, and the Galapagos Islands.

Reef cornetfish (pez corneta) *Fistularia commersonii*   To about 4 feet. An expert
at stalking other fishes by floating sticklike around the reef until it is close enough
to attack. This allows it to prey on such smaller fishes as herrings, halfbeaks,
needlefishes, and snake eels. The tubular snout is an efficient pipette—it can suck
small or large morsels of food into the mouth with great accuracy. Recognized by
the pair of bluish stripes running along the back and sides, it can quickly change
color to a mottled or barred pattern when motionless or feeding. **Range:** widely
distributed through the Indo-Pacific; here, Bahía Magdalena (Baja California) and
the entire Gulf of California to Panama, including most offshore islands.

plates on their sides and a very long second dorsal spine.

The sticklebacks of the family Gasterosteidae are fascinating, industrious little fishes that have gained much
attention in recent years, owing to their nest-building activity. They are anadromous, spawning mostly in fresh
water. There the red-breasted male builds a nest and
guards the eggs.

The tubesnout, family Aulorhynchidae, closely related
to the stickleback, is elongate with a tiny mouth at the end
of a long snout. This fish also builds a nest, usually in a
kelp bed, and the male guards the eggs. ♦

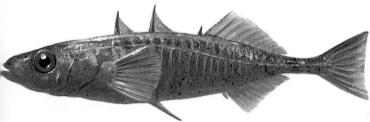

Trumpetfish (corneta) *Aulostomus chinensis*
To 2 feet. Like the cornetfish, a sociable
opportunist, expert at stalking smaller fishes
and crustaceans in the shadows of larger fishes or
divers. It has various colorations but shades often seen
are orange to golden yellow or light gray as shown. It resembles the cornetfish, but lacks the long filament on the end
of the tail; it has a series of isolated spines in front of the dorsal
fin and a barbel at the tip of the snout. It is found around shallow
reefs in the same general habitat as the cornetfish. **Range:** Indo-
Pan-Pacific, Red Sea to Japan and Hawaii; so far recorded in the tropical
eastern Pacific only in Panama, the Galapagos Islands, and Isla del Coco.

Threespine stickleback *Gasterosteus aculeatus*   To 4 inches (average: 2 inches).
Through most of the year, sticklebacks school up to a mile offshore. At breeding
time males break away and move inshore to establish territory in streams, backwaters, and tidal flats. Breeding males develop a reddish head, breast, and belly as
shown. The male builds a nest of plant matter and sand, glues it all together with
kidney secretions, and makes small entrance and exit holes. He ferociously defends
his nest against other males and even females not yet welcome. Finally, when a
gravid female enters his territory, he swims in zig-zag movements, driving and
leading her into the nest to lay eggs. When she leaves, he fertilizes the eggs with
his milt, then prepares for another female. Some males may manage several nests
simultaneously. Over the six-day incubation period the male vigorously fans the
nest with his pectoral fins to aerate the eggs. Even after hatching, the male tries
to keep his offspring near the nest for protection. Note the three isolated dorsal
spines, the thin bony plates on the side, and the keel on the caudal peduncle.
Range: holarctic; in the Pacific from Korea to the Bering Sea and Aleutian Islands
190   to northern Baja California.

Tubesnout *Aulorhynchus flavidus*
To 7 inches. Closely related to the stickleback,
the tubesnout ranges from Alaska to northern Baja
California and is the only member of its family. It looks like
an elongated stickleback with about 24 to 27 spines in front
of the soft dorsal fin. A nest builder, the male binds seaweed
together in the lower areas of giant kelp beds. Females, outnum-
bering males by 10 or 20 to 1, deposit eggs around the seaweed which is
closely guarded by the male. Eggs hatch in two to three weeks. Tubesnouts
school throughout life except at spawning time. In 1950, California Fish and
Game biologists found a dense school of tubesnouts a quarter mile in diameter and
40 feet deep off Santa Rosa Island. **Range:** Sitka (Alaska) to northern Baja California.

Slender snipefish *Macroramphosus gracilis*   To 6 inches. Called the bellows fish
in some parts of the world, these little fishes swim head downward over soft bottoms—backward and forward—searching for invertebrates, fish eggs, and other
morsels. Also found from the surface to near the bottom, sometimes in large
schools. They have long tubular snouts with tiny mouths and jaws at the tip. Noteworthy for the deep body, greatly enlarged second dorsal fin spine, and abdominal
pelvic fins. **Range:** circumtropical; here, Santa Monica (southern California)
southward.

GOBIES AND JAWFISHES

Gobies, of the family Gobiidae, are among the smallest fishes of the sea. Most of them are under 3 inches long and many grow no longer than an inch. The tiniest vertebrate animal known, the Luzon goby of the Philippines, *Pandaka pygmaea*, is full grown at less than half an inch. Because gobies are small, they have little commercial value and tend to be overlooked, but close inspection reveals them to be a fascinating group of fishes. Their small size means that gobies are often at the mercy of turbulent water in the surge zone where many of them live. Almost all have pelvic fins that are joined into a suction cup or disc. The disc is a very handy anchor to hold a tiny fish fast to the bottom or to a rock face as the surge rushes in and out.

Most gobies are marine, but many enter brackish and freshwater estuaries, rivers, and streams. Many are quite colorful, with flattened heads, eyes that seem to pop out of the top of the head, and blunt snouts. Almost all have two dorsal fins, most live on the bottom exclusively, and many can change color and pattern rapidly to match their background or to signal breeding readiness.

Blackeye goby, crested goby, bluespot goby (gobio) *Coryphopterus nicholsi*   To 6 inches. First taken on July 26, 1881, in Departure Bay, British Columbia. This pale, beautiful goby is easily identified by the black eyes, black tip on the spiny dorsal fin, the dusky pelvic disc (jet black in breeding males), and the fleshy crest on the head. There is a small blue spot below the eye. It prefers sandy bottoms near reefs and rocky areas, usually in deep quiet water. It ranges from the intertidal zone to 348 feet. Often abundant but not noticed by divers because it will freeze on the bottom until closely approached, and then dash to a crevice or burrow into sand or mud. The breeding male cleans a spawning nest under a rock or other object. Then he rises and descends with all fins flared until a female is attracted. After eggs are laid, the male guards the nest. **Range:** Queen Charlotte Islands (British Columbia) to Punta Rompiente (central Baja California).

Bluebanded goby, Catalina goby (gobio bonito) *Lythrypnus dalli*   To 2½ inches.
The four to nine electric-blue bars on a coral-red body surely make this the most
brilliant of all gobies. Originally described in 1890 when a 1¼-inch specimen was
dredged from 210 feet in the harbor at Catalina Island (southern California), it was
thought to be very rare. For many years very few additional specimens were found.
Then in 1938, Vernon Brock, California's first diving ichthyologist, made the surprising discovery that the "rare" goby is quite common. It is found around steep,
rocky slopes in reef cracks and crevices from the intertidal zone down to 250 feet.
Although very territorial, perching boldly on exposed rocks out in the open, they
retreat to reef holes when threatened, or hide among the spines of sea urchins.
Females lay a clutch of oblong eggs in an empty shell, then leave the male to guard
the nest. They feed on plankton, crustaceans, and other small invertebrates. **Range:**
Morro Bay (central California) to Isla de Guadalupe (off central Baja California),
including the Gulf of California.

Though small, gobies are extremely abundant, especially in the tropics around coral reefs. There are an estimated 2,000 species worldwide, including about 1,000 that
have not even been described yet. Our Pacific Coast is favored in having some of the most beautiful gobies in the
world, as well as others with quite unusual life styles. The
brilliant, iridescent bluebanded and zebra gobies are favorites of aquarists for their spunky, pugnacious character
as well as their colors. Since almost all other fishes are
larger than gobies and many prey on them, gobies must
live where safe retreats are only a dash away. The bluebanded and zebra gobies live in or near reef holes and
crevices. Other species can burrow quickly into the sand
or mud bottom, or change their colors to exactly match the
background and become almost invisible. The arrow goby
lives an odd-couple arrangement in the burrow of the
ghost shrimp, where it dives for cover when threatened.
The ghost shrimp is the loser, since the goby eats the
shrimp babies, and although the shrimp will occasionally
nip the goby, it can do little else in defense of its burrow.

The banded cleaner goby looks like a red-headed underwater honeybee and maintains a cleaning station around a   193

rocky reef hole or crevice. Larger predatory fishes such as eels and groupers come and sometimes wait in line to be cleaned of parasites. The redhead goby, which is often found living commensally with the club urchin in a common hole in the reef, is territorial and very aggressive. Fights between adults sometimes end in jaw wrestling and much thrashing about.

Jawfishes are not gobies but belong to the family Opisthognathidae. They are interesting, industrious, secretive fishes that may be seen hovering or tail-standing just outside their burrows. When danger approaches, they dart into their burrows tail-first until only the head protrudes.

The Pacific fat sleeper is gobylike in shape and structure, but grows to 1 foot and is reported (but not confirmed) to reach 2 feet—which is most un-gobylike. It belongs to the Eleotridae—a gobylike family of fishes. ♦

Redlight goby (gobio semáforo) *Coryphopterus urospilus* To 2½ inches. Frequently seen by divers in the Gulf of California over sand bottoms near the base of rocky reefs where the rock merges with sand. The sandy, spotted coloration and translucent body enable this goby to virtually disappear over patches of sand. Even so, it will dart to a reef crevice for safety if approached. It forages across the sand patches for small crustaceans and other invertebrates. A subtidal species, it has been taken occasionally in large tidepools and out to depths of 125 feet. Named for the prominent dark spot on the caudal fin. **Range:** Bahía Magdalena (Baja California) and northern Gulf of California to Colombia, including most offshore islands.

Banded cleaner goby (gobio barbero) *Elacatinus digueti* To 1¼ inches. Looking a bit like a red-headed underwater honeybee, this goby stations itself near a rocky reef hole or crevice and cleans large predatory fishes such as jacks, groupers, and moray eels of external parasites. The fish to be cleaned will often assume a head-down position, open its mouth and gill covers, flare its fins, and sometimes change color to signal its readiness for servicing. Thomson et al. (1979) report that it will even service aquanauts and will swarm over a diver's legs or swim fins in search of parasites, sometimes nipping at body hairs. Very common in the central and lower Gulf of California along rocky shores with steep slopes. **Range:** upper Gulf of California to Colombia.

Zebra goby (gobio) *Lythrypnus zebra*   To 2¼ inches. First discovered in 1890, when dredged from 216 feet of water off the Mexican coast. Like the bluebanded goby this splendid fish was assumed to be a rare species until the advent of SCUBA diving revealed that it was not rare, just secretive. It retreats to reef cracks and crevices or hides among the spines of sea urchins when threatened. It is found from the intertidal zone to 318 feet. The zebra goby is very like the bluebanded goby, except that it has many more (13 to 18) blue bars on its sides, with short, narrow bars in between. Even though the two gobies are often found together, the zebra is more secretive and not seen as often as the bluebanded goby. Both species are favorites of aquarists and are captured regularly for the aquarium market. Females lay eggs which are aggressively guarded by the male. Usually retiring and secretive, males become territorial and pugnacious during the breeding season. **Range:** Carmel Bay (central California) to Isla Clarión (Mexico), including the central and southern Gulf of California and Isla de Guadalupe.

Arrow goby (gobio) *Clevelandia ios*   To 2¼ inches. Unique because, when threatened, it dives for cover into the burrow of a ghost shrimp or occasionally a mud shrimp—an unwelcome intrusion, since the goby feeds on the young of the shrimps and often gets nipped in retaliation. Hart (1973) reports this fish will place pieces of food too large to handle near crabs to be torn up, and the goby then takes the smaller pieces. They also burrow into mud and sand until hidden; only spurts of water from the gills reveal their presence. Found in sheltered bays, lagoons, estuaries, and tidal sloughs in marine and fresh water. Adults eat diatoms, green algae, tintinnids, and eggs, and in turn are eaten by rockfishes, sculpins, greenlings, and terns. Males display a conspicuous black band across the anal fin. **Range:** Strait of Georgia (British Columbia) to northern Baja California.

Redhead goby (gobio de cabeza roja) *Elacatinus puncticulatus* To 1¾ inches. A territorial and extremely aggressive fish. Thomson et al. (1979) state that adults engage in jaw wrestling accompanied by much thrashing about. Breeding males turn almost black in color and lure females by approaching, quivering, and then returning to the male's shelter. If the female follows, egg-laying and fertilization ensue. These gobies occasionally remove parasites from other fishes but are not obligate cleaners, as is the banded cleaner goby. Frequently found living with the club urchin (*Eucidaris thouarsii*) in holes in the reef. Distinctive for the red head and pale body with a line of black spots at midbody. Quite common in the central and lower Gulf of California. **Range:** upper Gulf of California to Ecuador.

Longjaw mudsucker (chupalodo) *Gillichthys mirabilis* To 8¼ inches. Easily recognized by the long upper jaw, especially in large males, reaching almost to the gill opening. No other goby has such a huge jaw. The pectoral fin is rounded; the anal fin is quite short. Found over tidal flats, bays, and sloughs; it seeks out mud bottoms in shallow water. Exploited because it is legally used as a bait fish in fresh water, at one time it was scarce in California and reinforcement stocks were imported from Baja California to satisfy fishermen. The fish is extremely hardy, reported to live for several weeks in fresh water. The similar shortjaw mudsucker (*G. seta*) has a slightly shorter jaw, a more depressed head, and a more pointed snout. It also has a more southerly range. **Range:** longjaw mudsucker, Tomales Bay (northern California) to the Gulf of California; shortjaw mudsucker, endemic to northern and central Gulf of California.

Bay goby, finescale goby (gobio) *Lepidogobius lepidus* To 4 inches. As its name implies, the bay goby is found in quiet water bays and inlets and especially over muddy bottoms from near-shore habitats to 660 feet. For recognition, note the olive coloration, black margin on the first dorsal fin, small mouth (ending below the eyes), and scales so fine they are difficult to see. It has dark or dusky edges on all fins. First recorded at Victoria, British Columbia, in 1881. **Range:** Welcome Harbour (northern British Columbia) to central Baja California.

Pacific fat sleeper (guabina) *Dormitator latifrons* To 1 foot; reported to 2 feet. Sleepers (family Eleotridae) resemble gobies in many respects. They have the goby shape; a flat, blunt, gobylike head; and have two dorsal fins and an anal fin with one weak spine. The Pacific fat sleeper is not gobylike in two other ways, however: it is surely one of the largest gobylike fishes known; and its pelvic fins are separate and not joined into a sucking disc as in most gobies. The fat sleeper earned the name because of its shape and its habit of lying motionless on the bottom, rarely moving unless disturbed. It frequents shallow inshore areas, usually in fresh water, but can swim freely in salt water. **Range:** Palos Verdes Peninsula (southern California) to Ecuador; rare north of Baja California.

Finespotted jawfish (boca grande) *Opisthognathus punctatus* To 16 inches. Occurs in much shallower water than other jawfishes; thus a popular resident of seaside aquariums. Few other fishes are so preoccupied with keeping their homes so clean and tidy. The jawfish seems always busy, excavating and cleaning its burrow, chasing intruders away, spitting sand and aggregate, and wrestling bits of rock and shell around like a miniature bulldozer. Recognized by the fine, dark spots covering the head and the larger, dark, evenly spaced spots on the body and fins. It appears to be more active at night and may be a nocturnal predator. Feeds on small fishes, crustaceans, and other invertebrates. **Range**: Bahía Magdalena (Baja California), throughout the Gulf of California, and south to Panama.

Splitbanded goby (gobio blanco y negro) *Gymneleotris seminudus* To 2 inches. Striking for the zebralike markings and long, flowing, pointed pectoral and tail fins; also distinctive for the separate pelvic fins, not joined into a disc as on most gobies. Juveniles start out with only about six wide body bands, which increase to 12 or 13 on the adult. It is quite secretive, almost always found under rocks, and thus poorly known. It seems to prefer areas of reef rubble and cobble covered with algae. It ranges from 3- to 75-foot depths, usually from 15 to 30 feet. **Range:** Bahía Magdalena (Baja California) and central Gulf of California south to Ecuador.

197

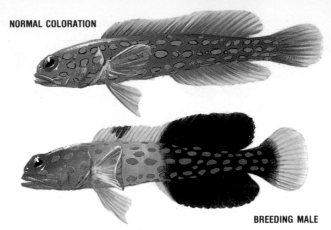

NORMAL COLORATION

BREEDING MALE

Bluespotted jawfish (boca grande) *Opisthognathus* sp. (species undescribed)   To about 4 inches. This brilliant, colorful jawfish seems restricted to offshore islands, where it congregates in large colonies. Jawfishes construct deep burrows for shelter, and a colony is usually chaotic; each fish tries to steal stones from its neighbor's burrow, amid much mock battling and threat display, but little actual biting. Thomson et al. (1979) observed the male during courtship display: it hovers motionless with pelvic and dorsal fins extended, over its burrow, then, with a whip of its tail, will suddenly dive into the burrow. During this display, the rear half of the body becomes dark blackish-brown, as illustrated. The courting display, often involving dozens of males bobbing up and down over their burrows, may last for several hours. They feed on small fishes and crustaceans that venture near their burrows. Juveniles are overall bright yellow, with no spots. **Range**: throughout the Gulf of California, especially near offshore islands.

Panamic frillfin (guaseta, mapo) *Bathygobius ramosus*   To 4½ inches. This familiar fish is often seen leaping from one rocky tidepool to another; it is also found on mud bottoms in rivers and streams. It is closely related to the similar Atlantic Coast frillfin (*B. soporator*) and was at one time identified as that species. The frillfins are widely considered the most common shore fishes of tropical America. The Panamic frillfin, like the Atlantic frillfin, is often found in rocky tidepools when the tide is out; it can return to the sea by jumping from one pool to another, if required. It cannot see the next pool when it leaves the first, yet leaps precisely and without error. It is theorized that the fish memorizes the location of pools when swimming above them at high tide, and thus leaps them with precision at low tide. Distinctive for having the upper five pectoral fin rays flexible and free, hence the name frillfin; the body is large and deep, with a strong sucking pelvic disc and six spines in the dorsal fin. **Range:** Bahía Magdalena (Baja California) and northern Gulf of California to Peru.

BLENNIES, KELPFISHES, FRINGEHEADS, AND WOLF EELS

Like the gobies, many of the blennies and blennylike fishes are denizens of the rocky-shore intertidal zones throughout the world. The beachgoer and tidepooler can easily find them when the tide is out, hiding under stones or seaweed or darting around rockpools. Most are small, less than 6 inches long, with elongated bodies. The dorsal fin extends from in back of the head almost to the tail or may be continuous with it. Pelvic fins are very reduced or absent. They are grazing fishes, feeding mainly on algae and sessile invertebrates.

Blennies lead a very precarious existence living on the lip of the ocean, at the mercy of surging waves, high and low tides, high and low temperatures, large predatory fishes, birds, and even rats and mice. Yet they have adapted perfectly to the intertidal zones and have become so successful that their families and species are among the most numerous of the ocean. Back in 1877, a Mr. Ross of Topsham in Devon, England, noticed that his shanny, a species of blenny, became restless in his aquarium as the time for high tide approached. Mr. Ross placed a large

Bay blenny (pez de roca, trambollito) *Hypsoblennius gentilis*   To 5¾ inches.
A common blenny in rocky tidepools, especially in bays and estuaries, ranging out to 80 feet. Though small, they are fiercely territorial and will attack anything approaching their hole or burrow, including divers. The male of the species is shown in breeding colors. The bright red throat is especially noticeable. The female has a smaller head, much less prominent cirri over the eyes, and a large blue spot between the first and third dorsal spines. Males attract females to their burrows by quivering and head-jerking. The female then attaches eggs one by one to the burrow walls with a special adhesive disc. The male chews and rubs the eggs after fertilizing them, and guards them until hatching. Bay blennies feed on invertebrates and algae. **Range:** Monterey Bay (California) to Bahía Magdalena (Baja California), with a disjunct population from the northern to the central Gulf of California.

Rockpool blenny, notchbrow blenny
(pez de roca) *Hypsoblennius gilberti*
To 6¾ inches. An expert color changer,
this blenny can be mistaken for the
bay blenny or mussel blenny, but the
rockpool has a distinct notch in its head
just behind the eye (hence "notchbrow blenny"). Also the cirrus over
the eye is larger and divided into several filaments. Note the dark streaks
below the eye and the eight dark saddles at the base of the dorsal fin. Frequents intertidal and subtidal areas out
to 60 feet. Like the bay blenny, the
male rockpool blenny guards the egg
cluster until hatching. **Range:** rocky
tidepools from Point Conception
(southern California) to southern Baja
California, but not the Gulf of California.

Mussel blenny (pez de roca, trambollito) *Hypsoblennius jenkinsi* To
5 inches. Often shares the same rockpool with the bay blenny. It is territorial and closely guards its own
rockpool hole or crevice; it will not
hesitate to nip at trespassers, including human fingers. Eschmeyer et al.
(1984) report that it also moves into
the burrows of boring clams or tubes of
marine worms, and into mussel beds.
Shore tidepools out to 70-foot depths.
Distinctive for the crescent-shaped
mark on the cheek, often tinged with
red, and the large cirrus over the eye
divided into filaments at the tip.
Range: Santa Barbara County (southern California) to Bahía Magdalena
(Baja California), with a disjunct population in the upper Gulf of California.

Panamic fanged blenny (trambollito negro) *Ophioblennius steindachneri* To about
7 inches. Closely related to the redlip blenny of the Atlantic Coast, *O. atlanticus*,
which is superabundant on West Indian reefs. The Panamic fanged blenny is the
most abundant combtooth blenny along rocky coasts in the tropical eastern Pacific. It
seeks out the surge zone of rocky headlands where it takes cover in a hole or
crevice. From a steep nearby slope it will defend this home vigorously against attackers. It is omnivorous, feeding on algae and sessile invertebrates. Note the blunt
head, the red circle around the eyes, the dark spot in back of the eye, and the cirri
on the head. It is equipped with a formidable pair of canine teeth far back in the
lower jaw (hence "fanged blenny") and it will bite if handled. **Range:** central Baja
California and the upper Gulf of California to Peru. **Edibility:** poor.

stone in the tank with its top out of water. At times for low tide, the fish would leave the water and lie on the rock. It flopped back into the water and became active at high tide. With its biological clock, the shanny always knew the state of the tide. In nature, each blenny finds a hole or makes a crevice under a rock, often wriggling and twisting to dig a depression in the sand. Then its time is spent in dashing out, finding food, and darting back to shelter. Much effort is devoted to defending its crevice against other blennies. Dominant, larger blennies push out smaller ones until each has a hole or crevice in the rocks. Those who can find no shelter are soon eaten by predators.

A wide range of diversity in anatomy and behavior is found among the many blenny and blennylike families. Two families treated here are the scaleless or combtooth blennies of the family Blenniidae and the scaled blennies of the family Clinidae, which have patches of fixed, conical teeth. Crests, fringes, and ridges on the head are often helpful identification marks of many of the Blenniidae. Included here are such representatives as the bay blenny, rockpool blenny, mussel blenny, Panamic fanged blenny, and sabertooth blenny. Members of the Clinidae live in temperate as well as tropical and subtropical seas, and include the giant kelpfish and the striped, crevice, and island kelpfishes. Two members of the tube-dwelling blennies (family Chaenopsidae), the orangethroat pikeblenny and the signal blenny, are described. Also treated are two blennylike fishes with very big mouths and bad tempers: the sarcastic fringehead and the onespot fringehead make homes in empty beer bottles, beer cans, pipes, or auto tires and will often charge and snap menacingly with gap-

Sabertooth blenny (diente sable) *Plagiotremus azaleus*   To about 4 inches. This strange little blenny has gone to surprising lengths to mimic the Cortez rainbow wrasse, *Thalassoma lucasanum* (see page 109). Hobson (1968) states that by night these very territorial blennies live in mollusk tubes in rocks; by day, they join loose groups of rainbow wrasses, copying their swimming motions and appearance. Using this cover, the blenny darts after other nearby fishes, nipping and biting off mucus, perhaps bits of skin. They sometimes nip the legs of divers with their comblike teeth. Note the inferior, sharklike mouth and cone-shaped snout. **Range:** central and lower Gulf of California to Peru, including most offshore islands.

ing jaws at anything, man or fish, going by their burrows. Wolf eels of the wolffish family are related to the blennies. They like cold-water habitats and grow to over 6 feet of coiled power lurking in rocky dens and crevices. Yet like the moray, they will emerge from their dens and take food from a diver's hand gently and carefully. ♦

Sarcastic fringehead *Neoclinus blanchardi* To 1 foot. A bad-tempered, big-mouthed, aggressive fish that charges and snaps at anything passing its burrow. Feder et al. (1974) report vicious attacks on divers grabbed by the cavernous mouth of this fringehead. Upon winning the struggle, divers are astounded to find that the loser is only 6 or 7 inches long. The huge jaws and two blue ocelli on the first dorsal fin are unmistakable. Females have smaller jaws and a larger cirrus over the eye than males do. Found along open coastlines on sand or hard mud bottoms beyond the breaker zone out to 200 feet, often living in discarded bottles or other manmade debris. Also favors empty mollusk shells, vacated geoduck (*Panope generosa*) or horse clam (*Tresus nuttalli*) burrows; wanders over beds of sand dollars. Eggs are deposited in clam burrows or crevices, or under rocks; the male guards them. **Range:** San Francisco (California) to central Baja California.

Onespot fringehead *Neoclinus uninotatus* To 9¾ inches. Similar to the sarcastic fringehead, but has one blue spot at the front of the dorsal fin rather than two, and much larger, longer, and more branched cirri on the head. A very aggressive, territorial fish, often seen at the mouth of its burrow with only head and large mouth protruding. Found in empty gastropod shells, bottles, auto tires, beer cans, and various other debris. Intruders, whether man or fish, may be met with a charge, and snapping of the gaping jaws. Spawns in April and May, cementing an orange egg mass to the upper inside surface of its bottle, beer can, or hollow. Male and female guard the eggs, fan and oxygenate them, and keep the burrow clean.
Range: Bodega Bay (northern California) to northern Baja California.

Giant kelpfish *Heterostichus rostratus*   To 2 feet. A master of camouflage; even divers inches away have difficulty seeing it in the kelp forest. The color varies widely to match kelp or seaweed backgrounds. It can be confused with other kelpfish species, but has a forked caudal fin, a pointed snout, and a short pectoral fin. It feeds on mollusks, crustaceans, and small fishes. When spawning, a male establishes a nest area in seaweed or kelp; male and female perform quivering motions during which the female attaches pink to greenish eggs to feather boa kelp, giant kelp, or surf grass. The male stays to guard the eggs. **Range:** British Columbia to southern Baja California.

Signal blenny (trambollito señal) *Emblemaria hypacanthus*   To about 2 inches. Like the orangethroat pikeblenny, the signal blenny is also a member of the tube blennies (family Chaenopsidae), all of which make their homes in the unused tubes of dead or departed invertebrates. According to Thomson et al. (1979), signal blennies seek out mussel holes in limestone or gastropod tubes, or any suitable hardwalled tube. Illustrated is the male signal blenny in breeding coloration. Males darken at breeding time, and jerk in and out of their tubes with saillike dorsal fin erected high, to attract females. Eggs are laid in their tube burrows. Males are unmistakable, but females are colored quite differently, with contrasting black and white patches and reticulations along the sides, and the fins are streaked and spotted with black. Females usually remain in the open but will dive for shelter in the nearest tube when threatened. **Range:** endemic to the Gulf of California, from Puerto Penasco to Cabo San Lucas.

Striped kelpfish *Gibbonsia metzi* To 9½ inches. Lives in the seaweed in shallow water and in the kelp canopy, much like the crevice kelpfish. It has bold stripes which can change from kelp browns to lavender to seaweed green or fade when the fish relocates from one home site to another. Note the very short pectoral fin. Feeds mostly on small crustaceans. Transparent young appear in April and school in the kelp canopy and inshore. As they mature, they become opaque and move into the seaweeds. **Range:** Vancouver Island to central Baja California.

Crevice kelpfish *Gibbonsia montereyensis* To 4½ inches. An expert color changer, adept at precisely matching its background whether algae green, kelp brown, lavender-red, or silvery, in the urchin- or algae-covered rocks where it makes its home. The color-change may be slow, sometimes taking a week to exactly match the hue of a new home site. Note the very long dorsal fin, raised at both ends, and the line of dark ocelli or "eye" spots that run along the lateral line. **Range:** Ucluelet (Vancouver Island) to northern Baja California.

Island kelpfish *Alloclinus holderi* To 4 inches. A common kelpfish in seaweed, kelp, rocky tidepools, and other subtidal areas ranging out to 162-foot depths. Very abundant around such islands as Santa Cruz Island and Isla de Guadalupe, hence the name. Distinguished by the long pectoral fin reaching well past the front of the anal fin, and the six to eight irregular bars on the sides. The dorsal fin is red-orange and has a greenish blotch at the front. An accomplished color changer. **Range:** Santa Cruz Island (southern California) to central Baja California.

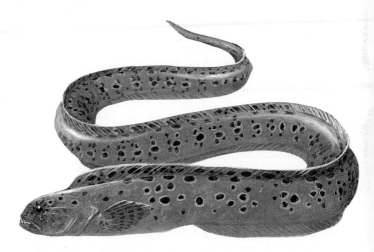

Wolf eel, wolffish *Anarrhichthys ocellatus* To 6 feet, 8 inches. Wolf eels (family Anarhichadidae) are related to the blennies and prefer the cold waters of the North Pacific and North Atlantic. Some are commercially important for food. They are eellike, and grow very large; with their powerful canine teeth and stout molars, they can be quite dangerous. Yet divers in Oregon report that the wolf eel quickly grows accustomed to visitors, even greedily accepts hand-held food, much like morays. Wolf eels feed on fishes and hard-shelled organisms such as mollusks, crabs, and sea urchins. They live in crevices and holes in rocky reefs and wrecks, in subtidal areas and to 740 feet. They have no pelvic fins, no lateral line; the dorsal fin is long and flexibly spined (no soft rays); the body and fins are adorned with pale-ringed dark ocelli. Young are orange, with dark stripes at the rear of the body. **Range:** Sea of Japan and Aleutian Islands to Imperial Beach (southern California).

Orangethroat pikeblenny (trambollito lucio) *Chaenopsis alepidota* To 6 inches. A tube dweller (family Chaenopsidae); closely related to the bluethroat pikeblenny of the Florida coast, *C. ocellata*, and known for its aggressiveness in maintaining the parchment worm tube home, it appropriates in sandy inshore areas out to 35 feet. If one male invades the territory of a neighbor, he is met with large, gaping jaws and raised dorsal fin; males may stay locked mouth-to-mouth until one bites the other, usually ending the stalemate. Distinctive for the slender, long, scaleless body, and large jaws. Note the spot at the front of the dorsal fin, the orange throat, and the pearly spots along midbody. **Range:** Anacapa Island (southern California) to Puerto Vallarta (Mexico), including the Gulf of California; a subspecies, *Chaenopsis a. alepidota*, is endemic to the Gulf of California from Sonora to Cabo San Lucas. 205

PRICKLEBACKS, GUNNELS, AND WRYMOUTHS

"Eellike blennies" describes the elongated pricklebacks, gunnels, and wrymouths. Most are colorful, shallow-water, cold-water fishes of the North Pacific and North Atlantic. All three families are distinctive in having very long dorsal fins made up of all-spinous rays, though a few of the pricklebacks do have some soft rays at the rear of the dorsal fin. The name "prickleback" comes from the spiny dorsal surface, which is prickly to the touch.

Pricklebacks and gunnels, like their cousins the blennies, are most often seen when the tide is out, dashing for cover under a rock or in a clump of seaweed. They may wriggle snakelike over wet stones and kelp fronds—but as a rule they are secretive and rarely venture out of cover. They are most active at high tide when the reefs are fully submerged; they feed on mollusks, crustaceans, algae, and seaweed. Spawning occurs from December to March. Pricklebacks and gunnels are unique in the manner of laying and caring for the eggs. The female lays her eggs in a cluster, usually in a rock crevice or cavity or in an empty bivalve shell. She curves her body into a loop as she lays the eggs, encircling and rolling the egg mass into a ball roughly an inch in diameter. Once laid, either the male or the female (depending on the species) takes care of the eggs, fanning and oxygenating them until they hatch

Mosshead warbonnet *Chirolophis nugator*   To 6 inches. Well-named for the mossy growth of cirri on this prickleback's head resembling an Indian warbonnet. A secretive fish like most pricklebacks, usually found hiding under rocks or in crevices or tubeworm holes in rocky subtidal areas. You may see only the mossy head protruding from a hole or crevice. They are found from shore out to 264-foot depths. Note the distinctive 12 or 13 eyespots on the dorsal fin and the white bars along the belly. **Range:** Aleutian Islands to San Miguel Island (southern California).

High cockscomb *Anoplarchus purpurescens*   To 7¾ inches. A beautiful prickleback, with a fleshy crest on its head and roguish stripes radiating out from the eyes. An accomplished color changer, it can switch from purple to brown or red or black, depending on background and lighting. At breeding time the male sports orange fins, as shown here. The female produces a mass of around 2,700 eggs in late winter, guarding them in rock or shell crevices. She bends her body around the egg mass and fans the eggs with her body to oxygenate them. A similar prickleback, the slender cockscomb (*A. insignis*), is much more slender, with a crest that is not so pronounced as that of the high cockscomb. Both species prefer inshore rocky areas and seek cover under rocks or in crevices. **Range:** high cockscomb, Pribilof Islands (Alaska) to Santa Rosa Island (southern California); slender cockscomb, Aleutian Islands to Point Arena (northern California).

Monkeyface prickleback *Cebidichthys violaceus*   To 2½ feet. Thought to be an eel by many shore fishermen and often called the ''monkeyface eel'' or the ''blenny eel.'' Like most pricklebacks, they are secretive and rarely seen. They frequent rockpool areas between the tide lines, taking cover in holes, crevices, and under rocks. Tidepoolers using a pole and a short wire leader with baited hook will poke around rocks and crevices to hook the fish, said to be good eating. Spawning occurs in the spring when eggs are deposited on a rock, gathered into a ball, and carefully guarded and oxygenated by a parent until hatching time. They feed mostly on crustaceans and algae. Distinctive for the large size, fleshy ridge on the adult head, and two dark streaks running back from the eye. They have no pelvic fins; half the dorsal fin is made up of spines, half of soft rays. Note the red-orange spots on the sides. **Range:** southern Oregon to north-central Baja California; common only from the Oregon-California border to Point Conception (southern California).

Bluebarred prickleback *Plectobranchus evides* To 5¼ inches. The name *evides* means comely; and this is a handsome fish with smart blue (often white) bars on its side, three black "eye" spots on the rear of the dorsal fin, and dusky barred and striped fins. Unfortunately it is not seen by divers owing to its preference for mud or sand bottoms at 276- to 900-foot depths. It has long, substantial pelvic fins and large pectoral fins with elongated lower rays. **Range:** central British Columbia to San Diego (California).

Rock prickleback *Xiphister mucosus* To 23 inches. Very like the black prickleback, it has four lateral line canals, no pelvic fins, and tiny, almost invisible pectoral fins. Two dusky lines fan out from the eye, but the lines on this fish are bordered by black—not white as on the black prickleback. The dorsal fin of the rock prickleback starts near the head, whereas on the black prickleback it is well separated from the head. This fish can change color from greenish black to brownish to reddish black but, since it feeds principally on algae inshore and out to 60 feet, it is often greenish in color to match its surroundings. The female of the species lays eggs in a ball in a rock crevice, and the male encircles the eggs with his body, guarding them until they hatch. **Range:** southeast Alaska to Santa Barbara (southern California).

Black prickleback *Xiphister atropurpureus* To 1 foot. Quite common along shallow coastlines. Young are found under rocks in the intertidal zone; adults may range out to 25-foot depths. Color can change from blackish brown to reddish brown or greenish black, often with the white stripe at the tail base. Two dark stripes edged with white radiate out from the eye. It has tiny pectoral fins and no pelvic fins; and four lateral-line canals. Females lay egg masses usually under a rock. The male guards the eggs by encircling them with his body. Hart (1973) reports that young black pricklebacks ¼ inch to 1 inch long were taken at the surface in May and June in the southern Strait of Georgia (British Columbia). They were eating copepods and clam larvae. **Range:** Kodiak Island (Alaska) to northern Baja California.

some weeks later. In some species, such as penpoint gunnels and saddleback gunnels, both males and females encircle the eggs and guard them. After hatching, the larvae become free-swimming members of the plankton swarm. When they reach about an inch in length, they sink to the bottom and become bottom dwellers like their parents.

Pricklebacks (family Stichaeidae) are similar in appearance to gunnels, but have a longer anal fin. Some pricklebacks have pelvic fins and at least one lateral line, and a few have up to four lateral lines. Most are under 10 inches, but the monkeyface prickleback grows to $2\frac{1}{2}$ feet and is sometimes taken by shore fishermen as a food fish.

Gunnels (family Pholididae) have no lateral line and have either tiny pelvic fins or none at all. Scales are tiny, cycloid, almost invisible, and are covered with a thick mucus. The slippery bodies of some gunnels give rise to the name butterfish. The dorsal and anal fins join the caudal fin. Most gunnels are shorter than 1 foot. The largest, the penpoint gunnel, grows to $1\frac{1}{2}$ feet.

Wrymouths (family Cryptacanthodidae) closely resemble pricklebacks, with long dorsal fins made up of stiff spines. They have no pelvic fins—the dorsal and anal fins join the caudal fin. They have broad, flat heads, and upward-pointing mouths with projecting lower jaws. They range in size from 1 to 4 feet. ♦

Giant wrymouth *Delolepis gigantea*   To 3 feet, 10 inches. A large fish found over soft bottoms from 20 to 420 feet. Wrymouths resemble pricklebacks in being long, eellike fishes with long dorsal fins made up of stout spines. They are occasionally classed in the prickleback family (Stichaeidae) but more often placed in a separate family, the Cryptacanthodidae. They are distinctive in having long anal fins with only two spines and no pelvic fins. Their heads are broad and flat and mouths are almost vertical with projecting lower jaws. The similar but much smaller dwarf wrymouth (or red devil), *Lyconectes aleutensis*, grows to 1 foot, has upward-pointing eyes, is pink or reddish in color, and lives at 150- to 1,150-foot depths, partly buried in the muddy bottom. **Range:** giant wrymouth, Bering Sea to Humboldt Bay (northern California); dwarf wrymouth, Bering Sea to Eureka (northern California).   209

Longfin gunnel *Pholis clemensi* To 5 inches. Beautifully clad in shades of magenta and silver with 15 light, speckled "targets" running along the dorsal fin base. Found around rocky areas from 24 to 210 feet. The name "longfin" refers to the anal fin, which is longer in this fish than in any other gunnel on the Pacific Coast. Notice the very tiny pelvic fins and the relatively large pectoral fins. Color is variable; some are pale. **Range:** Alaska to Point Arena (northern California).

Saddleback gunnel *Pholis ornata* To 1 foot. Named for the unique saddles or U- (or V-) shaped marks along the dorsal fin; the minute pelvic fins, each with one spine and one ray, are distinctive. Frequents the mouths of streams over muddy bottoms and eelgrass and seaweed beds ranging out to 120 feet. Changeable in color from greenish to brownish, depending on surroundings. Feeds on small crustaceans and mollusks. Both male and female guard the egg clusters. The crescent gunnel (*P. laeta*) resembles the saddleback gunnel closely and the two fish are often confused—but the crescent gunnel has a series of crescent-shaped or nearly circular marks at the base of the dorsal fin, instead of the U- or V-shaped marks. **Range:** saddleback gunnel, Vancouver Island to Carmel Beach (central California); crescent gunnel, Bering Sea to Crescent City (northern California).

Penpoint gunnel *Apodichthys flavidus* To 1½ feet. This splendid, vividly colored fish was first taken in the Strait of Georgia, British Columbia, by H.M.S. *Plumper* in 1859. That first specimen, a female, was presented to the British Museum by the Lords of the Admiralty—a worthy introduction! The single, grooved spine shaped like a penpoint in the anal fin gives it its name. Several pairs of these gunnels were found coiled around masses of white eggs at low tide in January. The green color blends perfectly with its eelgrass habitat, but it can change gradually to brown or red depending on background, diet, and habitat. Pectoral fins are large for a gunnel, and pelvic fins are absent. The row of white "porthole" spots at midbody can darken. The similar rockweed gunnel (*Xererpes fucorum*) occupies the same habitat but lacks the bar below the eye, has tiny pectoral fins, and grows to only 9 inches. **Range:** penpoint, Kodiak Island (Alaska) to Santa Barbara Island (southern California); rockweed, Banks Island (British Columbia) to central Baja California.

FLYINGFISHES, NEEDLEFISHES, AND HALFBEAKS

The leaping, gliding, skittering needlefishes, halfbeaks, and flyingfishes are all members of the order Synentognathi, and are true masters of life at the ocean's surface. If you have never stood at the rail of a fishing boat and seen a needlefish leaping after a smaller fish, then you have a treat in store. Looking very much like jet-propelled silver javelins, these 2- to 6-foot fishes can execute startling high-speed twisting, turning, diving, and resurfacing leaps across 100 feet of water. They are quite possibly the fastest fishes in and out of the water. Like living arrows, leaping needlefishes sometimes impale boaters with their beaks.

The needlefishes (or garfishes) of the family Belonidae are voracious predators and use their agility and swept-wing speed either to attack smaller prey with fearsome,

California flyingfish (pez volador) *Cypselurus californicus* To 19 inches. These magnificent sailors of the sea are seen everywhere along our coasts from Oregon to southern Baja California; common around offshore islands and often gill-netted in summer in southern California. Visitors and tourists on boat trips watch them glide over the water with delight. Gliding, flying, and skittering over the waves is crucial to these fishes, since they are often pursued and eaten by such giant predators as marlin, swordfish, dolphin, and tuna. Distinguished by the very long pectoral fins, short snout, silvery belly, and dark blue back. Note the enlarged pelvic fins, which help to raise this fish and keep it airborne. **Range:** see above.

211

slashing jaws, or to escape from larger predators. They are protectively colored for life at the surface with green or blue backs and silvery white sides and belly. Thus their needlelike shapes are extremely difficult to discern either from the surface or from below. Their dorsal and anal fins are placed opposite each other, just in front of the V-shaped tail. If you shrink a needlefish by about 1 or 2 feet and remove the long upper jaw, you have a halfbeak. Halfbeaks (family Hemiramphidae) are ancestors of the flyingfishes and some can glide 40 feet.

Passengers on ocean liners never tire of watching the "bluebirds of the sea," flyingfishes (family Exocoetidae), as they scull violently with their tails, taxiing to attain flight speed. They spread their pectoral fins, glide a few seconds, then splash back into the sea. When swimming, their long fins are folded against the body. At night, open illumined portholes on ships bring an occasional flyingfish soaring inside. A 1-pounder in flight can deal a man a knockout punch. Flight speeds of 35 miles per hour have been clocked, and flights as long as 13 seconds covering 450 feet have been timed. For many years a debate raged as to whether flyingfishes actually flapped their fins in flight or merely glided. Finally, stroboscopic photography showed conclusively that they are gliders, not true flyers. ♦

Ribbon halfbeak (pajarito) *Euleptorhamphus longirostris*   To 1½ feet. A fish of the open sea. It feeds to a large extent on fish larvae, zooplankton, small fishes, and floating seagrasses. Note the long lower jaw and very short upper jaw—hence halfbeak. Distinctive for the very long pectoral fins and the dorsal and anal fins placed far back by the tail. The lower portion of the tail is elongated. **Range:** circumtropical; here, southern California to the Galapagos Islands.

MEXICAN NEEDLEFISH

CALIFORNIA NEEDLEFISH

Mexican needlefish, houndfish (agujón) *Tylosurus crocodilus* To over 6 feet. This is the common, sometimes very large needlefish seen in the tropical Pacific and Atlantic oceans. They move like javelins in pursuit of smaller fishes. Note the greenish-blue back, the keel on the caudal peduncle, the saberlike beak, and jaws lined with sharp green teeth. Note the dark-colored keel near the tail; the California needlefish has no keel on its caudal peduncle. A tasty fish in spite of the green flesh and bones. **Range:** widespread in the Indo-Pacific; here, Cabo San Lucas and Mazatlán (Mexico) south to Panama.

California needlefish, garfish (agujón) *Strongylura exilis* To 3 feet. Often seen cruising the surface of bays and harbors in small squadrons. It will sometimes leap in and out of the water, skipping along the surface with its head and forebody out of the water, the tail vibrating and beating forcefully. Note that both jaws form a long beak lined with sharp, often green teeth, not for chewing but to prevent smaller fishes, which are swallowed whole, from escaping. Dorsal and anal fins are set far back on the body, near the tail. **Range:** San Francisco (California) to Peru, including the Gulf of California and the Galapagos Islands.

Sharpchin flyingfish (pez volador) *Fodiator acutus* To 9½ inches. Not as common as the California flyingfish, though often seen. The pectoral fins ("wings") are much shorter and less developed than those of the California flyingfish, and this fish does not glide nearly as well. Some researchers place this fish in the halfbeak family. Note that the lower jaw extends well beyond the upper jaw; the dorsal fin is high and rounded. **Range:** worldwide in warm seas; here, southern California to Peru, including the Gulf of California and the Galapagos Islands.

California halfbeak (pajarito) *Hyporhamphus rosae* To 6 inches. A beautiful fish with a red-tipped lower jaw or beak. Occurs near shore and is often seen around docks and piers in coastal bays swimming in small schools. They make very fast and sudden movements and, because they are so slender, they can dart right through all but the finest-meshed nets. They feed on small crustaceans, mollusks, and seagrass. **Range:** Santa Ana (southern California) to Costa Rica.

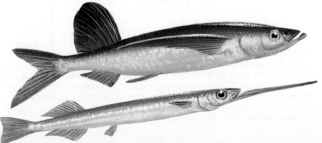

213

MARLINS, SAILFISHES, SWORDFISHES, AND DOLPHINFISHES

Back around 1910, when Zane Grey's westerns and novels brought him fame, fortune, and the freedom to do what he wanted, he decided that what he really wanted was to go fishing. So he did. His surprising catches, and the stories and books on fishing that followed, brought fame and fishermen to the fishing grounds of Florida, the South Seas, New Zealand, Australia, and California. At one time Grey held the world records for striped marlin (450 pounds), dolphinfish (63 pounds), Pacific sailfish (171 pounds), and broadbill swordfish (582 pounds). Grey's biggest catch, a 1,040-pound Pacific blue marlin, was the first fish over 1,000 pounds ever taken on rod and reel. Unfortunately, all of these records were later disallowed under updated regulations of the International Game Fish Association.

The majestic billfishes are the most sought after of all the big-game fishes—true fighting aristocrats of the sea. Blue-water fishermen comb the Pacific coast from southern California's Channel Islands and San Diego to the famed waters of Cabo San Lucas and the Gulf of California to the rich billfish grounds off Peru and Chile.

The principal targets of all this activity are the representatives of two fish families: the Istiophoridae, comprising

Sailfish (pez vela) *Istiophorus platypterus*   To 10 feet, 9 inches and 180 pounds. A beautiful fish, unmistakable with its huge fanlike dorsal fin and the 15 to 25 light-blue bars on the side. A very fast swimmer, clocked at 68 miles per hour, and one of the most popular game fishes on both the Atlantic and Pacific coasts of America. On Florida's east coast, at the Masters Angling Tournament held at Palm Beach each January, close to 200 sailfishes may be caught and released in a 5-day period. **Range:** circumtropical; here, taken as far north as Monterey (California) and occasionally in San Diego, most common in the Gulf of California and Panama, ranging to Chile. **Edibility:** poor—release when caught.

Black marlin (marlin negro) *Makaira indica*   To 14 feet, 9 inches and 1,560 pounds. A giant found almost entirely in the Indian and Pacific oceans and much prized by sport and commercial fishermen. The record 1,560-pounder was landed in Cabo Blanco (Peru), and this size even surpasses the "big blue marlin" rod-and-reel record of 1,282 pounds. It is easily identified and separated from all other marlins by the rigid pectoral fins which are held out firmly, at right angles to the body, and cannot be folded flat against the sides as they are in most marlins. It usually has no stripes or spots on its sides. It is a deep-bodied fish, similar in girth to the blue marlin. The color is highly variable, ranging from slate-blue above to silvery white below, to an all-milk-white, hence the Japanese name *shirokajiki* or "white marlin" and in China *pu-pi* or "white skin." Sometimes pale blue stripes are seen on the sides, but these colorations seldom persist after boating. All fins are dark. **Range:** southern California to Chile. **Edibility:** good.

the marlins and sailfishes, and the Xiphiidae, or swordfish. Billfishes all possess a sword or bill—a bony projection from the upper jaw—that is used in subduing smaller fishes. They use the sword as a club to maim their victims as they rush through a school of mackerel or similar prey. Small squadrons of sailfishes have been seen to herd schools of smaller fishes into compact balls, then slash their way through them, killing and eating in well-coordinated teams.

The special attraction for big-game fishermen along the Pacific Coast is the abundance of splendid striped, blue, and black marlins. The blue and black marlins attain a weight of 2,000 pounds, though the average taken is between 150 and 400 pounds.

All marlins are impressive fighters, noteworthy for their individuality in fighting. Some will fight the hook to the   215

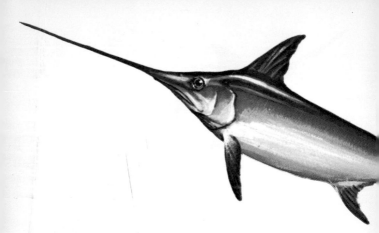

Striped marlin (marlin) *Tetrapturus audax* To 13½ feet and 692 pounds. A valuable sport and commercial fish of the Pacific and Indian oceans. A fish of 406½ pounds was taken at La Jolla, southern California, in 1955, though the usual weight is around 200 to 250 pounds. The striped marlin cannot be fished commercially in California waters; they are usually caught offshore or near islands by sport fishermen, and commercial fisheries take them all the way across the Pacific. Easily distinguished by the high, pointed dorsal fin, highest for all marlins and higher than the greatest depth of the body. The sides of the body are marked with 15 to 25 prominent pale bluish or lavender or whitish bars—hence the name. All fins are dark except for the brilliant cobalt-blue first dorsal and first anal fins. **Range:** Point Conception (southern California) to Chile. **Edibility:** good.

Blue marlin (marlin) *Makaira nigricans* To 14 feet, 8 inches and 1,805 pounds. One of the largest marlins, ranging the warm waters of the Pacific and Atlantic oceans and highly valued by sport fishermen for the spectacular fight it provides when hooked. The largest Pacific blue marlin taken by anglers was a 1,085-pound fish caught off Hawaii in 1972. Japanese longline fishermen report blue marlins reaching (unverified) weights of over 2,000 pounds. Seems to feed mainly on fish, squid, and octopus, and large tuna and bonito are sometimes found in their stomachs. Distinguished from the black marlin by its movable pectoral fin (the black marlin's is rigid) and from the striped marlin by its relatively low first dorsal fin, high anal fin, and fewer bars (15) on the side (15 to 25 on the striped marlin). **Range:** worldwide in warm and temperate seas; here, southern California to Peru. **Edibility:** poor—release when caught.

216

Swordfish, broadbill swordfish (pez espada, espadon) *Xiphias gladius*   To 15 feet and 1,182 pounds, though the average caught is 250 pounds. One of the strongest, most aggressive, and valuable fishes, pursued worldwide by sport and commercial fishermen. In addition to its magnificent fighting qualities, it is one of the finest food fishes, commanding very high prices in the world fish markets. Thus, to compensate a sport fisherman for a night searching and hooking up with the broadbill, a sale at dockside can more than make up for expenses. Its aggressiveness is legendary, and many a skipper has limped home with gaping holes in the side of his boat after a hooked swordfish had punched it repeatedly with the massive beak. One skipper broke his ankle after a struggle with a swordfish that charged his boat 14 times. The upper jaw of the swordfish is shaped into a powerful, broad, flattened bill or sword. It has no pelvic fins; the pectoral fins are placed low on the body. The first dorsal fin is high but stubby with a small base. There is a single keel on the caudal peduncle. Color is very dark blackish-blue or brown above, lighter tan or white below. **Range:** worldwide in tropical and temperate seas; here, Oregon to Chile, occasionally the Gulf of California. **Edibility:** excellent.

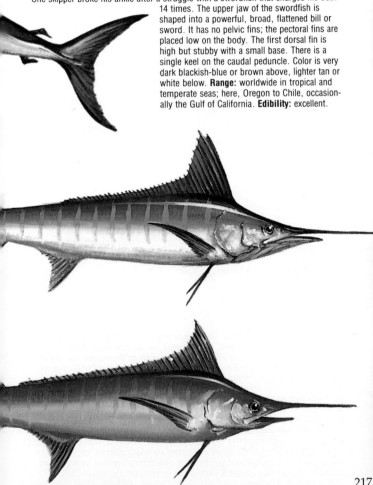

217

surface, twisting and tailwalking; others will sound deep, which means a long, tedious battle. They are sought more for their fighting spirit than for their strong and oily flesh. Each year more conservation-minded fishermen are releasing billfishes and other game fishes before boating them, so that the fishes can live to breed again. In California, commercial fishing of billfishes is prohibited, except for the swordfish. They can be taken only by sport fishermen on hook and line.

A much smaller billfish is the Pacific sailfish, a strikingly beautiful animal with a huge, fanlike dorsal fin. The sailfish is such popular game off Panama that a sailfish club has formed, devoted to catching these fishes from April to November. The broadbill swordfish rivals the shark in both size and strength. Dolphinfishes or dorados of the family Coryphaenidae are beautiful, active fishes that range all warm seas. They are common in the tropical eastern Pacific and are taken by offshore fishermen all year, but are most numerous from May to December. ◆

Dolphinfish, mahi mahi (dorado) *Coryphaena hippurus*   To 6 feet, 9 inches and 87 pounds (average: about 3 feet). Dolphinfishes are beautiful active fishes that range all warm seas. They have been taken as far north as Washington, but are rare north of Baja California, being commonly caught around Cabo San Lucas in spring and Panama in summer. In Hawaii, they are called *mahi mahi* and are popular restaurant fare; also a favored food in Pacific Coast markets and restaurants. Dolphinfishes feed on sardines, anchovies, and mackerel, but their favorite prey seems to be flyingfishes. The speed of the dolphinfish enables it to flush flyingfishes like quail, catching them as they fall after a fumbling start or a full flight. It is gorgeous when caught, with iridescent shades of purplish-bluish gold, sea green, and emerald. At death it quickly becomes plain gray. The name dolphin is confusing, since it is applied to this fish and the porpoise. The two are totally different: the dolphinfish is water-breathing, the porpoise dolphin is an airbreathing mammal closely related to whales. **Range:** circumtropical; here, Grays Harbor (Washington) to Chile, including the Gulf of California and the Galapagos Islands. **Edibility:** good.

SHARKS AND RAYS

For the interested swimmer who contemplates skin or SCUBA diving as a sport, probably one of the greatest fears is the shark attack. Popular misconceptions engendered by such films as *Jaws*, as well as countless TV, book, and newspaper stories, all contribute to the image of the shark waiting offshore to pounce on anyone who enters the water. I have talked with numerous people who would not consider diving or fishwatching because of fear of sharks. Yet actual shark sightings around coasts and shallow reefs are rare, and attacks by sharks on humans near most of the world's beaches are extremely rare. According to figures gathered by Jacques Yves Cousteau, of the countless millions who enter the world's oceans, only about 50 are attacked by sharks each year. In 1985, only four people were reported killed by sharks worldwide. This compares with about 125 people killed by lightning each year in the U.S. alone and 50 to 75 people who die yearly from insect stings.

Most sharks are not reef-dwelling animals, but make occasional visits to the reef to feed on resident fishes. Div-

Bonito shark, shortfin mako (tiburón bonito) *Isurus oxyrinchus* To 12½ feet and 1,102 pounds. A prized and fast-swimming game fish known for tackle-busting runs and leaps. Dangerous in the boat or in the water because very aggressive. Implicated in attacks on man and boats. Shown here is a mako shark in a typical threat display just prior to attack. A roving, offshore shark, but it is also encountered near shore. Note the long, pointed snout. The first dorsal fin is much larger than the second. The tail is symmetrical and there is a prominent keel on the caudal peduncle. Gill slits are relatively small. **Range:** worldwide in warm seas; here, Oregon to the Gulf of California and Ecuador to Chile.

Great white shark, white shark, maneater shark (tiburón blanco, jaquetón) *Carcharodon carcharias*   To 25 feet. Undoubtedly the world's most dangerous and widely known shark, it has been implicated in numerous attacks on people and even boats. Often found near islands and offshore colonies of seals and sea lions—its favorite food. Divers in wet suits and surfers should avoid reefs or islands where sharks might mistake them for resident seals or sea lions. Attacks along the West Coast average about two per year. Along the California-Oregon coast the number of great white attacks since the 1920's, when records were first kept, through 1984 is 59. Note the heavy, stout body, broad, triangular, serrated teeth, and large keellike tail fin. **Range:** worldwide in all seas; most often found in cooler, temperate areas; here, the Gulf of Alaska to Chile.

Blue shark (tintorera, tiburón azul) *Prionace glauca*   To 13 feet. Colorful, with a brilliant dark blue back shading to iridescent blue on the sides. Abundant along the West Coast. The blue shark is slim—a 9-footer will weigh only about 164 pounds. Potentially dangerous, common offshore and occasionally comes inshore and has been known to attack humans, though rarely. Often seen at sea with dorsal and tail fins out of the water. It will strike back if struck with an oar. Common around offshore islands and oil drilling rigs. Note the large eye, long narrow pointed snout, and long saber-shaped pectoral fins. Blue sharks give birth to live pups in litters of from 4 to 82, each about 19 inches long. **Range:** worldwide in warm seas; here, the Gulf of Alaska to Chile.

ers who spear or maim fish may attract sharks to the area because the wounded fish generate scent trails and low-frequency vibrations. Areas where seals and sea lions abound should be avoided by divers and surfers since, from below, it may be difficult for a shark to distinguish between a seal or sea lion and a black-suited diver or surfer. Of about 350 species of sharks, only 25 are known to have been implicated in attacks on humans. Forty other shark species are potentially dangerous but no attacks by them have ever been recorded. Most shark researchers find that, unless provoked or threatened, sharks will almost always retreat rather than confront a creature as large as man. When they do attack, many bite once and let go. This occurrence is so common that Dr. H. David Baldridge (1981), after analyzing the U.S. Navy's shark attack file, believes that 50 to 75 percent of all assaults are not caused by hunger but result from a perceived threat to an animal's territory or courting ritual. To guard himself against sharks, man is taking extraordinary measures to rid the ocean of these animals. In Queensland, Australia, nets strung under water to protect bathing beaches killed 20,500 sharks over a 16-year period. Alarmingly, the nets also claimed 468 highly endangered dugongs, 317 porpoises, 2,654 sea turtles, and 10,889 rays. Sadly, most of the 20,500 sharks would never have gone near a swimmer in the first place. According to Eugenie Clark (1981), a first pioneer step in the protection of sharks was taken by Israel's Nature Reserve Authority, which established a series of underwater preserves and parks along the Sinai Peninsula. Although Israel no longer controls the Sinai, the preserve would have protected the splendid coral reefs and all their inhabitants, including sharks. It is hoped that, as man loses his unreasoning fear of sharks, the move to protect them may spread.

Sharks and rays, fishes of the class Elasmobranchii, are distinct from all bony fishes because their skeletons are composed of cartilage instead of bone. Sharks all have five gill slits on each side—with two exceptions, the rather primitive sixgill and sevengill sharks. All male sharks and rays have claspers just behind the pelvic fins. It was previously thought that these were used to clasp the female during copulation, but it was learned that these are long, intromittent organs used to transfer sperm to the female's oviduct. Ovoviviparous or live-bearing females nurture eggs in the oviduct until hatching time; oviparous sharks

Bull shark (gambuso, chato) *Carcharhinus leucas* To 11 feet. This inshore shark is never far from land. Often hooked by game fishermen but bull sharks do not rise to the surface like other sharks but stay deep and fight long, tiring battles. Commonly enters tropical rivers and lakes (Lake Nicaragua), reaching 2,000 miles inland. A very dangerous shark—has attacked humans in both fresh and salt water. Notable for the massive, bull-like head and jaws and heavy body, as well as the triangular upper teeth and large first dorsal fin. **Range:** Baja California and Gulf of California to Peru.

Oceanic whitetip shark *Carcharhinus longimanus* To 11½ feet. Distinctive for the gray body with white tips on almost all fins of adult fishes. Epipelagic, hence usually encountered at or near the surface well offshore. Not fast moving but potentially dangerous all the same, and implicated in attacks on humans. **Range:** circumtropical; here, the Cortez Banks (off San Diego, California) to Islas Revillagigedo.

Blacktip shark (volador, sardinero) *Carcharhinus limbatus* To 8 feet. Like the mako, a popular game fish owing to the leaping, spinning, and rotating antics it performs when hooked. Occasionally encountered swimming in packs of 6 to 12. Note the black tips on all fins (the color fades on older fish). Epipelagic, feeding on squid and fishes on or near surface. Common in the Gulf of California where a shark fishery exists for blacktips. **Range:** Baja California and Gulf of California to Peru.

Pacific sharpnose shark (bironche) *Rhizoprionodon longurio*   To 3½ feet, rarely to 5 feet. One of the smaller requiem sharks, with small fins and a very long, pointed snout. Quite common in the Gulf of California and a frequent catch of the shark fisheries there. An inshore coastal fish. **Range:** rare in southern California (only one or two records) but common off southern Baja California and southward to Peru.

Tiger shark (tintorera, tiburón tigre, alecrín) *Galeocerdo cuvier*   To 24 feet (rare over 14 feet). This shark is well named for the tigerlike stripes on its sides and the voracity that makes it one of the most dangerous sharks. Much like the great white, it will eat or snap at almost anything, from other sharks to mammals, garbage, and metal. But unlike the great white shark, it is a big-headed, slow species, abundant in the tropics. It swims well offshore and in coastal areas, including river mouths, bays, and estuaries. **Range:** circumtropical; here, southern California (rare) to Peru; uncommon in the Gulf of California.

and skates lay egg cases that hatch later on the reef or ocean bottom. Viviparous females nourish the young in the oviduct until live birth some months later.

Most sharks are unmistakable, but some, like the angel sharks, look more like rays than sharks. Sharks breathe much like normal fishes, taking water in through the mouth and expelling it out over the gills. But since skates and rays spend so much time on the sea bottom, they are equipped with spiracles in back of their eyes on top of their heads. Thus they can draw water in through the spiracles and expel it through the gill slits on the underside of the head, and so avoid swallowing sand or mud from the bottom. Many shark species are moderate in size but some are gigantic, rivaling the great whales. The basking shark reaches 45 feet in length and the whale shark grows 223

[*text continues on p. 228*]

Soupfin shark *Galeorhinus zyopterus*   To 6½ feet. The soupfin, smoothhound, and leopard sharks are all members of the smoothhound family of sharks (Triakididae). A popular food fish, once pursued intensively for its liver oil, and now taken commercially for the fish market and for the Chinese to use in shark fin soup. The fin rays are gelatinous and give the soup a special flavor and consistency. Wide ranging, soupfin sharks travel in schools covering up to 35 miles per day. Very abundant offshore; they also come in to coastlines, bays, and shallows. A very slender, fusiform fish distinguished by the long, pointed snout, black-tipped tail fins, and the large terminal lobe on the tail fin. **Range:** nearly worldwide in temperate seas; here, northern British Columbia to Bahía San Juanico (Baja California).

Common thresher shark (tiburón coludo, zorro) *Alopias vulpinus*   To 20 feet. Unmistakable with the giant caudal fin with which it herds, corrals, and even stuns smaller fishes into submission for an easy mealtime. Because of the recent popularity of thresher shark steaks in the marketplace, now actively pursued by commercial shark fishermen. The California Department of Fish and Game has procured legislation reducing commercial gill netting to prevent overfishing. Threshers feed on anchovies, herrings, squid, and other fishes. Young in litters of 2 to 6 are nourished by uterine cannibalism: the dominant infant consumes others and often emerges as the only offspring. They are members of the Alopiidae or thresher shark family. **Range:** worldwide in warm seas; here, British Columbia to Chile.

224

Leopard shark (tiburón leopardo) *Triakis semifasciata* To 7 feet. These active, fast-moving, nomadic sharks with leopardlike spots roam inshore sand flats and rocky areas in schools, often in the company of smoothhound sharks. They seem to be in constant motion, moving in a snakelike fashion. They are not considered dangerous to swimmers and seem wary of divers—not aggressive. They feed on fishes and crustaceans. Often sought by commercial fishermen as food fishes; sport fishermen take them from 12 feet inshore out to 300 feet. Numbers have declined lately, possibly because of increased spear fishing. **Range:** Oregon to Mazatlán (Mexico), including the Gulf of California.

Gray smoothhound shark (tiburón mamón, gatuso) *Mustelus californicus* To 5 feet, 4 inches. Closely related to the leopard shark and frequently seen swimming along in schools with them. It is a small fish found only off the California-Mexican coastline and prefers inshore shallow-water habitats often of 12 feet or less, but ranges out to 150 feet. Due to its small size, it is not a dangerous animal. Another close cousin, the brown smoothhound shark (*M. henlei*) is similar to the gray, but more bronze-brown in color. It has dorsal fins that are frayed at the rear edge (the gray's are smooth) and teeth that are pointed (the gray's are blunt). The brown smoothhound is smaller, growing to only 37 inches, and has a much wider range than the gray smoothhound. **Range:** gray, Cape Mendocino (California) to Mazatlán (Mexico); brown, Coos Bay (Oregon) to the Gulf of California, and to Ecuador and Peru.

Sevengill shark *Notorynchus maculatus* To 9 feet. Distinctive for the seven gill slits (most sharks have five), the single dorsal fin placed well back on the body, and the long upper lobe of the tail fin. A closely related species, the sixgill shark (*Hexanchus griseus*), has a similar profile, no spots, and grows larger (to 16½ feet). Both are found off open coastlines, inshore over soft bottoms, and in bays, as well as offshore (adults) at considerable depths. Neither is considered aggressive but both become snappish and dangerous when hooked and boated. Thought to be worthy game by some sport fishermen because of their fighting prowess and often taken commercially. The Chinese are very fond of sevengill meat. A member of the cow shark family (Hexanchidae). Females are ovoviviparous, bearing live, self-sustaining young. **Range:** sixgill, British Columbia to Punta Banda (outer Baja California); sevengill, British Columbia into the Gulf of California; both also found off Chile.

Lemon shark (tiburón chato, amarillo) *Negaprion brevirostris* To 11 feet. A southern inshore shark common in very shallow water either singly or in loose aggregations of 4 to 6 fishes. Both juveniles and adults take hooks baited with fish and feed almost indiscriminately on any available fish. Distinctive for the yellow coloration, two large dorsal fins, and the short rounded snout. Large specimens can be dangerous, and they have been implicated in attacks on humans. A valuable shark: its skin makes fine leather, the flesh is good eating, and even the fins are used in table delicacies. **Range:** Atlantic and Pacific coasts of the Americas; here, southern Mexico to Ecuador, including the Gulf of California.

Swell shark (gata) *Cephaloscyllium ventriosum*   To 3 feet, 3 inches. An unusual little shark with colorful saddles, blotches, and spots which inhabits shallow reefs, kelp beds, caves, and crevices along the coast and offshore islands. Catlike, with catlike eyes, it belongs to the cat-shark family, the Scyliorhinidae. As the name implies, this swell shark can inflate its stomach with water when disturbed, thus wedging itself tightly into caves and crevices, safe from attackers. Harmless and sluggish, it emerges at night to forage for fishes and crustaceans. The female lays a large, purse-shaped egg case with one egg, often attached to kelp strands by curling tendrils. It hatches seven to nine months later. When these egg cases wash onto shore and are found by humans, they are often called "mermaids' purses." **Range:** Monterey Bay (California) to Acapulco (Mexico); also Chile.

Nurse shark (gata, gata manchada) *Ginglymostoma cirratum*   To 14 feet. A southern, inshore, sluggish shark found around shallow sand flats, channels, and coral reefs and often apparently sleeping inside reef caves and crevices. Young have dark spots on body which fade as they mature. Although thought to be harmless, unprovoked attacks have been recorded in Florida and the Caribbean, as well as attacks on people foolish enough to spear it or grab it by the tail. Note the blunt head, barbels in front of each nostril, two large dorsal fins, and the long, low, single-lobed tail. The only North American member of the carpet shark family (Orectolobidae). **Range:** both coasts of tropical America; here, the Gulf of California to Ecuador.

to over 60 feet—the largest fishes in the world. Other sharks are very small, reaching only 1 foot. Some, like the great white, mako, and blue sharks, must swim constantly; others, like the nurse and angel sharks, are sluggish and spend much of their time on the bottom. The largest family, the requiem or carcharhinid sharks, are represented here by the tiger, blue, whitetip, blacktip, bull, sharpnose, and lemon sharks.

The skates and rays are flattened fishes related to sharks. The pectoral fins are greatly enlarged and are attached to the sides of the head. The gills and mouth are on the underside of these fins. All skates lay eggs and all rays bear live young. There are about 400 species of skates and rays, 23 in our area. ◆

Scalloped hammerhead shark (cornuda, pez martillo, cruz) *Sphyrna lewini* To 13 feet, 9 inches. A tropical shark, this hammerhead seems to school in great numbers around offshore islands, reefs, and seamounts in the Gulf of California. The reason for schooling is not known, but the behavior has attracted wildlife photographers. Although reputed to be dangerous, the schooling hammerheads seem quite passive and no attacks have yet been recorded. Elsewhere in tropical seas, attacks do occur and hammerheads are carefully avoided. Found offshore and inshore, they feed primarily on fish and to a large extent on other sharks and rays. Many theories explain why the head of this strange shark is drawn out into a hammer shape—including easier turning and better ability to locate odors—but no one knows for sure. Nine species worldwide in tropical seas—four off the Pacific Coast, all rare or uncommon north of San Diego. They have distinctive head profiles: the scalloped hammerhead has three notches on the leading edge of the head (viewed from above or below); the smooth hammerhead (*S. zygaena*) has two notches at the front edge of the head; the great hammerhead (*S. mokarran*) has a single notch at the center of the head; the bonnethead shark (*S. tiburo*) has a smooth spade-shaped head (viewed from above). The bonnethead is a small harmless shark, reaching 6 feet; but the other three grow to be quite large (to 18 feet), active, and dangerous.
Range: scalloped hammerhead, southern California and the Gulf of California to Ecuador; smooth hammerhead, central California to Chile; great hammerhead, southern Baja California to Ecuador; bonnethead, San Diego (California) to Peru.

Horn shark (tiburón cornudo) *Heterodontus francisi* To 3 feet, 2 inches. Distinctive for the large bull-like head with piglike snout, bony ridges over the eyes, tan-spotted body, and formidable, venomous spines ("horns") in front of each dorsal fin. Slow, sluggish, and relatively harmless, but, like the swell shark, will bite if handled or provoked. Found in kelp beds, shallow reefs, sandy areas, and reef caves and crevices. Emerges most often at night to feed on fishes and crabs, and has both cutting and crushing teeth in each jaw to grind up sea urchins and mollusks. Courting activity is initiated by the male using only one of his claspers. This activity puts a 45-degree elbow in the clasper that lasts for several days. Females enclose eggs in augerlike egg cases—one egg to a case—and these are then tightly wedged and "augured" into reef crevices. A member of the bullhead shark family, the Heterodontidae. **Range:** central California to Gulf of California.

Pacific angel shark (tiburón angel) *Squatina californica* To 5 feet. It has many characteristics of both sharks and rays and demonstrates their close relationship. It is a flattened bottom dweller with winglike pectoral fins and a disclike head. It lies partially buried in the sand, as rays do, changing colors to perfectly match its background, from rusty red to pearl-white, gray, brown, or black. The eyes and mouth are at the front of the head, sharklike, and the wide, flat pectoral fins are not attached to the head, as they are in rays. It has sharp, shark teeth and Feder et al. (1974) report that it may turn on a spear and attack a diver and should be considered potentially dangerous. Found over sand and mud bottoms near reefs, kelp beds, and rocky areas from 10 to 150 feet. **Range:** southern Alaska to Baja California and the Gulf of California.

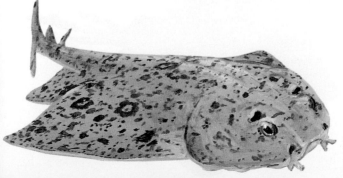

229

Big skate (raya) *Raja binoculata*   To 8 feet. First taken in 1880 at Victoria, British Columbia, and recorded in that year by D. S. Jordan and C. H. Gilbert. The largest skate on the Pacific Coast, frequently caught by sport fishermen and discarded, but commercially fished; the pectoral wings are sold as food. Note the distinctive ''eye'' spots on the back, long pointed snout, and the row of spines running mid-dorsally from head to first dorsal fin. Large females lay 1-foot-long egg cases containing two to seven eggs. Very abundant on the Pacific Coast from 10 to 360 feet and often caught by shrimpers in the Gulf of California. **Range:** Bering Sea to Bahía de San Quintin (northern Baja California) and the Gulf of California.

California skate (raya) *Raja inornata*   To 2½ feet. A small skate identified by the long, pointed nose and deeply notched pelvic fins. Quite common, it is often taken inshore, around shallow bays, and ranges out to 2,000-foot depths. A target of commercial fishermen, it is a prime food fish. Note the twin claspers on this male at the rear of the pelvic fins. **Range:** Strait of Juan de Fuca (British Columbia) to Bahía Tortugas (central Baja California).

Starry skate, prickly skate (raya) *Raja stellulata*   To 2½ feet. Most of its topside and underside are covered with prickly spines and denticles, which make it unappetizing to larger predators. Prefers deeper water at depths from 60 to 2,400 feet. The eggs, like those of other skates and some sharks, are laid in striated egg cases, with long hooks or "horns" for attachment to reef bottom in crevices or in kelp beds or seaweed flats. Distinctive for the very short, blunt nose, the two "eye" spots often but not always visible on the rounded pectoral wings, and the large spines down the middle of the back. **Range:** Gulf of Alaska to northern Baja California.

Shovelnose guitarfish (pez guitarra, pez diablo, viola) *Rhinobatos productus*   To 5½ feet and 40 pounds; uncommon over 3 feet. The familiar shovelnose shark frequently seen near shore and caught by shore anglers. It often occurs in large numbers in bays, sloughs, and estuaries in the southern part of its range. They eat crabs, worms, clams, and small fishes, and sometimes get so engrossed in feeding that receding waters leave them stranded. They must wiggle back into the water like grunion. Often buries itself in the sand for protection. Females bear up to 28 young, each 6 inches long. Note the spade-shaped head with very long, pointed nose, large tail fin, and row of spines on back. **Range:** San Francisco (California) to the Gulf of California; rare north of Monterey Bay.

Banded guitarfish (pez guitarra, pez diablo) *Zapteryx exasperata*   To 3 feet. Like the shovelnose guitarfish but has dark bars and light spots on its back. Note the rounded snout and wide pectoral wings. Occurs over rocky areas and seeks out reef caves and crevices. This is the unfortunate guitarfish that is caught, mutilated, dried in the sun, and sold from Mexico to Panama to gullible tourists as "diablos" or "sea monsters." **Range:** La Jolla (southern California) to Panama; rare in California but common in the Gulf of California.

Round stingray (raya de espina) *Urolophus halleri*   To 22 inches. Much smaller than the diamond stingray but the most common stingray off California beaches. It sometimes clusters in shallow inlets, bays, and lagoons in great numbers in summer when water temperatures rise. Like most rays, the round stingray is not aggressive but will sting if stepped on. Many bathers and waders are stung each year. Wounds are not fatal, but can be quite painful, depending on depth of sting. Distinctive for the round pectoral wings, short, stout tail, large sting, and large tail fin. Feeds on worms, mollusks, and crustaceans. **Range:** Eureka (northern California) to Panama and throughout the Gulf of California.

Diamond stingray (raya de espina) *Dasyatis brevis*   6 feet long, 4 feet wide. This ray is one good reason for swimmers and divers to learn the "stingray shuffle" (dragging your feet so as not to step on the ray) when wading around Pacific sand or mud bottoms. Its large size, long whiplike tail, and venomous sting can mean serious injury, intense pain, and slow recovery. Eschmeyer, Herald, and Hammann (1983) report that at least one Gulf of California death was stingray caused. Prefers sandy areas near rocks or kelp beds from 7 to 55 feet. It burrows and covers its back with sand to become almost invisible on the bottom. Note the diamond shape of the pectoral wings. **Range:** Kyoquot Sound (British Columbia) to Paita (Peru); common from San Diego (California) south, and abundant in the Gulf of California.

Bullseye stingray (raya) *Urolophus concentricus*   To 22 inches. A common ray occurring on rocky bottoms as well as beaches, bays, and sloughs in the Gulf of California. Some researchers believe that this ray and the round stingray may be the same species, since they differ only in color. However, the bullseye stingray seems to be confined to the Gulf of California, and the round stingray has a much wider range. **Range:** central and lower Gulf of California.

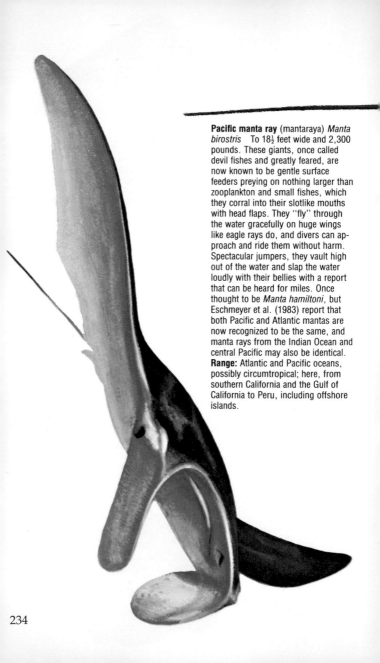

Pacific manta ray (mantaraya) *Manta birostris*   To 18½ feet wide and 2,300 pounds. These giants, once called devil fishes and greatly feared, are now known to be gentle surface feeders preying on nothing larger than zooplankton and small fishes, which they corral into their slotlike mouths with head flaps. They ''fly'' through the water gracefully on huge wings like eagle rays do, and divers can approach and ride them without harm. Spectacular jumpers, they vault high out of the water and slap the water loudly with their bellies with a report that can be heard for miles. Once thought to be *Manta hamiltoni*, but Eschmeyer et al. (1983) report that both Pacific and Atlantic mantas are now recognized to be the same, and manta rays from the Indian Ocean and central Pacific may also be identical. **Range:** Atlantic and Pacific oceans, possibly circumtropical; here, from southern California and the Gulf of California to Peru, including offshore islands.

Spotted eagle ray (chucho, raya pinta) *Aetobatus narinari*   To 9 feet wide. One of the most striking and attractive rays of the order, especially when seen winging singly, in pairs, or in large aggregations just beyond the breaker line or along the perimeter of patch reefs in the Gulf of California. Although beautiful, they have powerful jaws, grinding teeth, and a whiplike tail with two spiny stingers at the tail base, so do not mishandle. When pursued, they make startling leaps in the air to escape the pursuer. Females are ovoviviparous and young are born tail first with wings rolled up like a Mexican tortilla. **Range:** circumtropical; here, Gulf of California to Panama and the Galapagos Islands.

California butterfly ray (raya mariposa) *Gymnura marmorata*   To 5 feet wide. A handsome ray with huge spotted wings shaped not unlike a giant butterfly. It does have a stinging spine but it is small and positioned at the base of the tail, making this ray relatively harmless. Found along sandy beaches, in shallow bays, and out to 180 feet. A frequent catch of shrimpers in the Gulf of California. **Range:** Point Conception (southern California) to Peru, including the Gulf of California.

Bat ray (raya gavilán) *Myliobatis californica*   To 6 feet wide and 200 pounds. This ray has an unmistakable large, raised head, heavy jaws, dark brown-black color, and a long whiplike tail with a caudal fin and stinger at its base. Large aggregations of these rays can be seen swimming gracefully around the Channel Islands off southern California and also along the perimeter of patch reefs in the Gulf of California. They seek out inshore bays and sloughs, flat rocky bottoms, and kelp beds with sandy patches, where they dig and flap their wings to uncover the worms, shrimps, clams, abalone, and crabs they feed on. They like to bury themselves in the sand with just the eyes protruding. Handle carefully; the stinger and powerful crushing jaws are potentially dangerous. Found from shore to 150-foot depths. **Range:** Oregon to Gulf of California.

Pacific electric ray (torpedo, raya electrica) *Torpedo californica*   To 4½ feet. This unusual ray is said to pack an 80-volt charge for any aggressor touching it. Feder et al. (1974) state that this ray seems to realize it has a potent weapon. If a diver comes too close, blocks its path, or irritates it with a spear, the ray may turn on the diver. It may swim directly at the diver with its small mouth open. It is a slow mover, however, and there is no record of a diver being bitten or shocked. Fishermen also report taking this fish without being shocked. Yet it is wise not to mishandle this ray. It seeks out a fine-sand bottom but also occurs around reef rocks and kelp beds, where it hovers over the bottom in order to stun fishes coming up beneath it. **Range:** southern British Columbia to central Baja California.

MORAYS, CONGERS, AND SNAKE EELS

The moray eel has a far worse reputation than it deserves. It is thought by some to be vicious, dangerous, and even venomous. Yet recent contacts between divers and morays show that these eels can be docile and almost puppylike. They will emerge from their caves and gently take food from a diver's bare hand. Although the moray opens and closes its mouth continuously, making it appear menacing and aggressive, these movements are the moray's way of breathing by pumping water across its gills. Nevertheless, divers and fishermen should exercise caution when approaching morays, since they can bite with fanglike teeth if threatened. They feed almost exclusively on small fishes, octopuses, and crustaceans. The moray is a night-active fish and will forage across the reef hunting for small, wounded, or sleeping fish. Certain wrasses and parrotfishes wrap themselves in a mucous cocoon at night as a protection against marauding morays and other predators. Morays have the reputation of being venomous, but no evidence has ever been offered to support this.

Moray eels, of the family Muraenidae, have long been esteemed as food in many parts of the world. In the Mediterranean the ancient Romans kept moray and conger eels in specially built reservoirs or *piscinae* near the sea to serve at their banquets. Morays are found in all warm seas, usually in shallow tropical areas, sheltering in reef or coral crevices. They have no pectoral fins (unlike most eels) and usually possess powerful canine teeth. They have no scales, no lateral line, and a gill opening that is almost round.

Burton and Burton (1975) report that morays can throw their bodies into a knot and move this knot forward or backward from the head, a very handy device to shake off attackers like octopuses. When hooked on a line, a moray will try the same trick, sometimes climbing the line tail-first. One memorable fishing trip in Florida was ended abruptly when three fishermen jumped overboard as a large brown moray came twisting, tail-first, aboard the boat.

Conger eels, of the family Congridae, are easily separated from the morays by their usually prominent pectoral fins. Congers have very strong jaws but lack the long canine teeth of the morays. Garden eels are a subfamily of the congers, famous for their burrowing habits and the 237 "eel gardens" they form when several (sometimes hundreds) have their burrows in one patch or garden.

Snake eels (family Ophichthidae) are also burrowing eels, and are named for their long, cylindrical snakelike bodies. Some have spikelike tails, which they use to burrow tail-first into the sand for cover. ◆

Panamic green moray (morena verde) *Gymnothorax castaneus*   To over 4 feet. Common in the central and lower Gulf of California. As with most eels, especially morays, divers should approach this eel cautiously. It has large canine teeth and can injure unwary fishermen or divers when hooked, speared, or boated. This moray forages for fishes and crustaceans at night and is able to sense wounded, distressed, or sleeping fishes; it even leaves its crevice in daylight to seize likely prey. It is greenish brown, often with fine white spots; note the sharply pointed snout. **Range:** northern Gulf of California and Baja California to Colombia, including Islas Revillagigedo and Isla de Malpelo.

California moray (morena) *Gymnothorax mordax*   To 5 feet. This shallow-water eel stays in or near its rocky burrow or crevice during the day, with only its head protruding. At night it becomes active and forages across the reef for octopuses, crustaceans, and small fishes. Use caution around this eel. The name *mordax* means "prone to bite," and if the fish is hooked, boated, or speared, like most morays it may bite anything around it with large fanglike teeth. Divers and hunters of abalone and lobster are often bitten when sticking a hand into a hole that turns out to be the home of this moray. It ranges from 2 to 65 feet in depth. Note the lack of pectoral fins and pelvic fins. Older morays live to be 30 years or older. **Range:** Point Conception (southern California) to southern Baja California.

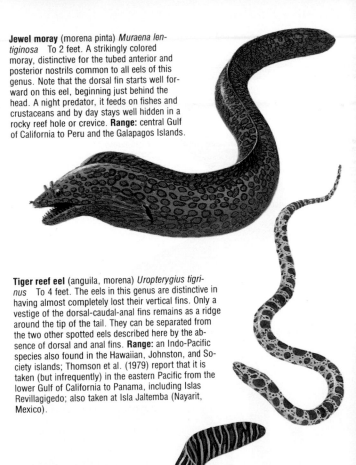

Jewel moray (morena pinta) *Muraena lentiginosa* To 2 feet. A strikingly colored moray, distinctive for the tubed anterior and posterior nostrils common to all eels of this genus. Note that the dorsal fin starts well forward on this eel, beginning just behind the head. A night predator, it feeds on fishes and crustaceans and by day stays well hidden in a rocky reef hole or crevice. **Range:** central Gulf of California to Peru and the Galapagos Islands.

Tiger reef eel (anguila, morena) *Uropterygius tigrinus* To 4 feet. The eels in this genus are distinctive in having almost completely lost their vertical fins. Only a vestige of the dorsal-caudal-anal fins remains as a ridge around the tip of the tail. They can be separated from the two other spotted eels described here by the absence of dorsal and anal fins. **Range:** an Indo-Pacific species also found in the Hawaiian, Johnston, and Society islands; Thomson et al. (1979) report that it is taken (but infrequently) in the eastern Pacific from the lower Gulf of California to Panama, including Islas Revillagigedo; also taken at Isla Jaltemba (Nayarit, Mexico).

Zebra moray (morena cebra) *Echidna zebra* To 2½ feet. A secretive eel, rarely found out of its burrow. Eels of this genus are unique in having blunt, molarlike teeth, and the zebra is equipped with rows of pebblelike grinding teeth reportedly used for crushing the hard-shelled crustaceans and mollusks on which it feeds. Hobson (1974) found that in Hawaii these eels feed primarily on crabs. **Range:** central Gulf of California to Panama and the Galapagos Islands, and widely distributed through the Indo-West Pacific.

Catalina conger (congrio) *Gnathophis catalinensis* To 16½ inches. Note the large pectoral fin, which helps to separate the conger from the morays and other marine eels. The conger is usually found over soft sand or mud bottoms where it preys on fishes and invertebrates. It will burrow tail-first into the sand if necessary and ranges over depths from 30 to 1,200 feet. When it moves, it is true poetry in motion as undulating ripples flow down the fins and the body snakes gracefully through the water. Congers have strong jaws but lack the long canine teeth of the morays. **Range:** Santa Rosa Island (southern California) to the Gulf of California.

Cortez garden eel (anguila jardin) *Taenioconger digueti* To 25 inches. Garden eels, a subfamily of the congers (Heterocongrinae), are sociable fishes, unique for their burrowing habits and the "eel gardens" they produce. A large colony is an unusual sight, each eel bending and swaying with the tides, picking zooplankton from the drifting swarm. If approached by a predator or a diver, they slide back into their burrows, then quickly reappear when danger is past. At night they retreat inside, covering the burrow opening with sand. They range over moderate depths from 12 to 20 feet. The Cortez garden eel has minute dark-brown pectoral fins and conspicuous lateral-line pores circled by white areas. **Range:** central and lower Gulf of California to Puerto Vallarta (Mexico).

240

Pacific worm eel, estero worm eel (morena) *Myrophis vafer* To 18¼ inches. Found in tidepools, estuaries, and near-shore habitats out to 36-foot depths, this eel is rare off southern California but fairly abundant from the Gulf of California to Peru. The body is wormlike, the pectoral fins are small, and the dorsal fin begins far behind the pectoral fins. The color is light brown. There are tubes on the anterior nostrils; the teeth are pointed and sharp. **Range:** San Pedro (southern California) and the Gulf of California to Peru.

Spotted snake eel, Pacific snake eel (morena) *Ophichthus triserialis* To 44½ inches. Grows quite large and is easily recognized by its large mouth, assortment of large and small black spots covering the body, and the spiked, pointed tail. Like the yellow snake eel, it is adept at burrowing and disappearing tail-first into the sand, where it can travel backward and forward with ease. Usually inhabits intertidal and shallow shore areas, but has been taken at depths of 60 feet. **Range:** Klamath River (northern California) to Peru, including the Gulf of California and the Galapagos Islands; rare north of Baja California.

Yellow snake eel (morena) *Ophichthus zophochir*   To 34½ inches. Another bottom-dwelling eel that prefers sandy areas near rocky outcroppings where it can find cover by burrowing quickly in the sand tail-first with its reinforced, pointed, spike-like tail. It ranges from near shore out to 210 feet. Note that the origin of the dorsal fin is far forward, close behind the pectoral fin base. **Range:** Eureka (northern California) to Peru; uncommon north of Baja California.

Tiger snake eel (anguila, vibora, culebra) *Myrichthys maculosus*   To 18 inches. Similar to the spotted snake eel, but it has uniform (rather than large and small) spots, a smaller mouth, short pectoral fins, and molar-like teeth. It is often seen moving freely about the reef by day, picking and probing its way through sand and seagrass areas. Its eyesight is bad; it hunts by smell; it is quite harmless and may be easily observed by divers. Note the small pectoral fins and long, tubed nostrils. **Range:** San Francisco (California) to Ecuador, including the Gulf of California and the Galapagos Islands.

SEA SNAKES

The yellow-bellied sea snake is one of the most widely distributed venomous sea snakes in the world. It is fairly common in some Central American Pacific coastal areas, and it is covered here, along with the eels one might mistake it for, to familiarize divers, swimmers, and fishermen, so that they can give it a wide berth. ◆

Yellow-bellied sea snake (vibora, culebra) *Pelamis platurus* To 2½ feet. A very venomous sea snake occasionally reported along the Pacific Coast. All who frequent the coast, especially the area from Baja California to Ecuador, should learn to recognize this sea snake so as to avoid it. A live adult was found on the beach at San Clemente (southern California) in 1972. More recent sightings have been made in Bahía Magdalena (southern Baja California), the Gulf of California as far north as San Felipe, in Bahía de Los Angeles (the central Gulf), and along the mainland Gulf coast. Some may have been carried northward by the warm Davidson Current (the northernmost breeding population was found in Bahía Banderas, Jalisco, Mexico). Although not particularly aggressive, the yellow-bellied sea snake has caused fatalities in the Indo-Pacific. It is unmistakable with its bright yellow underside.
Range: the most widely distributed of all sea snakes; here, from San Clemente (southern California) and throughout the Gulf of California to Ecuador; also ranges from the west coast of Central America across the South Pacific and Indian oceans to eastern Africa, and in the Indo-Pacific area from southern Siberia to Tasmania.

DIVING TIPS AND MAPS OF THE
EASTERN PACIFIC

The eastern Pacific is a fish watcher's paradise. Whether you are diving off British Columbia, Oregon, Washington, California's superb coastline, or the immense, varied, and fascinating Mexican coast, the underwater world of the reefs is only minutes away. All that is needed is the ability to swim and the effort required to adjust to swimming with a face mask and snorkel tube. These can be purchased at most sporting goods stores for around $20. Swim fins, which give you the added push necessary for effortless cruising around the reefs, are advised for longer skin-diving excursions. In northern waters, a wet suit is required to ward off the cold.

This guidebook treats the fishes found in the coastal waters of the Eastern Pacific from Alaska to Peru. As you will see, however, many species are not restricted to that vast range—some reach across the Pacific to Japan and Korea, and others range down the coast to the waters of Chile. A few fishes are circumtropical or even worldwide in distribution.

To aid the fishwatcher interested in tracking the range of the many fishes covered here, the book provides quite detailed maps showing (1) the complete area covered, from Alaska to Peru (pp. 246–47); (2) the Pacific Northwest coast, from Vancouver Island to San Francisco (p. 248); (3) the central coast, from San Francisco to the Mexican border (p. 249); and (4) the coasts and islands of Baja California and the Gulf of California, a veritable treasure-trove of fishes (p. 250). The maps show most of the key landmarks and points of interest (bays, beaches, capes, islands, and cities), but clearly it was not possible to show them all. The maps also highlight those areas that are of special interest to divers and fishwatchers, such as state marine parks, many with underwater diving trails.

Without doubt, the best areas for the diver are the warm, clear waters of southern California, Mexico's Cabo San Lucas, and the magnificent Gulf of California. To cruise slowly over a reef or around a kelp bed in 60° to 75° water with good visibility is an unforgettable experience. Thousands of animals swarm through forests of kelp or coral, and half an hour of slow and watchful cruising will reveal 244 many of the fishes shown in this book.

Highly recommended for beginning and experienced aquanauts are the California underwater parks, which range from Mendocino County in the north to San Diego near the U.S.-Mexican border (see the maps on pages 248 and 249). Many of the parks offer breathtaking underwater vistas. In the Northwest, the San Juan Islands of Washington's Puget Sound offer superb skin- and SCUBA-diving tours.

A few words of caution are called for, however, before you plunge into the surf. Skin diving is easy and pleasurable when practiced in calm, clear-water bays and beaches, but be sure to exercise caution when swimming near kelp, rock cliffs or outcrops, or coral reefs. If you are not careful, wave action can pitch you unexpectedly into reef heads that may inflict painful scratches, or wounds that are difficult to heal. At all times, watch where you are in relation to the shore and nearby reefs, and make allowances for wave action. Stay clear of thick kelp beds: entanglement in kelp strands can be very dangerous for any diver. Avoid overtiring yourself, and always swim accompanied by a capable companion. Keep hands and feet out of reef holes and crevices, and avoid areas of high surf, turbulence, and choppy water. SCUBA (self-contained underwater breathing apparatus) diving will provide even greater and deeper access to the underwater world, but the beginner requires detailed instruction and certification by a skilled diver before crossing this frontier. Qualified SCUBA instructors abound up and down the Pacific Coast; consult the phone book or your hotel registrar for information.

SOME SPANISH/ENGLISH EQUIVALENTS

bahía	bay	playa	beach; shore
cabo	cape; head	puerto	port
pez	fish	punta	point
golfo	gulf	rio	river
isla(s)	island(s)	roca	rock; cliff

245

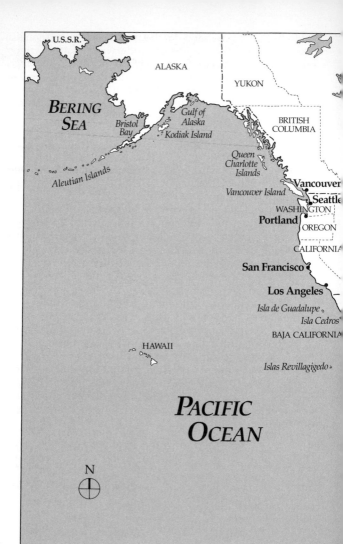

THE PACIFIC COAST, ALASKA TO PERU

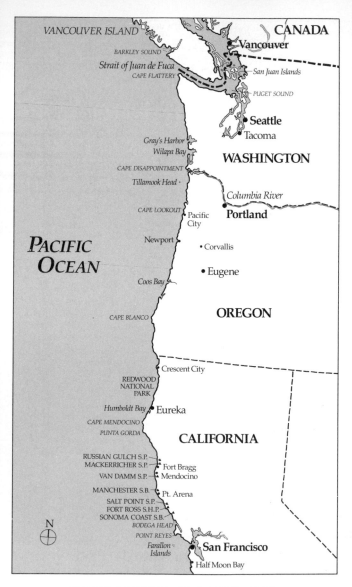

WASHINGTON, OREGON, AND
NORTHERN CALIFORNIA

CENTRAL AND SOUTHERN CALIFORNIA

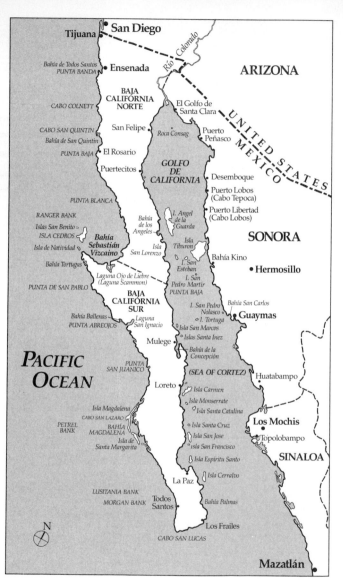

BAJA CALIFORNIA AND THE
GULF OF CALIFORNIA

BIBLIOGRAPHY

American Fisheries Society. 1980. *A List of Common and Scientific Names of Fishes from the U.S. and Canada*. 3rd ed. Wash., D.C.

Baldridge, H. D. 1981. "Sharks—Magnificent and Misunderstood." *Nat. Geographic*. August, Vol. 160(2). Wash., D.C.

Baxter, J. L. 1980. *Inshore Fishes of California*. 5th revision. Calif. Dept. of Fish and Game, Sacramento.

Bohlke, J. E., and C. C. G. Chaplin. 1968. *Fishes of the Bahamas and Adjacent Tropical Waters*. Livingston Publ. Co., Wynnewood, Pa.

Burgess, W. E., and H. R. Axelrod. 1984. *Fishes of California and Western Mexico*. T.F.H. Publications, Neptune City, N.J.

Burton, M., and R. Burton. 1975. *Encyclopedia of Fish*. Octopus Books, London.

Cannon, R. 1973. *The Sea of Cortez*. Lane Magazine and Book Co., Menlo Park, Calif.

Carl, G. C. 1975. *Some Common Marine Fishes of British Columbia*. Handbook 23, B.C. Provincial Museum, Victoria.

Castro-Aguirre, J. L. 1978. *Catálogo Sistemático de los Peces Marinos que Penetran a las Aguas Continentales de México con Aspectos Zoogeográficos y Ecológicos*. Serie Científica No. 19, Instituto Nacional de Pesca, México, D.F.

Clark, E. 1981. "Sharks—Magnificent and Misunderstood." *Nat. Geographic*. August, Vol. 160(2). Wash., D.C.

Clemens, W. A., and G. V. Wilby. 1961. *Fishes of the Pacific Coast of Canada*. 2nd ed. Bull. 68, Canada Fisheries Research Board, Ottawa.

De Manzanos, J. A. 1966. *Diccionario de Pesca y Marina*. Editorial Pesca y Marina, Tijuana, B.C., Mexico.

Dewees, C. M. 1984. *The Printer's Catch—An Artist's Guide to Pacific Coast Edible Marine Life*. Sea Challengers, Monterey, Calif.

Eschmeyer, W. N., E. S. Herald, and H. Hammann. 1983. *A Field Guide to Pacific Coast Fishes of North America*. Houghton Mifflin, Boston.

Farley, M. B., and L. K. Farley. 1978. *Diving Mexico's Baja California*. Marcor Enterprises, Port Hueneme, Calif.

Feder, Howard M., C. H. Turner, and C. Limbaugh. 1974. *Observations on Fishes Associated with Kelp Beds in Southern California*. Fish Bull. 160, Calif. Dept. of Fish and Game, Sacramento.

Fitch, J. E., and R. J. Lavenberg. 1971. *Marine Food and Game Fishes of California*. Univ. Calif. Press, Berkeley.

———. 1975. *Tidepool and Nearshore Fishes of California*. Univ. Calif. Press, Berkeley.

Gallo, P. 1973. *Guidebook to Saltwater Fishing in Southern California*. Anderson, Ritchie & Simon, Los Angeles.

Garrison, C. 1977. *Offshore Fishing in Southern California*. Chronicle Books, San Francisco.

Goodson, G. 1973. *The Many-Splendored Fishes of Hawaii*. Stanford Univ. Press, Stanford, Calif.

———. 1976. *Fishes of the Atlantic Coast*. Stanford Univ. Press, Stanford, Calif.

Gotshall, D. W. 1981. *Pacific Coast Inshore Fishes*. Sea Challengers, Los Osos, Calif.

———. 1982. *Marine Animals of Baja California*. Sea Challengers, Los Osos, Calif.

Halstead, B. W. 1978. *Poisonous and Venomous Marine Animals of the World*. Rev. ed. Darwin Press, Princeton, N.J.

Hart, J. L. 1973. *Pacific Fishes of Canada*. Bull. 180, Canada Fisheries Research Board, Ottawa.

Herald, E. S. 1972. *Living Fishes of the World*. Doubleday, Garden City, N.Y.

Hobson, E. S. 1965. "Diurnal-nocturnal activity of some inshore fishes in the Gulf of California." *Copeia* 1965 (3).

———. 1968. *Predatory Behavior of Some Shore Fishes in the Gulf of California*. Res. Rep. 73, Bur. Sports Fish and Wildlife, Sacramento.

———. 1972. "Activity of Hawaiian reeffishes during the evening and morning transitions between daylight and darkness." *U.S. Fishery Bull.* (70) 3. Wash., D.C.

———. 1974. "Feeding relationships of teleostean fishes on coral reefs in Kona, Hawaii." *U.S. Fishery Bull.* (72) 4. Wash., D.C.

Holder, C. F. 1910. *The Channel Islands of California*. McClurg, New York.

International Game Fish Association. 1984. *World Record Game Fishes*. Ft. Lauderdale, Fla.

Jordan, D. K. 1963. *The Genera of Fishes and a Classification of Fishes*. Stanford Univ. Press, Stanford, Calif. (reissue of 1917–1923 publications).

Jordan, D. W., and B. W. Evermann. 1896–1900. *The Fishes of North and Middle America. Parts I, II, III and IV*. Bull. 47, U.S. Nat. Mus., Wash., D.C.

———. 1902. Reprinted 1969. *American Food and Game Fishes*. Dover Publications, New York.

Kessler, D. W. 1985. *Alaska's Saltwater Fishes and Other Sea Life*. Alaska Northwest Pub. Co., Anchorage, Alaska.

Kumada, T., and Y. Hiyama. 1937. *Marine Fishes of the Pacific Coast of Mexico*. Nissan Fisheries Inst., Odawara, Japan.

Lord, J. K. 1866. *A Naturalist in Vancouver Island and British Columbia*. British Museum, London.

McClane, A. J. 1974. *McClane's New Standard Fishing Encyclopedia*. Holt, Rinehart and Winston, New York.

Miller, D. J., and R. N. Lea. 1972. Reprinted 1976 with addendum. *Guide to the Coastal Marine Fishes of California*. Fish Bull. 157, Calif. Dept. of Fish and Game, Sacramento.

Mowat, F. 1984. *Sea of Slaughter*. Atlantic Monthly Press, Boston.

National Geographic Society. 1965. *Wondrous World of Fishes*. Wash., D.C.

Phillips, J. B. 1957. *A Review of the Rockfishes of California (Family Scorpaenidae)*. Fish Bull. 104, Calif. Dept. of Fish and Game, Sacramento.

Pietsch, T. W., and D. B. Grobecker. 1987. *Frogfishes of the World: Systematics, Zoogeography, and Behavioral Ecology*. Stanford Univ. Press, Stanford, Calif.

Ramirez-Hernandez, E., and A. Gonzales Pages. 1976. *Catálogo de Peces Marinos Mexicanos*. Instituto Nacional de Pesca. México, D.F.

Randall, J. E. 1963. "Notes on the systematics of parrotfishes (Scaridae) with emphasis on sexual dichromatism." *Copeia* 1963 (2).

Ricketts, E. F., J. Calvin, J. Hedgpeth, and D. Phillips. 1985. *Between Pacific Tides*. Stanford Univ. Press, Stanford, Calif.

Roedel, P. M. 1953. *Common Ocean Fishes of the California Coast*. Fish Bull. 75, Calif. Dept. of Fish and Game, Sacramento.

Roessler, C. 1976. "Ocean gallery: The grouper family." *Skindiver Magazine*, December. Petersen Pub. Co., Los Angeles.

Rosenblatt, R. H., and E. S. Hobson. 1969. "Parrotfishes (Scaridae) of the Eastern Pacific, with a generic rearrangement of the Scarinae." *Copeia* 1969 (3).

Rosenblatt, R. H., and B. Zahuranec. 1967. *The Eastern Pacific Groupers of the genus* Mycteroperca; *Including a New Species*. Calif. Dept. of Fish and Game, 53 (4), Sacramento.

Simon, A. W. 1984. *Neptune's Revenge*. Bantam Books, New York.

Smith, C. Lavett. 1971. *A Revision of the American Groupers:* Epinephelus *and Allied Genera*. Bull. 146 (2), Am. Mus. Nat. Hist., New York.

Snodgrass, R. E., and E. Heller. 1905. "Papers from the Hopkins-Stanford Galapagos Expedition, 1898–1899. 17. Shore Fishes of the Revillagigedo, Clipperton, Cocos and Galapagos Islands." *Proc. Wash. Acad. Sci.* (6), Seattle.

State of California. Underwater Parks Master Plan. 1984 (updated). Dept. of Parks and Recreation, Sacramento.

Steinbeck, J., and E. F. Ricketts. 1941 (Reissued 1971). *Sea of Cortez: A Leisurely Journal of Travel and Research*. Paul P. Appel, Mamaroneck, New York.

Stillwell, H. 1948. *Fishing in Mexico*. Alfred A. Knopf, New York.

Thomson, D. A., L. T. Findley, and A. N. Kerstitch. 1979. *Reef Fishes of the Sea of Cortez*. John Wiley & Sons, New York.

Thomson, D. A., and N. McKibbin. 1976. *Gulf of California Fishwatcher's Guide*. Golden Puffer Press, Tucson, Arizona.

Walford, L. A. 1932. *Handbook of Common Commercial and Game Fishes of California*. Bull. 28, Bur. Commercial Fisheries, Sacramento.

———. 1937. *Marine Game Fishes of the Pacific Coast from Alaska to the Equator*. Univ. Calif. Press, Berkeley.

Warner, R. R. 1975. "The adaptive significance of sequential hermaphroditism in animals." *American Naturalist* (109).

Warner, R. R., D. R. Robertson, and E. G. Leigh, Jr. 1975. "Sex change and sexual selection." *Science* (190).

INDEX OF FISH NAMES

(A page number in boldface type identifies the primary treatment of that entry.)

259

NOTES